Unthinking Social Science

Unthinking Social Science

The Limits of Nineteenth-Century Paradigms

Immanuel Wallerstein

Polity Press

Unthinking Social Science

The Limits of Nineteenth-Century Paradigms

Immanuel Wallerstein

Polity Press

Copyright © Immanuel Wallerstein 1991

First published 1991 by Polity Press
in association with Basil Blackwell

Editorial office:
Polity Press, 65 Bridge Street,
Cambridge CB2 1UR, UK

Marketing and production:
Basil Blackwell Ltd
108 Cowley Road, Oxford OX4 1JF, UK

ISBN 0 7456 0876 0
ISBN 0 7456 0911 2

British Library Cataloguing in Publication Data
A CIP catalogue record for this book is available from the British Library.

Library of Congress Cataloging in Publication Data
A CIP catalogue record for this book is available from the Library of Congress.

Typeset in 10½ on 12pt Times
by Graphicraft Typesetters Ltd., Hong Kong
Printed in Great Britain by T.J. Press, Padstow, Cornwall

Contents

Acknowledgements

The author and publisher gratefully acknowledge permission from the original publishers of the material contained in this book to reproduce the essays here. Unless otherwise stated, the original publisher of each essay, or the journal in which the essay originally appeared, holds copyright in the essay.

1 *Social Research*, LVI, 1, Spring 1989.
2 A. Bergesen (ed.) 1983: *Crises in the World-System*. Beverly Hills: Sage. Reprinted by permission of Sage Publications, Inc.
3 *Thesis Eleven*, 13, 1986.
4 J. Kocka and G. Ránki (eds) 1985: *Economic Theory and History*. Budapest: Akadémiai Kiadó.
5 *International Sociology*, I, 1, March 1986.
6 *Cooperation and Conflict*, XXIV, 1, 1989.
7 *Economic and Political Weekly*, XXIII, 39, September 1984.
8 *Canadian Journal of African Studies*, XXII, 2, 1988.
9 Session paper: 'Historical Sociology of India,' XI World Congress of Sociology, New Delhi, August 18–23, 1986. © Immanuel Wallerstein.
10 *Geography*, LXXIII, 4, October 1988.
11 S. Resnick and R. Wolff (eds) 1985: *Rethinking Marxism*. Brooklyn, NY: Autonomedia.
12 *American Journal of Sociology*, XCI, 6, 1986.
13 *Radical History Review*, 26, 1982.
14 *Monthly Review*, XXXVII, 9, February 1986.
15 *Journal of Modern History*, LXIII, 2, June 1991. © 1991 by the University of Chicago.

16 *Radical History Review*, 49, December 1990.
17 *European Journal of Operational Research*, XXX, 2, June 1987.
18 A. Giddens and J. Turner (eds) 1987: *Social Theory Today*. Cambridge: Polity Press. Original title of essay, 'World-Systems Analysis.'
19 H. van der Wee (ed.) 1990: *Studies in Social and Economic History*, 15: Erik Aerts, Thomas Kuczynski, and Vladimir Vinogradov (eds) *Methodological Problems*. Leuven: Leuven University Press.
20 *Review* XII, 2, Spring 1990 (Fernand Braudel Center).

Introduction: Why Unthink?

I have entitled this book, "unthinking social science" and not "rethinking social science." It is quite normal for scholars and scientists to rethink issues. When important new evidence undermines old theories and predictions do not hold, we are pressed to rethink our premises. In that sense, much of nineteenth-century social science, in the form of specific hypotheses, is constantly being rethought. But, in addition to rethinking, which is "normal," I believe we need to "unthink" nineteenth-century social science, because many of its presumptions – which, in my view, are misleading and constrictive – still have far too strong a hold on our mentalities. These presumptions, once considered liberating of the spirit, serve today as the central intellectual barrier to useful analysis of the social world.

Let me be very clear from the outset. I am *not* proposing here a new paradigm for our collective work in what I prefer to call the historical social sciences. Rather, I am trying to expose what I consider to be highly dubious and narrow-minded in the dominant viewpoints. I hope thereby to encourage the search for a new paradigm which will take considerable time and effort by many to construct. I see this book as part of an effort to clear away the underbrush of a very dense and organizationally quite well-defined forest which is blocking our vision.

No doubt many will disagree with my description of the epistemology of nineteenth-century social science, and with my analysis of the social history of this epistemology. I have the sense that the defenders of the existent dominant epistemology are neither self-effacing nor timid in the expression of their views. I have the sense as well that those who criticize the existing dominant epistemology, even when their criticisms are serious and pertinent, often remain nonetheless less than fully liberated from the *Weltanschauung* they renounce. I feel I am not exempt from this backsliding myself. This has only confirmed me in my views of how strong a hold these methodological assumptions have on us, and therefore how critical it is to "unthink" these assumptions.

I have divided these essays into six themes. The first deals with the social history of the epistemology in question. I seek to locate the invention of the historical social sciences as an intellectual category within the historical development of the modern world-system. I seek to account not only for why the historical social sciences became institutionalized as a mode of knowledge in the nineteenth century, and only in the nineteenth century, but also why they developed the particular epistemology they did, centered around what I think of as the false nomothetic-idiographic antinomy. I then seek to account for why, in the last 20 years, and only really then, this epistemology has begun to come into question, presenting us with the intellectual dilemmas of the present.

Once the historical context is argued, I turn my attention to what seems to me the key, and most questionable, concept of nineteenth-century social science, the concept of "development." To be sure, the word "development" only became commonplace after 1945, and then initially in what seemed the marginal realm of explicating current developments in the "Third World," or the peripheral zones of the capitalist world-economy. I believe nonetheless that the idea of development is simply an avatar of the concept of an "industrial revolution," and that this idea in turn has been the axis not only of most historiography but of all the varieties of nomothetic analysis. Here is an idea which has been eminently influential, highly misleading (precisely because, in its partial correctness, it has seemed so persuasively self-evident), and consequently generative of false expectations (both intellectually and politically). And yet there are very few indeed who are ready truly to unthink this central notion.

I then shift from development, which, if misleading as a concept, is at least widely discussed, to time and space, or to what I call TimeSpace. One of the most remarkable achievements of the epistemology that has dominated social science has been to eliminate TimeSpace from the analysis. It is not that geography and chronology were never talked about. Of course they were, and quite extensively. But they have been considered to be physical invariants, and hence exogenous variables, rather than highly fluid social creations, and hence variables not merely endogenous but critical to the understanding of social structure and historical transformation. Even today, we rarely consider the multiplicity of TimeSpaces that confront us, and therefore rarely concern ourselves with which ones we use, or should use, in the deciphering of our social realities.

Having attempted to show the limits of the concept of development central to the nineteenth-century paradigm(s), and the absence therein of what ought to have been a central concept, TimeSpace – the two things being logically and intimately related – I then turn my attention to two major thinkers who may be of some assistance in liberating us from the constraints of nineteenth-century social science: Marx and Braudel.

Karl Marx was of course himself a major figure of nineteenth-century social science. He has been called – with some justice, in my view – the last of the classical economists. He shared a very large part of the epistemological premises of the European intellectual world of his time. When Engels said that Marx's thought had its roots in Hegel plus Saint-Simon plus the British classical economists, he was confessing as much. And yet Marx claimed to be engaged in a "critique of political economy," a claim that is not without some serious basis.

Marx was a thinker of his time who sought to rise above the limitations of his time. I am not concerned here with assessing the degree to which Marx did or did not succeed in this task. Rather, I observe that Marx's ideas have entered into our common discourse largely in the version that was assembled by the Marxism of the parties, and that this version, rather than pursuing the critique of political economy, participated in the dominant epistemology fully. I am concerned here with revisiting the other Marx, that Marx who resisted the dominant perspectives of nineteenth-century social science.

I believe it is also useful to revisit Fernand Braudel. Braudel was a very different figure from Marx. He was not self-consciously a "theorist" or a "methodologist." He was a historian engaged in archival research out of which he hoped to build a *"histoire pensée."* He seldom talked of epistemological issues per se. But he had sure instincts which led him in fact to question historiographical verities, and thereupon (sometimes explicitly, sometimes only implicitly) to indicate new ways out of old dilemmas. I have revisited him, to see to what degree he helps us to unthink nineteenth-century social science, and in particular to arrive at an understanding of capitalism in the *longue durée* that is not based on the premise of "development" and the absence of TimeSpace.

Finally, I turn to world-systems analysis, as a contemporary perspective on the social world, one that makes central the study of long-term, large-scale social change. World-systems analysis intends to be a critique of nineteenth-century social science. But it is an incomplete, unfinished critique. It still has not been able to find a way to surmount the most enduring (and misleading) legacy of nineteenth-century social science – the division of social analysis into three arenas, three logics, three "levels" – the economic, the political, and the socio-cultural. This trinity stands in the middle of the road, in granite, blocking our intellectual advance. Many find it unsatisfying, but in my view no one has yet found the way to dispense with the language and its implications, some of which are correct but most of which are probably not.

Perhaps it is that the world must change some more before the scholars are able to theorize it more usefully. But I am convinced that it is this conundrum which ought to be preoccupying us, before any other, and that overcoming this aporia, unlocking this mystery, unthinking this metaphor is essential if we are to reconstruct the historical social sciences.

Part I
The Social Sciences: From Genesis to Bifurcation

1

The French Revolution as a World-Historical Event

The significance or importance of the French Revolution has usually been analyzed in one of two ways: as an "event" in French history which has its course and consequences; or as a phenomenon which had a specific influence on the history of other countries. I wish in this essay, however, to view the French Revolution as a world-historical event in the very specific sense of its significance and importance in the history of the modern world-system as a world-system.

As we know, the literature on the French Revolution of the last 30 years has reflected a gigantic intellectual battle between two principal schools of thought. On the one side, there has been the so-called social interpretation, of which Georges Soboul has been the central figure and which traces its lineage to Lefebvre, Mathiez, and Jaurès. This viewpoint has built its analysis around the theme that the French Revolution was essentially a political revolution of the bourgeoisie who were overthrowing a feudal *ancien régime*.

A second camp has emerged in "revisionist" criticism of the social interpretation of the French Revolution. This second camp has no accepted collective name. The two leading exponents of this view have been first Alfred Cobban and then François Furet. This camp rejects the concept of the French Revolution as a "bourgeois" revolution on the grounds that eighteenth-century France can no longer be meaningfully described as "feudal." Rather, they suggest that it can better be described as "despotic" and the French Revolution seen as a political explosion of anti-despotic libertarian demands.[1]

The key difference this makes in the analysis of the actual events revolves around the interpretation of the political meaning of the insurrection of August 10, 1792. For Soboul, this insurrection was a "second revolution" ushering in a democratic and popular republic. For Furet, it was exactly the opposite. It was the closure of the path leading to the liberal society. It was no doubt a second revolution, but one that represented not the fulfillment of the first but its *dérapage*. Thus, for Soboul, Robespierre and the Mountain represented the most radical segment of the French bourgeoisie and therefore a force for liberation; for Furet, Robespierre and the Mountain represented a new (and worse) despotism.

In this debate, the lines are clearly drawn and are certainly familiar ones in terms of twentieth-century European politics. Indeed, as has often been said, this debate is as much an argument about the Russian Revolution as it is about the French Revolution. It is important nonetheless to see what premises are *shared* by the two camps in rhetorical battle. They both share a model of history which is developmental and which assumes that the units that develop are states. (The Atlantic thesis also shares this model.) For the social-interpretation school, all states go through successive historical stages, the most relevant transition in this case being that from feudalism to capitalism, from a state dominated by an aristocracy to one dominated by a bourgeoisie. Ergo, the French Revolution is simply the moment of dramatic or of definitive transition, a moment that was, however, both necessary and inevitable. For the "liberal" school, the process of modernization involves the renunciation of a despotic state and its replacement by a state founded on liberal principles. The French Revolution was an attempt to make this (not inevitable) transition, but one that was abortive. The drive to freedom remained latent in the French polity and would be resumed later. For Soboul, since the revolution was bourgeois, it was the point of departure of liberal democracy in

---

[1]   The so-called Atlantic thesis is an amalgam of these two perspectives, although it was presented initially prior to the revisionist work. The Atlantic thesis is that the French Revolution was both bourgeois and antidespotic. It is furthermore world-systemic in that its origins and that of the other more or less simultaneous "Atlantic" revolutions were in the common fount of Enlightenment thought. One can see this as marrying either the best or the worst of the other two theses.

France. For Furet, after the *dérapage* the revolution became itself an obstacle to liberal democracy.

It is interesting to see how therefore each side treats the long war with Great Britain that began in 1792 and continued (with interruptions) until 1815, that is, long past the Jacobin period. For Soboul, the war was essentially launched from abroad by the French aristocracy, who, losing the civil war, were hoping to recoup their position by internationalizing the conflict. For Furet, the war was desired by the revolutionary forces (or at least by most of them) as a way of pursuing the revolution and strengthening it.

No doubt one can make a plausible case for each of these explanations of the immediate origins of the war. What is striking is that there seems to be, in these analyses, no consideration of whether or not a Franco-British war might not have occurred at this time in the absence of anything resembling an internal French revolution. After all, there had been three successive major wars between Britain (or England) and France over a period of a century, and from the perspective of today we might think of the 1792–1815 wars as simply the fourth and last of these major wars in the long struggle for hegemony in the capitalist world-economy.

I shall briefly summarize here an analysis expounded at length in chapters 1 and 2 of vol. 3 of *The Modern World-System* (1989b) without the supporting data found in the book. I do this merely as background for the argument I wish to make about the ways in which the French Revolution as a world-historical event transformed the world-system as a world-system. I start with the assumption that the capitalist world-economy existed as a historical system since the "long" sixteenth century with boundaries that from the beginning included England and France, and that therefore both countries had been functioning for all this time within the constraints of a capitalist mode of production and had been members of the interstate system that emerged as the political framework of the capitalist world-economy.

Such a "world-systems perspective" leaves little room for the most fundamental assumptions of the two main scholarly schools concerning the French Revolution. The French Revolution could not have been a "bourgeois revolution" since the capitalist world-economy within which France was located was already one in which the dominant class strata were "capitalist" in their economic behavior. The "capitalists" in that sense had no need of political revolution in particular states in order to gain *droit de cité* or to pursue their fundamental interests. This of course does not exclude that fact that particular groups of capitalists might have been more or less happy with the public policies of their states and might have been willing, under certain conditions, to consider political actions that ended up by being in some sense "insurrectionary," thereby changing the structures of given state institutions.

On the other hand, the world-systems perspective gives equally little place to the underlying assumption of the revisionist school (or schools), who take as central a putative macrostruggle between the tenets of political despotism and the tenets of political liberalism within each state, and see a sort of vector of modernity in the drive for liberalism. "Liberalism" in a world-systems perspective is seen rather as a particular strategy of the dominant classes utilizable primarily in core zones of the world-economy and reflecting among other things a lopsided intrastate class structure in which the working classes are a much lower percentage of the total population than in peripheral zones. At the end of the eighteenth century, neither England nor France yet had effective "liberal" institutional structures, and neither would have them for another century or so. The *dérapage* of 1792, if that is what one wants to call it, had no greater long-run significance than what might be thought of as the parallel *dérapage* of 1649 in England. Seen from the perspective of the twentieth century, Great Britain and France are not significantly different in the degree to which "liberal" political institutions prevail in the two centuries. Nor are they significantly different from, say, Sweden, which had no dramatic set of events comparable to the English or French revolutions.

What can be noted about England and France is that, once Dutch hegemony in the capitalist world-economy began to decline in the mid-seventeenth century, these two states were the competitors for the hegemonic succession. The competition could be seen in two principal arenas: in their relative "efficiencies" of operation in the markets of the world-economy, and in their relative military-political strengths in the interstate system.

In this long competition, 1763 marked the beginning of the "last act." The Peace of Paris marked Great Britain's definitive victory over France on the seas, in the Americas, and in India. But, of course, it simultaneously laid the bases for the acute difficulties that Great Britain (and Spain and Portugal as well) were to have with their settler populations in the Americas, and which led to the process of settler decolonization which originated in British North America and spread everywhere.

We know that the American War of Independence attracted

eventually a French involvement on the side of the settlers which, in the 1780s, greatly aggravated the fiscal crisis of the French state. To be sure, the British state also faced great budgetary dilemmas. But the 1763 victory made it easier for the British to resolve these difficulties in the short run than for the French state. Witness, for example, the role of "Plassey plunder" in relieving British state indebtedness to the Dutch.

The French state found it politically impossible to solve their fiscal problem through new modes of taxation and had no access to the equivalent of Plassey plunder. This explains their willingness to enter into the Anglo-French Commercial (Eden) Treaty of 1786 to which the French king agreed in good part on the grounds that it would create new sources of state revenue. Its immediate impact was in fact economically disastrous and politically unnerving. The *cahiers de doléance* were full of complaints about the treaty.

If one looks at the comparative efficiencies of French and British agricultural and industrial production in the eighteenth century, it is hard to make a case for any significant British lead. As of 1763, the French were if anything ahead. But despite the fact that the economic realities were very similar, at least up to the 1780s when Britain was perhaps doing a little better, it is true that there was an (incorrect) perception in France after 1763 of France falling behind. This was probably an illusion whose elaboration became a rationalization for the military defeat of 1763. There seems to have been a similar illusion prior to 1763 among the English that they were behind France, an illusion apparently effaced after 1763. In any case, this sense on the part of the French educated strata helped also to create the justification for the Eden Treaty.

When the king convened the Estates-General, the general atmosphere (the defeat of 1763, the fiscal crisis of the state, the error of agreeing to the Eden Treaty, all compounded by two successive bad harvest years) created the political space for the "runaway" situation we call the French Revolution, a "runaway" situation which basically did not end until 1815.

One could say that the period 1763–89 in France was marked by an unwillingness of French elites to accept defeat in the struggle for hegemony with Great Britain, exacerbated by a growing feeling that the monarchy was unwilling or unable to do anything about the situation. The wars of 1792–1815 were therefore part of the fundamental logic of the French revolutionaries, seeking to restructure the state so that it would be capable of finally overcoming the British foe.

From the strictly relational perspective of the Franco-British struggle in the interstate system, the French Revolution turned out to be a disaster. Far from permitting the final recouping of the defeat of 1763, France was beaten militarily more definitively in 1815 than it ever had been, because this time the defeat was on land, where French military strength lay. And far from allowing France to overcome the previously largely fictive economic gap with Great Britain, the wars created this gap for the first time. In 1815 it was true to say, as it had not been in 1789, that Great Britain had a significant "efficiency" lead over France in the production of goods for the world markets.

But were there not at least significant internal economic trans- formations in France as a result of the revolution? When the dust settled, it turned out that the transformations were less startling than is often asserted. The larger agricultural entities for the most part remained intact, although no doubt there was some change in the names of property owners. Despite the presumed "abolition of feudalism," such constraints on "agricultural individualism" (to use Marc Bloch's phrase) as *vaine pâture* and *droit de parcours* survived until late in the nineteenth century. The yeoman class (such as the *laboureurs*) emerged stronger than before, but largely at the ex- pense of the smallest producers (such as the *manoeuvriers*). The agricultural reforms were at times noisy, but they fit into a slow steady curve of parallel change in much of western Europe over several centuries.

As for industry, guilds were abolished to be sure. And internal tariffs disappeared, thereby creating a larger unfettered internal market. But let us not forget that before 1789 there already existed a zone without internal tariff barriers, the Five Great Farms, which included Paris and was approximately the size of England. The revolution did of course revoke the Eden Treaty and France once again, quite sensibly, returned to protectionism. The state did acquire a new administrative efficiency (the linguistic unification, the new civil code, the creation of the *grands écoles*) which no doubt was very helpful to France's economic performance in the nineteenth century.

But from a strictly French point of view, the balance sheet of the French Revolution is relatively meager. If it was the "exemplary" bourgeois revolution, this doesn't say much for the value or the force of such revolutions. As a struggle against despotism, we have the word of the theorists of this position that it did not turn in a stellar performance. Of course, we could celebrate it on Tocquevil- lian grounds: the French Revolution was France's fulfillment of its state creation, the achievement of bureaucratic centralization that Richelieu and Colbert sought but never quite completed. If so, one might understand French celebration of this event as the incarnation of French nationalism, but what could the rest of us celebrate?

I believe there is something for the rest of us to note, and perhaps to celebrate, if somewhat ambiguously. I believe the French Revolution and its Napoleonic continuation catalyzed the ideological transformation of the capitalist world-economy *as a world-system*, and thereby created three wholly new arenas or sets of cultural institutions that have formed a central part of the world-system ever since.

We must begin with the perceived meaning of the French Revolution to contemporaries. It was, of course, a dramatic, passionate, violent upheaval. In what might be called its primary expression, from 1789 (the fall of the Bastille) to 1794 (Thermidor), the Great Fear occurred, "feudalism" was abolished, church lands were nationalized, a king was executed, and a Declaration of the Rights of Man was proclaimed. This series of events culminated in a Reign of Terror, which finally ended with the so-called Thermidorian Reaction. However, of course dramatic events did not cease then. Napoleon came to power and French armies expanded throughout continental Europe. They were greeted originally in many areas as carriers of a revolutionary message, and then came to be rejected later in many areas as bearers of a French imperialist drive.

The reaction everywhere in Europe among the established authorities was one of horror at the undermining of order (real and potential) represented by the French revolutionary virus. Efforts to counter the spread of these ideas and values were implemented everywhere, and most notably in Great Britain, where a very exaggerated view of the strength of possible sympathizers led to an effective repression.

We should note in particular the impact of the French Revolution (including Napoleon) on three key zones of the "periphery" of the world-system: Haiti, Ireland, and Egypt. The French Revolution's impact on St-Domingue was immediate and cataclysmic. The initial attempt of White settlers to capitalize on the revolution to gain increased autonomy led rapidly to the first Black revolution in the world-system, a Black revolution which, over the succeeding decades, all other players (Napoleon, the British, the White settler revolutionaries in the United States and in Latin America) sought in one way or another to destroy or at least contain.

The French Revolution's impact on Ireland was to transform

what had been an attempt by Protestant settlers to gain autonomy (as had the analogous group in British North America) into a social revolution that for a time drew together both Catholics and Presbyterian Dissenters into a common anticolonial movement. This attempt, hitting at the very heart of the British state, was turned aside, undermined, and repressed, and Ireland was all the more closely integrated with Great Britain by the Act of Union of 1800. The result, however, was to create an endemic internal political issue for Great Britain throughout the nineteenth century, its equivalent *mutatis mutandis* of the US political issue of Black rights.

In Egypt, the Napoleonic invasion resulted in the emergence of Egypt's first great "modernizer," Mohammed Ali, whose program of industrialization and military expansion seriously undermined the Ottoman Empire and almost established a powerful state in the Middle East capable eventually of playing a major role in the interstate system. Almost, but not quite – Mohammed Ali's efforts were eventually successfully checked, as were all similar efforts in the periphery for a century.

To all of this must of course be added the settler decolonization of the Americas. No doubt, this was not the doing (alone) of the French Revolution. The American War of Independence predated the revolution. But its sources lay in the same post-1763 restructuring of the geopolitics of the world-system, and it made appeals to the same Enlightenment doctrines to legitimate itself as did the French Revolution. The Latin American independences of course then came in the wake of the same geopolitical restructuring, reinforced by the successful models of both the American and French revolutions, plus the devastating political consequences of Napoleon's invasion of Spain in 1808 and the abdication of the Spanish monarch.

All in all, it added up to a political whirlwind of a kind that had never been known before in the modern world. Of course there had been previous periods of turmoil, but their impact had been different. The English Revolution no doubt shared many features with the French Revolution – in England. But its effect outside of England was quite limited, in large part because there was no "Napoleonic" conquest associated with it. And no doubt the Reformation-Counter Reformation turmoil was every bit as wrenching as the French revolutionary turmoil. But it was not focused around issues of political order, and the ultimate outcome, while involving real political restructuring, seemed not to raise questions about political legitimacy of rulers and their structures per se.

I think the bourgeoisie, or if you prefer the capitalist strata, or if you prefer the ruling classes, drew two conclusions from the "French revolutionary turmoil." One was a sense of great threat, not from what might be done by the Robespierres of the world, but from what might be done by the unwashed masses, who seemed for the first time to be contemplating seriously the acquisition of state power. The French Revolution proper had several times almost "gotten out of hand" not because some "bourgeois" were seeking political changes but because some "peasants" or some "sansculottes" or some "women" began to arm themselves and to march or to demonstrate. The Black slaves of St-Domingue did more than demonstrate; they actually seized state power, a political development that turned out to be even more difficult to contain and turn back than the rebellions in France.

These "uprisings" might of course be assimilated analytically to the recurring food riots and peasant uprisings of prior centuries. I believe the world bourgeoisie perceived that something different was occurring, that these "uprisings" might better be conceived of as the first truly antisystemic (that is, anticapitalist system) uprisings of the modern world. It is not that these antisystemic uprisings were terribly successful. It was simply that they had occurred at all, and that therefore they were the harbinger of a major qualitative change in the structure of the capitalist world-system, a turning point in its politics.

The world bourgeoisie thereupon drew, I believe, a second and very logical inference. Constant, short-run political change was inevitable and it was hopeless to maintain the historical myth used by previous world-systems, and indeed even by the capitalist world-economy up to that point, that political change was exceptional, often short-lived, normally undesirable. It was only by accepting the normality of change that the world bourgeoisie had a chance of containing it and slowing it down.

This widespread acceptance of the normality of change represented a fundamental cultural transformation of the capitalist world-economy. It meant that one was recognizing publicly, that is, expressively, the structural realities that had in fact prevailed for several centuries already: that the world-system was a capitalist system, that the world-economy's division of labor was bounded and framed by an interstate system composed of hypothetically sovereign states. Once this recognition became widespread, which seems to me to have occurred more or less in the period 1789–1815, once this discourse prevailed, three new institutions emerged as expressions of and responses to this "normality of change." These three institutions were the ideologies, the social sciences, and the movements. These three institutions comprise the great intellectual/ cultural synthesis of the "long" nineteenth century, the insitutional underpinnings of what is sometimes inaptly called "modernity."

We do not usually think of ideologies as institutions. But this is in fact an error. An ideology is more than a *Weltanschauung*. Obviously, at all times and places, there have existed one or several *Weltanschauungen* which have determined how people interpreted their world. Obviously, people always constructed reality through common eyeglasses that have been historically manufactured. An ideology is such a *Weltanschauung*, but it is one of a very special kind. It is one that has been consciously and collectively formulated with conscious political objectives. Using this definition of ideology, it follows that this particular brand of *Weltanschauung* could be constructed only in a situation in which public discourse accepted the normality of change. One needs to formulate an ideology consciously only if one believes that change is normal and that therefore it is useful to formulate conscious middle-run political objectives.

Three such ideologies were developed in the nineteenth century – conservatism, liberalism, and Marxism. They were all world-systemic ideologies. It is no accident that conservatism was the first to emerge institutionally. It is clear that the new recognition of the normality of change posed urgent dilemmas to those of a conservative bent. Edmund Burke and Joseph de Maistre saw this clearly and quickly. They saw they needed to make an intellectual case for the slowest possible pace of change. But more importantly, they realized that some kinds of change were more serious than others. They gave priority therefore to preserving the structures which in turn could serve as brakes on any and all precipitate reformers and revolutionaries. These were of course the structures whose merits conservatives lauded: the family, the "community," the church, and of course the monarchy. The central motif of conservative ideology has always been "tradition." Traditions are presumed to be there, and to have been there for an indefinitely long time. It is argued that it is "natural" to preserve traditional values because they incarnate wisdom. Conservative ideology maintains that any tampering with traditions needs strong justification. Otherwise, disintegration and decadence follow. Hence conservative ideology is the incarnation of a sort of Cassandra-like cultural pessimism, inherently defensive in nature. Conservatives warn against the dangers of the change that now has become considered normal. The short-run political implications may vary enormously, but in the middle run conservatism's political agenda is clear.

Liberalism is the natural ideology of normal change. But it needed to become an ideology only after conservatism had emerged. It was English Tories who first called their opponents "liberals" in the early nineteenth century. To be sure, the idea of the individual's right to be free from the constraints of the state had a long history that predates this moment. The rise of the absolutist state brought in its train the advocates of constitutional government. John Locke is often considered the symbolic incarnation of this line of thought. But what emerged in the nineteenth century was liberalism as an ideology of consciously enacted reform, and this did not really exist in the seventeenth or eighteenth centuries. This is also why I believe the oft-cited difference between early-nineteenth-century "minimal state" liberalism and late-nineteenth-century "social state" liberalism misses the point. The exponents of both had the same conscious political agenda: legislative reform that would abet, channel, facilitate "normal change."

Marxism then came along quite late as the third ideology of the nineteenth-century world. Perhaps some would prefer to think of socialism as the third ideology. But over time the only variety of socialist thought that became truly distinguishable from liberalism as an ideology was in fact Marxism. What Marxism did, as an ideology, was to accept the basic premise of liberal ideology (the theory of progress) and add to it two crucial specifications. Progress was seen as something realized not continuously but discontinuously, that is, by revolution. And in the upward ascent to the good or perfect society the world had reached not its ultimate but its penultimate state. These two amendments were sufficient to produce an entirely different political agenda.

It should be noted that I have not discussed the social bases of these different ideologies. The usual explanations seem to me too simple. Nor is it at all clear that the emergence of these three ideologies depended on specific social bases, which is not to say that there has been no historic correlation between social position and ideological preference. What is important is that the three ideologies were all statements about how politically to deal with "normal change." And they probably exhausted the range of possibilities for plausible ideologies to be institutionalized in the nineteenth-century capitalist world-economy.

Political agendas are only one part of what one needs to deal with "normal change." Since these agendas represented concrete proposals, they required concrete knowledge of current realities. What they needed, in short, was social science. For if one didn't know how the world worked, it was difficult to recommend what one might do to make it work better. This knowledge was more important to the liberals and Marxists since they were in favor of "progress," and thus they were more prone than the conservatives to encourage and frequent social science. But even conservatives were aware that it might be useful to understand reality if only in order to conserve (and restore) the status quo (ante).

Ideologies are more than mere *Weltanschauungen*; social science is more than mere social thought or social philosophy. Previous world-systems had social thinkers, and we still today benefit by reading them, at least some of them. The modern world-system was of course the heir of a so-called "Renaissance" of (especially) Greek thought and built on this edifice in many ways. The rise of the state structures, and in particular of the absolutist state, led to a special flourishing of politicial philosophy, from Machiavelli to Bodin to Spinoza, from More to Hobbes and Locke, from Montesquieu to Rousseau. Indeed, this was a stellar period in the production of such thought, and nothing quite matches it in the post-1789 era. Furthermore, the middle and late eighteenth century saw the emergence of work in economic philosophy almost as rich as that in political philosophy: Hume, Adam Smith, the Physiocrats, Malthus. One is tempted to add: Ricardo, John Stuart Mill, Karl Marx.

But none of this represented the insitutionalization of social science. Social science, as it came to be defined in the nineteenth century, was the empirical study of the social world with the intention of understanding "normal change" and thereby being able to affect it. Social science was not the product of solitary social thinkers but the creation of a collective body of persons within specific structures to achieve specific ends. It involved a major social investment, which was never previously the case with social thought.

The principal mode of institutionalizing social science was by differentiation within Europe's traditional university structure which, by 1789, was virtually moribund. The universities, which at that point in time were scarcely vital intellectual centers, were still largely organized in the traditional four faculties of theology, philosophy, law, and medicine. There were, furthermore, relatively few universities. In the course of the nineteenth century, there occurred a significant creation of new chairs, largely within the faculty of philosophy, to a lesser extent within the faculty of law.

These chairs had new names and some of them became the forerunners of what today we call "departments."

At first it was not clear which "names" of putative "disciplines" would prevail. We know the outcome, however. By the end of the nineteenth century, six main "names" had survived and more or less become stabilized into "disciplines." They had become institutionalized not only within the university system, now renewed and beginning again to expand, but also as national scholarly associations, and in the twentieth century as international scholarly associations.

The "naming" of the disciplines – that is, the structure of the presumed division of intellectual labor – reflected very much the triumph of liberal ideology. This is of course because liberal ideology was (and is) the reigning ideology of the capitalist world-economy. This also explains why Marxists were suspicious of the new social science, and why conservatives have been even more suspicious and recalcitrant.

Liberal ideology involved the argument that the centerpiece of social process was the careful delimitation of three spheres of activity: those related to the market, those related to the state, and those that were "personal." The last category was primarily residual, meaning all activities not immediately related to the state or the market. Insofar as it was defined positively, it had to do with activities of "everyday life" – the family, the "community," the "underworld" of "deviant" activities, etc. The study of these separate spheres came to be named political science, economics, and sociology. If political science was the last name to be accepted, it was primarily the result of an archaic jurisdictional dispute between the faculties of philosophy and of law, and not because the operations of the state were deemed less worthy of study. All three of these "disciplines" developed as universalizing sciences based on empirical research, with a strong component of "applied science" attached to them.

Parallel to this, the "name" history was manifestly redefined. This is the great transformation represented by the work of Ranke. Ranke's great critique of what had been previously produced under the "name" of history is that it was too "philosophical," insufficiently "historical." This is the import of writing history *wie es eigentlich gewesen ist*. History had really occurred. What had happened could be known by turning to the "sources" and reading them critically. The history that now became institutionalized was rigorously idiographic.

What is to be noted in the emerging institutionalization of these four so-called disciplines, as they developed in the nineteenth century, are three things. One, they were concerned empirically primarily, almost exclusively, with the core countries of the capitalist world-economy – indeed, primarily with just a few of them. Two, almost all scholars worked on empirical materials concerning their own countries. Three, the dominant mode of work was empirical and concrete, even though for the three so-called nomothetic disciplines (economics, sociology, political science) the object was said to be the discovery of the "laws" that explained human behavior. The nationally based, empiricist thrust of the new "disciplines" became a way of circumscribing the study of social change that would make it most useful for and supportive of state policies, least subversive of the new verities. But it was nonetheless a study of the "real" world based on the assumption that one could not derive such knowledge deductively from metaphysical understandings of an unchanging world.

The nineteenth-century acceptance of the normality of change included the idea that change was normal only for the civilized nations, and that it therefore was incumbent upon these nations to impose this change upon the recalcitrant other world. Social science could play a role here, as a mode of describing unchanging customs, thereby opening the way to understanding how this other world could be brought into "civilization." The study of the "primitive" peoples without writing became the domain of anthropology. The study of the "petrified" peoples with writing (China, India, the Arab world) became the domain of Orientalism. For each field the academic study emphasized the elements that were unchanging, but was accompanied by an applied, largely extrauniversity domain of societal engineering.

If the social sciences became increasingly an instrument of intelligent governance of a world in which change was normal, and hence of limiting the scope of such change, those who sought to go beyond the limits structured by the world bourgeoisie turned to a third institution, the movements. Once again, rebellions and oppositions were not new. They had long been part of the historical scene, as had been both *Weltanschauungen* and social thought. But just as *Weltanschauungen* now became ideologies and social thought became social science, so did rebellions and oppositions become antisystemic movements. These movements were the third and last of the institutional innovations of the post-1789 world-system, an innovation that really emerges only after the world revolution of 1848.

The essential difference between the multiple prior rebellions and oppositions and the new antisystemic movements was that the former were spontaneous, short-lived, and largely uncoordinated beyond the local level. The new movements were organizations, eventually organizations with bureaucracies, which planned the politics of social transformation. They worked in a time frame that went beyond the short run.

There were, to be sure, two great forms of such antisystemic movements, one for each main theme of the "French revolutionary turmoil" as it was experienced throughout the world-system. There were the movements organized around the "people" as working class or classes, that is, around class conflict, what in the nineteenth century came to be called first the social movement, then the socialist movements. And there were the movements organized around the "people" as *Volk*, as nation, as speakers of a common language, what came to be known as the nationalist movements.

This is not the place to recount the arduous but effective institutionalization of socialist and nationalist movements as state-level organizations seeking state power within the states in which they were located or which they intended to establish. It is the place to note that, despite their appeal to "universal" values, the movements as they were constructed were all in effect state-level structures, just as the social sciences, despite their appeal to "universal" laws, de facto studied phenomena at the state level. Indeed, it was only the ideologies, of the three new "institutions," that managed to institutionalize itself somewhat at the world level.

What then can we say has been the true legacy of the French revolutionary turmoil? It clearly transformed the "cultural apparatus" of the world-system. But it did so in an extremely ambiguous way. For, on the one hand, one can say that it permitted the efflorescence of all that we have come to associate with the modern world: a passion for change, development, "progress." It is as though the French revolutionary turmoil allowed the world-system to break through a cultural sound barrier and permit the acceleration of the forces of "change" throughout the world that we know occurred.

But, on the other hand, the French revolutionary turmoil, by creating the three great new institutions – the ideologies, the social sciences, the movements – has created the containment and distortion of this process of change, and simultaneously has created the blockages of which the world has become acutely conscious in the last twenty years. The post-1789 consensus on the normality of change and the institutions it bred has now, perhaps, at last ended. Not, however, in 1917, but rather in 1968.

If we are to clarify our options and our utopias in the post-1968 world-system, perhaps it would be useful to reread the trinitarian slogan of the French Revolution: liberty, equality, fraternity. It has been too easy to pose liberty against equality, as in some sense the two great interpretations of the French Revolution have done, each interpretation championing if you will one half of the antinomy. Perhaps the reason the French Revolution did not produce either liberty or equality is that the major power holders and their heirs have successfully maintained that they were separate objectives. This was not, I believe, the view of the unwashed masses.

Fraternity, meanwhile, has always been a pious addition, taken seriously by no one in the whole long post-1789 cultural arena, until in fact 1968. What the "normality of change" has been interpreted, by all and sundry, to mean has been the increased homogenization of the world, in which harmony would come out of the disappearance of real difference. We have of course discovered the brutal fact that the development of the capitalist world-economy has significantly increased the economic and social disparities and therefore the consciousness of differences. Fraternity or, to rename it in the post-1968 manner, comradeship is a construction to be pieced together with enormous difficulty, and yet this fragile prospect is in fact the underpinning of the achievement of liberty/equality.

The French Revolution did not change France very much. It did change the world-system very much. The world-scale institutional legacy of the French Revolution was ambiguous in its effects. The post-1968 questioning of this legacy requires a new reading of the meaning of the popular thrusts that crystallized as the French revolutionary turmoil.

2

Crises: The World-Economy, the Movements, and the Ideologies

By crisis in a historical system I shall mean not conjunctural difficulties within a system but a structural strain so great that the only possible outcome is the disappearance of the system as such, either by a process of gradual disintegration (leading in unpredictable directions) or by a process of relatively controlled transformation (aiming in a predicted direction and therefore its replacement by one or several other systems). In this sense, a crisis is by definition a "transition," and "transitions" in large-scale systems tend to be (probably necessarily) medium-long in length, taking often 100–150 years (Wallerstein 1982). We are now living in such a transition – one from a capitalist world-economy to something else. This something else is probably a socialist world order, but by the nature of crises, it is impossible to do more than suggest probabilities of direction.

Samir Amin (1980; 1982) has suggested that it would be fruitful to observe that, whereas the transition from feudalism to capitalism was relatively controlled, a "revolution" in his language, the transition of Western Antiquity to feudalism had been rather a process of disintegration, or "decadence" in his language. Amin argues that the present crisis seems to have elements of both forms, but will in fact take more the form of a decadence or disintegration than of a controlled transformation. If this is true, this may in fact be actually a positive thing rather than a negative one, as it might at first consideration seem. For it must be remembered that the transition from feudalism to capitalism was indeed controlled – by the old upper strata to preserve their dominance in a new and improved form, precisely because their dominance had been threatened by a disintegration that was beginning. It may well be that disintegration is a mode of transition more favorable to creating a less hierarchical historical system than a controlled transformation, even if we have been taught the opposite for the past century or two (and what, we may ask, were the roots of this ideological presumption?).

I propose, therefore, to explore the actual modalities of transition, and what there is in the "real existing" structure of the capitalist world-economy that makes it more likely that transition will take the form of disintegration rather than one of controlled transformation. Indeed, I will argue that the major contemporary political debate is really over the modality of transition. This will enable me to address myself to the internal debates within the world family of antisystemic movements, and to the acute dilemmas they are currently facing. Finally, I shall suggest that these dilemmas of the movements may in fact be reflected in scientific discourse, in our epistemologies and our ideologies – which are beset by parallel and increasing internal debates.

What are the structural sources of the crisis of our historical system? I see a threefold process, which in summary language we might call the *economic squeeze,* the *political squeeze,* and the *ideological squeeze.* The economic squeeze goes back to two fundamental contradictions of capitalism as a mode of production. One is the contradiction between the thrust, on the one hand, of each entrepreneur to maximize competition and therefore profit by reducing costs (and in particular the real cost of labor), and the impossibility, on the other hand, of realizing profit in an expanding and competitive world-economy if there is insufficient effective world demand. The second contradiction is that caused by the anarchy of production, which has as its consequence the fact that the interests of any given entrepreneur as a competitor tend to run in the opposite direction from his or her interests as a member of a class. The two contradictions are, of course, intimately linked.

The result is well known: a pattern of cyclical expansion and stagnation phases in the world-economy in which the mechanisms that ensure the renewed phases of expansion always involve further commodification of the world-economy. Capitalism, however, is a system in which the base of profit making and the extraction of surplus-value are tied to substantial but nonetheless always partial commodification. As the commodification of land, labor, and capital increases, it moves inexorably toward an asymptote of 100 percent. Once we are in the upper ranges of this curve, each further step begins to put a squeeze on global profit and hence renders very acute the internal competition among the accumulators of capital.[1]

At such a point, it is no longer clear that further expansion of world production would actually increase the pie of the stock of accumulated capital. One sign that this is beginning to happen is the debate over the "limits of growth," a doctrine put forward by one set of accumulators and deeply resisted by a second set.

The process of global accumulation via the commodification of everything has of course had clear political consequences over time. First of all, it is what accounts for the tendency toward the polarization of distribution on a worldwide basis, which I believe a proper quantitative analysis will reveal to be absolute as well as relative. Polarization by itself is not, however, necessarily destabilizing. What creates the political turmoil is, as has long been noted, the corresponding commodification, which concentrates opposition elements physically and eventually removes the veils of the market that exist in the state of partial commodification.

The outcome has been the gradual but relatively spectacular rise of antisystemic movements as an organizational centerpiece of the politics of the world-economy since the middle of the nineteenth century. The family of these movements has grown collectively stronger over time, despite the pattern of systemic recuperation of individual movements (Wallerstein 1980b).

The growing strength of antisystemic movements has engendered, as might be expected, not only a rationalization of repressive machinery (including a strengthening of the formal structures of the interstate system), but also a systematic attempt to defuse these movements through concessions and cooptation. The concessions and cooptation have been directed not toward the masses of the world's work forces, but toward the significant intermediate stratum of cadres, within states and within the world-system as a whole. The revolutionary efforts of the world's work forces have led to significant reforms in the system of world redistribution, increasing the proportion of world surplus-value allocated to the world's intermediate strata.

The political payoff has been largely successful thus far, but it has come to a significant economic price for the largest accumulators of

[1] Insofar as I can understand it, this process seems to be parallel to a very general and recently discovered pattern of mathematical feedback loops wherein the feedback mechanism maintains order until it approaches a certain level, after which a very small further change induces a "chaotic pattern" (Hofstadter 1981).

capital. As long as the absolute level of world surplus-value was in fact increasing, the relative reallocation of shares *among* the world bourgeois strata did not cause too much strain. But the economic squeeze, which we suggest is in the process of coming about through the approach to the asymptote of commodification, must thereupon imply a political squeeze that will lead to acute internal conflicts among the upper strata, both among countries and within countries. This is exacerbated by the fact that as the sharing "at the top" has increased, there have been more and more insistent supplicants demanding to be admitted to that sector of the world population (in the order of perhaps one-tenth of the whole)[2] that shares in one way or another in the distribution of world surplus-value.

Thus we have three groups actively vying with each other to share in the spoils: a very small group who might be called the superaccumulators, the bulk of the cadres, and the supplicants to cadre status and reward. The second group is visibly threatened by the third (for example, the struggles around the New International Economic Order, or the 1982 debate over the US budget), and their struggles account for a good deal of what might be called the normal, open politics of the modern world. But the struggle of the first group (the superaccumulators) with the second group (the bulk of cadres) is no less important, even if it is less open. For the superaccumulators control largely economic sources of power (primarily the transnational corporations), while the bulk of cadres have come to control largely political sources of power (primarily the state-machineries), and the growing tensions are played out largely behind closed doors, as in the infighting over world financial manipulations (concerning currency exchange rates, interest rates, and the like).

The main point I am trying to make is that, as the economic processes move toward the asymptote of 100 percent commodification and therefore toward the constraints on the rate of profit, the political processes are pressing toward a three-way acute structural division *among the upper strata* for the division of a surplus whose rate of increase may already be declining and even whose absolute value (per capita) may soon begin to decline.

---

[2] Nathan Keyfitz (1976) has estimated the size of the "world middle class" today to be one-seventh of the whole. He has used as his criterion the proportion of persons having income over the US poverty line. Using a slightly more restrictive definition of those who are living off surplus-value, I arrive at my crude estimate of one in ten.

One would think that this infighting thus presents a marvelous opportunity for the antisystemic movement of the world-system. The defenders of order will increasingly be at war with each other, hence objectively weakened in their struggle against the forces of world revolution. No doubt it has been a marvelous opportunity, and no doubt the world's antisystemic movements have been taking advantage of it – but to a much lesser extent than one would have anticipated. As with so many phenomena that characterize the capitalist world-economy (such as commodification and urbanization), the thing to note about the strength of the world family of antisystemic movements, once one has made the primary observation that the secular curve is upward, is not that the rate of growth has been so rapid but that it has been so slow.

Yes, there has been uprising after uprising, mobilization after mobilization, victory after victory of antisystemic movements for the whole of the twentieth century. But why not many more? Why have the walls of Jericho not crumbled before the repeated blasts of the horns? There are only two possible answers to this question. One is the counsel of patience. The blasts were made too soon; the "objective conditions" have not yet been met; the walls are indeed crumbling, but slowly. In many ways, this has been the historic answer of both the Second and Third Internationals. Persist, they have said, in the appointed strategy, and a world shall rise on new foundations.

There is, however, a second possible answer, whose implications are at least worth exploring. The antisystemic movements are themselves institutional products of the capitalist world-economy, formed in the crucible of its contradictions, permeated by its metaphysical presuppositions, constrained by the working of its other institutions. Antisystemic movements are not free-floating avenging angels sent by Jehovah; they are mundane products of the real world. No doubt you will immediately think – of course, but this is a banality. It is not such a banality, however, for the very language in which we usually discuss the limitations of antisystemic movements – for example, the term "revisionism" – is a language of purity appropriate only to avenging angels.

Let us, therefore, explore the ways in which the operations of other institutions in the world-economy have systematically slowed the pace and distorted the impact of the antisystemic movements. The first and perhaps primary distortion derives from the fact that no enduring and relatively "successful" antisystemic movement has been constructed anywhere within the world-system that did not include within its leadership, and even to a significant degree in its

base, elements that belong to that third sector among the upper
strata – the aspirant cadres. (They have, of course, also included
elements from the other two sectors, but the latter have not been
numerically or organizationally significant.)

The fact that aspirant cadres have played a major role in antisystemic movements is an empirical statement. It is probably
theoretically deducible as well. In the first place, the antisystemic
movements have been by and large bureaucratic organizations and,
as such, have required skills that are unequally distributed among
the world's populations. Aspirant cadres tended to have these skills
and therefore often seemed welcome recruits. Secondly, in their
mobilization phase, antisystemic movements often found it tactically necessary in the short run to engage in trans-class alliances, and
such alliances then had consequences for the longer-run structuring
of antisystemic movements. Thirdly, when mobilization activities
led to imminent success, defined as effective participation of some
kind in state power, the movements by that very fact attracted an
opportunistic influx, which was massive and hard to stem. Furthermore, few movements thought it tactically wise even to try to
stem this influx, since the influx itself guaranteed the "success."
This is the so-called bandwagon effect.

Were all this not enough, the seizure of office (partial or even
total) within a given state-machinery represented only a partial
increase in real power. It also represented in some respects a
decrease in real power, since movements in power become im-
minently subject to the constraints on state-machineries inherent in
the working of the interstate system. One of the many forms that
such *raison d'état* takes is the rise in relative influence within antisystemic movements of aspirant cadres, and even their fresh re-
cruitment. This becomes part of the price of retaining state office
for the movement.

Finally, it should not be left out of consideration that what is
most dangerous to the superaccumulators is the disintegrative effect
of mass mobilization itself – both in the long run as politically
threatening to the system, and in the short run as causing turbulence and therefore interference with the smooth functioning
of world productive processes. While movements may have been
ignored in early stages of mobilization, there comes a point at
which prior mobilization has generated sufficient momentum to
seem to be able to ignite a real and prolonged political explosion,
one that could easily escape the control of the specific antisystemic
movement itself. Under such conditions, it often has seemed

advantageous both to the superaccumulators and to the leaders of the movement (themselves at least in part aspirant cadres) to strike a deal, precisely intended to cut off the process of mobilization. Under such circumstances, the arrival in state office of the anti-systemic movement would come in a way that maximizes the role, influence, and even the numbers of the aspirant cadre element in the movement. What the superaccumulators hoped to achieve was the transformation of the aspirant cadres into the major mechanism of political control of their own mass base.

Given all these structural factors at play, the surprising element to explain is no longer the slowness of the advance of antisystemic movements. Rather we should now look to explaining how they have advanced at all.

If in fact, as the governing ideology of the capitalist world-economy would have it, it were really true that the distributional gap was closing, it is hard to see where there would have remained a mass base of antisystemic movements. The fact is, however, that within the world-system as a whole, the gap has been widening and not closing. And it was this objective reality – the polarization of the world class structure, itself fed by the process of commodification, in turn fed by the driving motor of the endless accumulation of capital – that provided the material base for persistent political mobilization. Polarization tended to politicize the world's work forces, and tended to make the very organization of antisystemic movements an excellent tool for aspirant cadres to pursue their quite different self-interests. Hence, far from going away, the multiple mobilizations have been accelerating in number, duration, and quality, and it is hard to see anything that will counteract this trend in the immediate future.

The ambivalent role of the aspirant cadres has become ever more obvious by the mere repetition of the many instances of anti-systemic movements moving through their natural history. To some extent, these instances have bred disillusionment. But they have also bred experience and have encouraged experimentation with new tactics intended to avoid known pitfalls. There has been a decreasing quotient of naiveté among the militants of antisystemic movements.

What we have, then, is two trends within the world family of antisystemic movements themselves, moving in opposite directions. On the one hand, there has been an ever-increasing role within the movements for aspirant cadres whose activities in fact tended to strengthen, not weaken, the operations of the world-system (tempered somewhat nonetheless by the increasing world-systemic economic squeeze, which has made their upward mobility more difficult). On the other hand, there has been an ever-increasing base for antisystemic movements, and the historical process itself has been breeding greater sophistication, hence greater political strength, among the militants.

These two contradictory trends are in turn leading to an acute internal rattling in the world family of antisystemic movements. Thus it is that we can say that there are two political expressions of the systemic crisis that the capitalist world-economy is now traversing. There is first of all the intensified internal conflict among the three sectors of the upper strata which, when added to the endemic competition among entrepreneurs within capitalism as a system, may begin to approach the level of internecine strife among upper strata that was one of the celebrated features of the crisis of feudalism in the 1300–1450 period.

There is, however, also a real turning point in the evolution of the world family of antisystemic movements. The question in effect is which of these two contradictory trends is stronger. If it is the trend that is leading to the strengthening of the role within the movements of aspirant cadres, then the movements may come to be the major mechanism of the "controlled transformation" of the world capitalist system into something else that, however different, would permit the continuation in another guise of hierarchial exploitation of the world labor force. This is, let us remember, essentially what happened in the transition from feudalism to capitalism.

On the other hand, the trend of growing sophistication among the militants may gain the upper hand. If this is the case, it will probably take the form of a reevaluation of the basic strategy of the antisystemic movements that they have followed since the mid-nineteenth century – transition primarily through the successive acquisitions of state-office in the multiple states of the interstate system.

Before entering into what might be an alternative strategy, we must first review the third expression of the systemic crisis: the questioning of the basic metaphysical paradigms that have been the consequence and bulwark of the emergence of capitalism as a world-system. The system of knowledge that informed the modern world had no doubt a long and interesting heritage, but there seems little question that it was codified only in the seventeenth century with the intellectual triumphs of Newton, Locke, and Descartes: the conviction that by reason one could arrive at truth, at certitude, in the form of universal laws (Randall 1940; Hazard 1973).

It was in the physical sciences that this doctrine of universalism received its original justification via the concrete results it would offer in terms of the real world-economy. But from the beginning its implications for the social sciences were profound. As Randall points out:

> The two leading ideas of the eighteenth century, Nature and Reason ... derived their meaning from the natural sciences, and, carried over to man, led to the attempt to discover a social physics.... In all things the newly invented social sciences were assimilated to the physical sciences.... The rational order of the world, as expressed in the Newtonian system of nature, scientific method, and scientific ideals ... [was applied] in the comprehensive science of human nature that embraced a rational science of the mind, of society, of business, of government, of ethics, and of international relations. (1940: 255)

We have all lived on this basic legacy for three centuries.

One of the problems of the specialization of knowledge is not that specialists are unacquainted with other fields of knowledge, but that, on the whole, they have perforce an antiquated view of them. Hence it is that the very moment when the Newtonian world-view came under fundamental attack within the physical sciences, in the period following the Second World War, marked the highpoint of the influence of this world-view within the social sciences.

But the inexorable impact of the structural crisis of the world-economy has begun to force open a discussion of these premises of universalism, which are deeply ensconced in all the institutional structures of the world-economy, including to some extent even in the very antisystemic movements that exist presumably for the purpose of transforming the system. When social scientists challenge the metaphysical premises of the existing system, they are attacked as ideologues. It is harder to do this with physical scientists, which makes their attack so much more important and dangerous.

One of the spokespersons of this new basic atack, and one very aware of its implications for the social sciences, is Ilya Prigogine and his so-called Brussels school. Prigogine won the Nobel Prize in Chemistry in 1977 precisely for his work on "dissipative structures." Let us review some of his arguments in order to observe how close they are, in slightly different language, to the basic questioning of universalism that is occurring in the social sciences.

Dissipative structures, in contrast to equilibrium structures, are those that are maintained by the constant dissipation of energy and hence manifest self-organization. Prigogine argues that dissipative structures studied in physical and chemical systems evolve over time:

> In one phase the system behaves deterministically according to the average values involved, while in the other a fluctuation is amplified until it changes the entire structure, whereupon the former phase recommences in different circumstances. (Prigogine et al. 1977: 2)

What do we know of such dissipative structures? Unlike equilibrium structures, they have "a coherent behavior involving the cooperation of a large number of units" (Prigogine et al. 1977: 21). They thus "appear as a 'totality' with dimensions imposed by their own underlying mechanism." Furthermore, the dimensions are crucial. Small systems are dominated by boundary conditions. Only when the system is sufficiently large does it "acquire a degree of autonomy with respect to the outside world" (1977: 31). Unlike an equilibrium structure, in which, after equilibrium is reached, the initial conditions are "forgotten," in dissipative structures, "the macroscopic order which arises after an instability is determined by the fastest growing fluctuation." Prigogine calls this kind of order "order through fluctuation" (Prigogine et al. 1977: 38). He sums all this up in what he calls "the language of social sciences":

> Function can be viewed as being the "microstructure" of the system while the large scale spatial or spatiotemporal organization corresponds to a "macrostructure." A fluctuation leads to a local modification of the microstructure which, if the regulation mechanisms prove inadequate, will change the macrostructure. This in turn determines the "spectrum" of the future fluctuations that may occur.... Far from opposing "chance" and "necessity," we see that both aspects are essential in the description of nonlinear systems far from equilibrium. (Prigogine et al. 1977: 39)

It should be clear how this corresponds to the kind of holistic framework using a large-scale unit of analysis, paying close attention simultaneously to cycles (his microstructure, his necessity) and trends (his macrostructure, his chance), that we have been advocating. Lest anyone be unclear how far this is from the Newtonian model, Prigogine spells it out in various ways. There is first of all the issue of equilibrium structures. In classical thermodynamics, "nonequilibrium was considered as a perturbation preventing the appearance of structure identified with the order at equilibrium"

(Prigogine et al. 1977: 17). By contrast, it is now argued that nonequilibrium is a more usual source of order. Prigogine argues that the basic separation of "events" and "regularities" of classical physics, in which laws of dynamics pretended only to account for regularities, relegating events to "initial conditions" about which physics had no view, led inexorably to viewing living processes as a struggle "to maintain the highly improbable conditions which permit its existence." Quite the contrary, it is now argued, living processes and initial conditions "follow from the laws of physics appropriate to specific nonlinear interactions and to conditions far from equilibrium." Hence, a social structure is a phenomenon "both influenced by and [acting upon its] environment" and "occurring spontaneously in open systems maintained far from equilibrium" (Prigogine et al. 1977: 18–19).

Second, there is the question of the framework of analysis. Classical physics "conceived of units as having priority compared with interactions.... Each unit evolves separately as if it were alone in the world." But in fact, it is argued, individuals "are not separable from the entirety of their interactions, except in extremely simplified cases." Note then the radical conclusion: "The systems of classical physics correspond to borderline cases, and the modes of description appropriate to them generally do not permit extrapolation" (Prigogine et al. 1982: 61).

Third, there is the question of time. Time did not exist for classical physics (nor indeed for Einstein); put technically, time was thought to be reversible. Time was merely external duration. Against this, it is argued, there exists another time, time internal to structures. Modern physics has to recognize a "plurality of times" subtly interlinked – irreversible time moving towards equilibria, cyclical time nourished by the world in which it exists, the bifurcation time of evolutions through instability and the amplification of fluctuations. The classical science of flux is contrasted with "the science of turbulence," the science that demonstrates that "trouble can give birth to things, to nature, and to man" (Prigogine and Stengers 1979: 275, 281).

Fourth, Newtonian physics proclaimed the "theoretical extraterritoriality" of the scientists, which is now thought to be both theoretically and culturally impossible (Prigogine and Stengers 1979: 23). Far from social science having to model itself on physical science, it is now argued that all science is "human science, science made by man for man" (Prigogine and Stengers 1979: 281).

Finally, universalism is directly rejected. Science, recognizing time, innovation, and qualitative diversity as logically inherent in nature, "has concluded *theoretically* that it is impossible to reduce nature to the simplicity of a reality governed by universal laws" (Prigogine and Stengers 1979: 64). The Heisenberg Uncertainty Principle does not apply merely to microscopic phenomena. "The macroscopic equations themselves contain the element of stochasticity which leads to 'macroscopic indeterminacy'" (Prigogine et al. 1977: 57). We are thus adjured to reject the concept of science as the "disenchantment of the world" and to appreciate it as the "reenchantment of the world."

This massive questioning of the metaphysics underpinning our world-system has not evolved in a void. It has evolved from an intellectual squeeze, the impossibility of fitting an explanation of the now socially visible temporal transformations, the structural crisis in which we are living, into the ideological presuppositions of a universalism that extrapolated from limited conditions (physical, biological, and social) and, by seeking to interpret them as universal laws, sought to eliminate or slow down the processes of bifurcating turbulence (to use Prigogine's phrase).

Needless to say, the proponents of this metaphysical regeneration are still in a distinct minority, not only in the narrower arena that intellectuals inhabit but in the larger social arena. Nor, by the very logic of the position of those who reject universalism, can we clearly project where this scientific renewal is heading. But Prigogine is quite right to assert that, for precisely these reasons, "The role of knowledge is becoming more important. We are only at the beginning, at the prehistory of our insights" (Prigogine et al. 1982: 66).

The resolution of this scientific-metaphysical-ideological transition is, however, in my view, clearly linked to the resolution of the internal rattling of the antisystemic movements, and the two together will determine the direction in which the structural transition from a capitalist world-economy to something else will move. Hence, I am arguing that although we are indeed in a systemic crisis, this crisis is a long one that is unfolding at a visible but less hasty pace than we might wish. We can guess about its direction but we cannot be certain. We can nonetheless influence its direction. This systemic crisis plays itself out in the economic arena to be sure, in the long-term squeeze on the prospects for the further unending accumulation of capital.

But it also plays itself out in two other arenas, where we may more easily intrude our collective will, our energies, and such wisdom as we have. On the one hand, there is the political arena of the antisystemic movements. And on the other hand, there is the cultural arena of the metaphysical presuppositions of knowledge.

Both these latter arenas are in turmoil and will be in ever greater turmoil in the next 30 to 50 years. In both, the outcome of the turmoil is unsure. What seems to me to be on the agenda in the first case is a reconsideration of the basic strategy of the movements. What seems to me on the agenda in the second case is a reformulation of our basic conceptual apparatus, including the modes of measurement.

Let me, therefore, conclude with a brief specification of these two agendas for thought and action. The basic strategy of the world's antisystemic movements was set in the nineteenth century. It involved the creation of organizations that would take as their objective the obtaining of control over the state-machineries. This is the kernel on which virtually all the movements, of whatever tendency, tended to agree. We have already reviewed the ambiguities of this strategy, and the ways in which it permitted those in power in the world-system to negate partially the undoubted advantages that obtaining state-office involved for the antisystemic movements. We have also reviewed the increasing skepticism this strategy has aroused among the militants and potential militants of these movements.

What was limited in this strategy was, if I may say so, its Newtonian world-view. It viewed states as relatively autonomous structures and political power as located exclusively or at least primarily in the state-machineries. Both presumptions are empirically full of holes, and in their analyses (but seldom their strategic options), the antisystemic movements knew it. First of all, the state-structures are embedded (the word is not too strong) in the interstate system, and the degree of their autonomy is strictly limited. Second and perhaps even more important, it is not the case that the only locus of political power is in control of the state-machinery. Surely materialists, as many of these movements claimed to be, should know this. Do not transnational corporations have real political power? Of course. Their power is, to be sure, to some degree, their influence over state-machineries. But surely that is the least of it. Their real political power is their command over productive resources and their ability to make decisions about these resources – for example, to relocate them, or to withdraw them from use.

This somewhat obvious example should, however, give us an important clue. The elements of real political power are scattered in many loci. The state-machineries are an important such locus, but far from the only one. We have no quantitative measures of power, but I would guess that state-machineries account for less than half of the world-economy's real power concentrations, and if anything I suspect this estimate is high, not low. Power lies in control of economic institutions. Power lies in the control of veto-structures that have the power to disrupt. Power lies in the control of cultural institutions. Power lies in the movements themselves.

Yes, you will say, but the movements always knew this. Yes, they did, except that they always believed that power other than in state-machineries was a lesser form required *in order that* one be in a position to control the state. The strategic priority of achieving power in the state-structure was always there. It was the one objective that was always primary, and always held on to at all cost. Thus did all the movements in essence reject Gramsci's advice not to get mired down in the war of position and to remember the utility of the war of maneuver. What is on the agenda for the movements is, it seems to me, the development of a strategy of maneuver that relegates the acquisition of power in state-machineries to the level of a tactic, to a position into which one moves and out of which one may move, since it is in the process of *movement*, of mobilization, that the really constructive power of the movements lies. It is in the acceleration of the decadence of the present system and not in its controlled transformation, to use Amin's distinction, that the prospects of creating a truly socialist world-historical system lie.

This brings us to the intellectual reconceptualization. The antisystemic movements have bought far too large a portion of the universalist ideology (and its concurrent historiography). They have been critical, of course, but not critical enough. For example, they have analyzed capitalism as a fixed set of relations and structures that is there or not there, whereas in fact it is an incessantly evolving, unique single system whose usual descriptive parameters (free enterprise, the free market, free wage labor, alienable land, commodity exchange) are only, have only been, and will ever only be partially realized.

The institutional structures of the capitalist world-economy (the states, the classes, the peoples, the households, the movements) have been analyzed as though they were analytically self-contained entities that evolve from historical system to historical system in an evolutionary pattern parallel to that of the system as a whole. Thus we have conceptual aberrations such as "capitalist state," meaning that there is something analytically constant in the term "state" such that feudal state, capitalist state, and socialist state represent somehow three species of a single genus. In fact, the institutional structures of the capitalist world-economy are its collective product and cannot be analyzed, cannot even be identified, outside of an explanation of the operations of this particular large-scale whole.

What is, therefore, on the agenda is redoing the work of the social sciences of the last 200 years, perhaps not from scratch but almost so. The data we have collected are at best only partially relevant. The conceptual categories need to be built up anew. The methods of our research must be redefined in terms of this new objective: explaining a concrete, large-scale system that itself comes into existence, develops over time, and at a certain point enters into structural crisis. We must do this resisting reification, but nonetheless using concepts, which always involves reification. One may call this historical sociology if one wishes or sociological history or anything else, provided one realizes this is not a sub-discipline but the entire enterprise.

The two tasks – reorienting the strategy of the antisystemic movements and reorienting the strategy of social science – are equally difficult, equally important, and I believe intimately linked. Neither can succeed without the success of the other. The two tasks will interweave themselves in practice. Will the tasks be achieved? In my view, the struggle is an uphill battle, but the material base for succeess is there. This is, however, a guess, at best a probability. To repeat Prigogine's words, "We are only at the beginning, at the prehistory of our insights."

Part II

The Concept of Development

3

The Industrial Revolution:
Cui Bono?

One of the key concepts of the universalist thought that has been
produced by the West in the modern world is that of the (and/or
an) "industrial revolution." I wish to raise some questions about
the utility of this concept and its social function – both for social
science and for social ideology.

First of all, what is it supposed to mean? D. C. Coleman has
pointed out that the phrase covers three quite separate meanings. It
means firstly any sort of innovation which leads to the increased
mechanization of one or several branches of production. It is in this
sense that we can speak for example about the European industrial
revolution of the thirteenth century. It means secondly the so-called
first "real" industrial revolution, that of Great Britain, which is
usually dated as occurring more or less between 1760 and 1830. In
this sense, some authors suggest it represents a fundamental world
social transformation comparable to the Neolithic or agricultural
revolution of 5,000–8,000 years ago. It means thirdly all subsequent
national economic transformations considered to be similar to that
of Great Britain, and which are supposed to be in one way or
another a conscious imitation of Great Britain (Coleman 1966:
334–35).[1] It seems to me that the first usage is a mode of denying
the legitimacy of the second usage, and it would be simpler to say
so outright, while the third usage makes no sense unless one

---

[1] See also David Landes (1969: 42). "The technological changes that we
denote as the Industrial Revolution implied a far more drastic break with
the past than anything since the invention of the wheel."

already accepts the legitimacy of the second usage. Ergo the key usage is the second, the industrial revolution as the "first" great national transformation, the explanatory nexus for the analysis of the modern world.

The majority of authors who write on this subject pose the issues in the following way: why did this first industrial revolution take place in Great Britain (or England) rather than somewhere else? In fact, this somewhere else that is referred to is almost always France. There are three sorts of answers, often intertwined one with the other: a technological-economic explanation, a socio-political one, a "cultural" one. That is to say, usually the analysts seek to uncover in the specific traits of the two countries (comparing one to the other and to third countries) the factor or factors which could account for such a "revolution" or "take-off" (to revive the rather felicitous metaphor of Rostow, which was over-used and then discarded).

All the analyses begin by observing one basic fact. There was in that period of time a visible economic growth which consisted in a flourishing cotton textile industry (and also iron industry), a rise in agricultural production, an increase in population and its relative urbanization, all of these factors, as they were found in Great Britain at that time, were qualitatively in advance of the combination of analogous changes that were occurring in France at the same time, or had occurred anywhere else up to that time (and implicitly also those that occurred elsewhere later). Obviously, deciding exactly when quantity becomes quality is a thorny question, but that is an issue we will not discuss here. Although everyone agrees that it is extremely difficult to isolate a single decisive factor, nonetheless almost everyone gives priority sooner or later to his or her favorite explanatory variable. Deane for example refers to "the cluster of innovations" (Deane 1979: 106), that is, not one but several innovations, and not merely inventions but their utilization as innovations. Others speak rather of the new way of organizing manufacturing, the factory system which permitted the efficient use of machinery.[2] There are those who emphasize the existence of demand (either in the home market or abroad) great enough to attract innovations.[3] And on the other side, there are those who say

[2]   This is for example the central thesis of Paul Mantoux.
[3]   The key role of home demand is argued for example by D. E. C. Eversley (1967). The opposing view, emphasizing foreign demand, is put forward by W. A. Cole and Phyllis Deane (1966: 51) "The British case is the classic prototype of an industrial revolution based on overseas trade."

it is the availability of capital (either because of the low national interest rate or because of the primitive accumulation of capital of external and colonial origins) which explains the possibility of innovations. (Crouzet 1972).

Needless to say, each of these explanations has been refuted repeatedly and successively by someone or other. Bergier (1973: 42) suggests that far less production than is usually assumed took place at that time in factories. Hobsbawm is very skeptical about the presumed technological superiority of Great Britain,[4] and he receives very strong support in Daumas's magisterial *Histoire Générale des Techniques*, in which Daumas argues the thesis that, from the standpoint of technology, the moment of decisive change was in the mid-sixteenth rather than the mid-eighteenth century. The significant changes of the latter period were in "the change in the social organization of production, in the new system of commercial distribution, and in the system structures, rather than in a rapid transformation of the means of production" (Daumas 1965: xii). As for the famous home market, Mathias suggests that taxation was a particularly great handicap, especially in the home market, and more so in Britain than in France (Mathias 1969; Mathias and O'Brien 1976). For the moment, I shall not seek to evaluate the worth of these various objections. Rather I proceed.

Whatever be the nature of the explanations at this level, these technological-economic differences in turn need to be accounted for, leading to an analysis of the social structure or the politico-social structure. There are two main varieties of such analysis. One emphasizes the basic agricultural structure, contrasting a continuing "feudal" structure in France with an already "capitalist" one in England. The second, which is to be sure not totally separable from the first, looks at state structures and contrasts the presumed nonintervention of the British state in the economy with French absolutism. No one doubts that France and Great Britain were not identical in their structures in the eighteenth century, but in my view the differences have been vastly exaggerated.

Bloch reminds us that "the attempts at agrarian reform, via a break with collective servitudes, were a Europe-wide phenomenon

---

[4] "Whatever the British advance was due to, it was not scientific and technological superiority.... Fortunately few intellectual refinements were necessary to make the Industrial revolution.... Given the right conditions, the technical innovations of the Industrial Revolution practically made themselves, except perhaps in the chemical industry" (Hobsbawm 1962: 47–48).

in the eighteenth century" (Bloch 1930: 511), even if they succeeded somewhat more in Great Britain. Polanyi details how the Speenhamland law blocked the creation of a true labor market in England precisely between 1795 and 1834.[5] On the other hand, Le Roy Ladurie minimizes the economic significance of the feudal aspects of French rural life in the eighteenth century:

> As such, feudalism was in fact critical, in terms of the prestige, the desires and the pleasures of power experienced by the dominant strata; it was capable as well, as any organ of power, of generating indirect monetary advantage; but in the annual balance-sheet of the domains which continued by tradition to be called "seigniories," strictly speaking it counted for little, even very little. (Le Roy Ladurie 1975: 430)

For Le Roy Ladurie, as for Bloch[6] and Labrousse before him, the seigniory of the eighteenth century was first and foremost "one of the essential matrices of agricultural capitalism" (Le Roy Ladurie 1975: 534).

As for the state, it was its *insufficient* strength in France in the eighteenth century which accounts for her lesser ability to revise the rules of property compared to Britain where "faced with enclosure, the village had no freedom; once the Commons decided, the village had to obey" (Bloch 1930: 543). Scholars repeat, like a litany, that the British industrial revolution "occurred spontaneously, without ... government assistance" (Deane 1979: 2), but the very same

---

[5]   Karl Polanyi (1957: 83) draws the following conclusion: "[Before 1837] industrial capitalism as a social system cannot be said to have existed [in Great Britain]." Nor should we forget the picturesque analysis of Thorold Rogers about *The Act of Settlement* which governed the English labor market from 1666 to the enactment of Speenhamland in 1795: "The law of settlement not only fixed the tenant to the soil, but enabled the opulent landowner to rob his neighbour and to prematurely wear out the labourer's health and strength. All this, too, was done when the patriots and the placemen chattered about liberty and arbitrary administration, and fine ladies and gentlemen talked about the rights of men and Rousseau and the French Revolution, and Burke and Sheridan were denouncing the despotism of Hastings. Why at his own door Burke might have seen serfs who had less liberty than those Rohillas, whose wrongs he described so dramatically." Cited by Pierre Mantoux (1928: 444).
[6]   "In a world more and more dominated by a capitalist form of economy, the fact is that some favors, originally accorded to the heads of a few small self-sufficient village communities, took on bit by bit a value that had been hitherto unsuspected" (Bloch 1930: 517).

author, Deane, admits in the very same book that "as industrialization proceeded the state was intervening more deeply and more effectively in the economy than it had ever done before"[7] (Deane 1979: 23). If there was a political difference between France and Great Britain it was less in the role of the state than in the structure of internal political alliances. In France, the intermediate rural strata, the *fermiers*, allied themselves more with the small peasants than with the large landowners, a consequence according to Le Roy Ladurie not of the absence but of the presence of economic growth.[8]

For some scholars, in any case, the purely economic or sociopolitical aspects hide a still deeper reality or rather a still deeper "rationality." Landes is one of the spokesmen of this viewpoint. Analyzing the substitution of coal for wood in Great Britain, he asserts:

> Yet it is clear that the readiness to accept coal was itself indicative of a deeper rationality; such nations as France, confronted with the same choice, *obdurately* rejected coal – even where there were strong pecuniary incentives to switch over to the cheaper fuel. (Landes 1969: 54) [my emphasis]

Now we have it – the obdurate French and the British thirsty for progress. Crouzet can remind us that British industrialists of the

---

[7]   She adds on free trade (Deane 1979: 203), "The long wars which began in 1793, however, reversed the trend towards Free Trade by introducing a multitude of new uncertainties into the economic situation and by forcing the government to raise revenue-yielding tariffs in the effort to finance the war. The economic uncertainty and the search for government revenue continued into the post-war aftermath and although statesmen reared in the doctrine of Adam Smith paid lip-service to a more liberal commercial policy, producers had lost their nerve." See also Barry Supple (1973: 316), "The state did play an important, albeit indirect, role in the pioneer Industrial Revolution."

[8]   Le Roy Ladurie argues that France faced a choice, whose outcome was far from preordained, between a political alliance set he calls the English solution and the other one actually chosen which he calls the French solution: "A *unique* event as such, the French Revolution was not an inevitable event, or at least it would be difficult to prove that it was.... It was an expression of the final exasperated behavior of a society.... The French Revolution, in the countryside, was a direct consequence of the economic growth of the eighteenth century, even or especially when this growth was momentarily checked in the 1780s. It was sign of rupture and simultaneously of continuity (Le Roy Ladurie 1975: 591).

time, once they had made it, sought the "easy life" as quickly as possible, buying large estates on which they built castles (Crouzet 1972: 189). Goubert can on the other hand assure us that:

> A large proportion of [French] nobility, whether newly ennobled or of very old families, entered early on into the arena of the economy of the future, preparing its "take-off." Even in economic terms, progress was not the attribute of some class that preceded it. (Goubert 1969a: 234)

All in vain! Deane returns to the same theme-song about values: "One condition of an industrial revolution ... is a change in the attitude of mind of the representative producer" (Deane 1979: 123).

This example demonstrates the degree to which France in the Franco-British comparison plays the role of a symbolic target. Feudal France vs. capitalist, liberal, technocratic Great Britain is East vs. West, the barbarian who fails vs. the progressive bearer of civilization, poverty vs. happy prosperity, Caliban vs. Prospero. Let us see if there is not another way to pose the basic historiographical issue. Suppose we argue that between France and Great Britain, at the end of the eighteenth and beginning of the nineteenth centuries, there is very little difference in terms of the organization of the economy, and hence no difference to explain. Obviously, this is not the standard viewpoint, but it is nonetheless not one without some scholarly support.

First of all for the prior period, 1700–75, Ralph Davis has observed (and here there is widespread agreement) that the industrial growth of the two countries was more or less parallel, and even was greater in France towards the middle of the century (Davis 1973: 301). Indeed, Claude Fohlen calls the middle decades of the *eighteenth* century the time of French take-off which "comes just after that of the English" (Fohlen 1973: part 1, 12). I know there are contrary arguments. But are they carefully considered? For example Goubert, speaking of French economic expansion in the eighteenth century, sums up the situation in this manner:

> No "industrial revolution," no real "take-off," as long as the economy remained dominated by agriculture, as long as textiles (a consumer good) was far more important than metallurgy, as long as transport of goods continued to be slow and onerous, as long as the great majority of enterprises were still family-owned and small, as long as a pure stratum of wage workers, a true "proletariat," a

class-conscious "working class" did not exist in a concentrated mass. (Goubert 1969b: 234)

But for each of these items one could say the same for Great Britain, at the very least before 1830. Its economy was still primarily agricultural[9] (how in any case does one calculate the "domination" of a sector?); textiles were more important than metallurgy; its enterprises were mostly family-owned.

There is another way of approaching this issue. Morineau presents in great detail all the reasons why one should be skeptical that there was any agricultural revolution in France in the eighteenth century. Then, coming to the comparison with England, he finds the situation virtually the same, concluding:

> The take-off of the Western economy does not have its roots in an "agricultural revolution." It seems dubious to use this term to designate, even in England, a degree of progress so somnolent, so frightened by the very first frost? (Morineau 1971: 85)

In my opinion, we are stretching things to see at any cost some difference between British and French growth rates – in industry or agriculture – that could be called revolutionary, or even qualitatively significant. I will go further. There are scholars who will agree with me about Britain and France being about the same, but who insist all the same on an industrial revolution of northwest Europe in this era. But is it so clear that the changes at all levels that occurred over these 60–70 years were more significant, quantitatively or qualitatively, than what took place in several other epochs, earlier and later, that is, in every Kondratieff upturn? For my part, I agree with Schumpeter:

> It is necessary to guard against possible misunderstanding by making quite clear in what sense we accept the term industrial revolution and its implications. The writer agrees with modern economic historians who frown upon it. It is not only outmoded, but also misleading, or even false on principle, if it is intended to convey either the idea that what it designates was a unique event or series of events that created a new economic and social order, or the idea that, unconnected with previous developments, it suddenly burst upon the

---

[9] Louis Bergeron (1978: 226–27) asserts about agriculture: "Finally, if there was an 'agricultural revolution,'" was it English? In the eighteenth century, England merely overcame its backwardness vis-a-vis Flanders and Holland."

world in the last two or three decades of the eighteenth century.... We put that particular industrial revolution on a par with at least two similar events which preceded it and at least two more which followed it. (Schumpeter 1939: 253)[10]

Obviously, I shall not push my argument to say that nothing of importance happened at all. That Great Britain in the course of the nineteenth century dominated the world-economy and was its hegemonic power is an uncontested verity. But what conclusions shall we draw from this fact? In 1763, Great Britain had more or less definitively won its century-long war with France for the control of the high seas and therefore of extra-European commerce (Wallerstein 1980c: ch. 6). Despite this, French domestic output continued to surpass British in the 1780s, and "by an even greater amount than [it] did at the death of Louis XIV" (O'Brien and Keyder 1978: 60). If British productivity was slightly higher than French, it is nonetheless true that the two countries remained "essentially at the same stage" (Cole and Deane 1966: 11) of economic development in the 1780s. What brought about a change in this situation subsequently? The answer is simple: the French Revolution and the Napoleonic wars, a factor of economic advance for Britain and of regression for France. That the wars of 1793–1815 had this double effect seems to be certain – the consequence of deprivation of raw material resources for France, encouragement of agricultural innovation for Britain (Fohlen 1973: 13; Deane 1973: part I, 208; Cole 1952: 69) – to which the French Revolution added another element, a sort of sociological brake. As Eric Hobsbawm puts it, the French Revolution "took away with the hand of Robespierre much of what it gave with the hand of the Constituent Assembly."[11] It was Adolphe Thiers who expressed this most succinctly:

---

[10] Coleman (1966: 350) attempts to refute these arguments of Schumpeter, but I do not find Coleman convincing.
[11] (Hobsbawm 1962: 231). He explains this as follows (p. 93): "The Jacobins abolished all remaining feudal rights without indemnity, improved the small buyer's chance to purchase the forfeited land of emigres, and abolished slavery in the French colonies.... [They thereby] established the impregnable citadel of small and middle peasant proprietors, small craftsmen and shopkeepers, economically retrogressive but passionately devoted to Revolution and Republic, which has dominated the country's life ever since. The capitalist transformation of agriculture and small enterprise, the essential condition for rapid economic development, was slowed to a crawl."

We did not win the Battle of Trafalgar. We did not remain supreme
on the seas and we do not have 200 million consumers, as England
does. That is the whole secret of our inferiority. (Cited in O'Brien
and Keyder 1978: 76)

How did this come about? I think the appropriate historiographical question for this era is not how come Great Britain made the
world's first industrial revolution? but a quite different one: how
come, in the framework of a capitalist world-economy that had
been in existence already for over 200 years, Great Britain, at the
moment of this world-economy's second great geographical expansion, could become its hegemonic power for a short time, as
the United Provinces was earlier and the United States became
subsequently?

It may well be that the answers to this reformulated question are
not so different as those given to the classical question. The manner
of posing it pushes us, however, to looking more closely at a few
frequently neglected variables, which include the role of internal
repression in Great Britain, the impact of the Haitian revolution,
the renewal or increase of cereals production in peripheral zones of
Europe – and the list could continue.

But it is not only to include these largely neglected explanatory
variables that I wish to reformulate the question. It is also because
it has different implications for the present. If in the nineteenth
century the concept of an industrial revolution served the liberals as
a not very hidden ideological justification of British hegemony and
served the socialists as a slightly more subtle denegation of French
bourgeois revolutions, in the twentieth century this concept plays a
quite different role. For liberals and European social-democrats
alike, it is a way of placing the burden of guilt on the Third World
for its inability to match the West's economic living standards
unless they are ready to assimilate assiduously Western culture
(once again the East aligning itself with the more advanced West).
As for the militants of national liberation and revolutionary socialist movements, the concept has become a trap, virtually a definition
of socialism itself. Instead of seeing the struggle for socialism as a
struggle to transform the world capitalist system, with its world-
economy based on the law of value and its superstructural interstate
system based on the presumed sovereignty of states and balance of
power, they throw themselves willy-nilly into the game of seizing
state power in order to "catch up," that is, in order to make their
own "industrial revolution."

If we want to get back to the key elements in a critical analysis of modern history, the explanation of the growing gap between core and periphery of the capitalist world-economy and the polarization of classes at a world level, we must rethink the concepts we have hitherto used to write the history of this "age of revolutions" which were not all that revolutionary.

4

Economic Theories and Historical Disparities of Development

The phrase "economic theory" suggests a tightly organized set of interrelated disprovable hypotheses derived from a minimum set of axioms, and normally one that has survived a certain amount of rigorous empirical probing. If this were what we meant by economic theory, it would be hard to argue that economic history, as it has been written now for 150 years or so, has used any comprehensive economic theory for the explanation of large-scale, long-term socio-economic changes.

Rather, economic historians have built their work around organizing myths (more politely termed perspectives) which have informed, pervaded or underlain their work. An organizing myth is not a testable proposition. It is a tale, a metahistory, which seeks to provide a framework within which the structures, the cyclical patterns, and the events of a given historical social system may be interpreted. It can never be proven or disproven. It can only be propounded (and defended) as a heuristic device which explains more elegantly, coherently, and convincingly than some alternative myth the historical system under observation, and which leaves fewer puzzles unsolved or requires fewer *ad hoc* additional explanations to account for the empirical reality.

Perhaps the avowal that we build our work around organizing myths will upset some who will consider this as a call to return to the mode of writing history as a lesson in morality, which was presumably put aside forever in the nineteenth century by the new emphases on the search for sources and the development of a disciplined, specialized expertise. Let me allay these fears. I am surely not advocating a new form of disguised theology. Quite the contrary, I am suggesting that modern historiography has not yet discarded theology, it has merely substituted new organizing myths for the previous ones. If we are to make further significant progress, we must bring the dominant myths to the foreground and examine them openly, rather than hide behind the pretense of an unrealized scientificity.

John Nef, in his "reconsideration" of one of the central themes of the contemporary organizing myth, the "industrial revolution," expressed these sentiments quite splendidly, as early as 1943:

> Ideas are never photographs of actual scenes and expectations. When we speak of historical ideas as true, we are thinking of the general impression conveyed by a writer which corresponds most perfectly to the facts as they are revealed by the materials accessible to us. But in order to present such an impression, it is not enough to be in possession of a vast quantity of materials on some special aspect of history in some special period; it is necessary to understand the relation of this special subject and period to history as a whole .... Accurate specialization can produce inaccurate history no less than can the historical generalizations which preceded the age of accurate specialization. (Nef 1943: 4)

Our organizing myths are of course myths about "history as a whole." As we well know, one of the great intellectual shifts of modernity was the replacement of cyclical views of societal change with one which centered around the idea of progress.[1] Human progress was assumed to be, if not inevitable, at least highly probable; and it was assumed to be more or less continuous, that is, sequential.

The basic tale about the modern world was already well established by the middle of the nineteenth century. It was proclaimed by pundits, taught by schoolteachers, believed by most people (or at least most people who were "modern" and had some minimal "education"). Indeed this particular tale is so deeply rooted, still today, in our popular *and* our scholarly language and perceptions of the world that it is not the subject of serious analysis. What is this basic tale? It is rather simple. Once upon a time, Europe was feudal. It lived in the "Dark Ages." Most people were peasants.

---

[1] For an exciting reformulation of this well-worn theme, in ways directly relevant to the writing of economic history, see Pomian (1979).

Most peasants were ruled over by lords who owned much land. By some process (how and exactly when is still a subject of controversy), middle strata emerged, primarily the urban burghers. New ideas emerged or reemerged (a renaissance), economic production was expanded, science and technology flourished. Ultimately this brought about an "industrial revolution." Along with this great economic change went a political one. The bourgeoisie overthrew the aristocracy in one way or another and in the process expanded the sphere of freedom. All of these changes went together. However, they did not happen simultaneously everywhere. Some countries achieved progress before others. The favorite candidate for front-runner has long been Great Britain, as is natural in the context of a myth evolved under the aegis of British hegemony in the world-economy. Other countries were more "backward" or less developed. But, given the basic optimism of this tale, there was no need for despair, since the backward peoples could (and should) imitate the forward or progressive ones, and thereby taste too of the same fruits of progress.

It is interesting to note that in the great intellectual debates of the nineteenth century – conservatism vs. liberalism, liberalism vs. Marxism – all sides accepted this basic tale as credible; they merely argued about the implications of this organizing myth for political action. Liberals were those who celebrated the rise of the middle classes as the bearers of human freedom. They advocated extending the benefits of human progress to groups and countries which had to that point been left behind. Conservatives were those who deplored the decline of the aristocracy (a reality they could not accept) and argued that individualism was not freedom but a license for rapacity. Freedom was to be found in the restoration of tradition and authority. Marxists too belived that the middle classes had risen and defeated the aristocracy. They agreed with the liberals that the bourgeoisie had been the bearers of human freedom but they also argued that bourgeois freedom was, as the conservatives said, license for rapacity. However, they added, through the inevitable dialectics of history at a higher stage of progress, the proletariat would, in turn, overthrow the bourgeoisie as the bourgeoisie had overthrown the aristocracy. Once again, as with the conservative critics of dominant liberal thought, the Marxists did not challange the descriptive elements of the organizing myth.

To be sure this is all very simplified, and of course the full account of modern historiography shows great sophistication of analysis and unending questioning of each detail. I would still contend that this simplified account is not at all an unfair representation of how history has been written and thought. First there were lords and peasants; then somehow there were bourgeois and proletarians. The turning point in the historical life of the modern world, in terms of the centrality of the two pairs of acting groups, is thought to have been the end of the eighteenth, the beginning of the nineteenth century.

We tend to think that only Marxists believe in class polarization. Yet, liberals and conservatives too have asserted that the "aristocracy" and the "peasantry" have been slowly disappearing as social factors. Conversely, the concept that there have emerged new social strata – the "new middle classes" – is also to be found in other than non-Marxist writings. The persistence and amplification of the category of the petty bourgeoisie (often as a puzzle, to be sure) in even the most recent Marxist writings shows convergence here too.

Thus, I argue that in the analysis of the drama of the modern world there is a very wide consensus on the basic plot (the "rise of the middle classes") and the basic cast of characters – two disappearing groups (the defeated aristocracy and the traditional peasantry), two rising groups (the triumphant bourgeoisie and the expanding proletariat) and one hazy, ill-defined interloper (who seems to play an erratic role).

There is a second point of wide consensus. It is that this play is performed in numerous (but countable) variants – one for each country (or state, or people). The variation is both important (the stuff of history) and unimportant (the stuff of theory). The primordiality of these units of analyis – the countries – has been mostly unquestioned.

This organizing myth implied a certain intellectual agenda for historical social sceience. Question number one was how to account for the varying national itineraries. It took the form of a multitude of subordinate questions: how and why did the "transition from feudalism to capitalism" or the "industrial revolution" take place in this country or the other? Which country was first? (In other words: why was France so backward and Great Britain so successful? What made Europeans more "progressive" than Orientals?)

Question number two was how countries coped with the disarray caused by their "modernization." This also took the form of many subordinate questions: what is the optimal path to the creation of the modern "democratic" state that would permit wide "participation" in government but hold "anarchy" in check? How are individual countries able to cope with the individual "deviations" (crime, mental illness, etc.) caused by the "anomic" character of a non-traditional society? How can states deal (how have they dealt) with the interstate disarray caused by rapid economic growth (wars, imperialism, etc.)?

Finally, question number three, and the one by which historical social sciences proved to the policy makers the utility of answering the other two questions: how does a backward nation catch up? Since the answers to questions one and two have been asserted to lie largely in the particular, endogenous history of those "primordial" entities – the countries – the answer to question number three has essentially been: replicate! – obviously, to the extent possible. It is not always so easy to change one's "national character" in order to make progress, or to recreate the preexisting "class structure" in order to be able to move on to the "next stage." Nonetheless, easy or not, it is the only way. Here liberals and Marxists have been in profound accord. Conservatives don't disagree that replication would work. Ineed, this is precisely what they fear. They merely assert it is undesirable.

There have been, to be sure, some continuing difficulties about this organizing myth. Conceived in the nineteenth century, largely to explain why Great Britain was so much more powerful at the time than France or Germany, it seems to work best when applied to nineteenth-century western Europe. As one moves away in space and time (backwards or forwards), the anomalies in fitting empirical reality into the framework of this myth grow more apparent. But most analysts assume that the anomalies they find for their restricted space-time unit are exceptional, and can be handled by adding another "epicycle" to the "theory." There was industrialization before the industrial revolution? Let us call that "proto-industrialization," saving the term for the real thing. Nationalism or ethnicity or religious fanaticism is increasing in the late twentieth century instead of finally disappearing? Let us call that "regression," which has the flavor of a temporary aberration.

Still, whatever the gymnastics, let us admit that this organizing myth is a very powerful metahistory. It is first of all a familiar one. It explains very much of what seems to have happened. Otherwise, it would never have convinced so many. Furthermore, it is flexible (indeed a bit too flexible, perhaps). It suffers, however, from one major fault: it does not explain why, contrary to all the predictions inherent in the model, there is the widely recognized growing gap between the rich nations and the poor ones (since all were supposed to realize the "wealth of nations"). Nor does the prevailing myth explain (not even in its Marxist variant) the widely contested, but I believe very real, growing gap (polarization) between the bourgeoisie and the proletariat.

Suppose, however, that the problem with our analyses is not the accuracy of our data, nor the diligence of our research, nor even the sophistication of either our methods or our theorizing, but simply (simply?) the metahistory we have used to organize our data and formulate our generalizations. Suppose that all, or much, of what we have been collectively saying has not been true, not because the data were false, but because the mirrors in which we have been reflecting these data have been distorting more than was necessary.

On the wisdom of a reconsideration of our "theories" in a dialogue with active participation in the real world, let us call upon a committed believer in the centrality of experience as the datum of historians – E. P. Thompson:

> The appearances will not disclose this significance spontaneously and of themselves: does one need to say this yet again? It is not part of my intention to deny the seductive "self-evident" mystification of appearance, or to deny our own self-imprisonment within unexamined categories. If we suppose that the sun moves around the earth, this will be confirmed to us by "experience" every day. If we suppose that a ball rolls down a hill through its own innate energy and will, there is nothing in the appearance of the thing that will disabuse us. If we suppose that bad harvests and famine are caused by the visitation of God upon us for our sins, then we cannot escape from this concept by pointing to drought and late frosts and blight, for God could have visited us through these chosen instruments. We have to fracture old categories and to make new ones before we can "explain" the evidence that has always been there.
>
> But the making and breaking of concepts, the propounding of new hypotheses, the reconstructing of categories, is not a matter of theoretical *invention*. Anyone can do this. Perhaps the famine was some frolic of the devil? The blight in England a consequence of French witchcraft? Or perhaps it was in fulfilment of some ancient curse, consequent upon the Queen's adultery? Appearance will confirm each one of these hypotheses as well: the devil is well known to be abroad, the French well known to be witches, and most queens to be adulterous. And if we suppose the Soviet Union to be a Workers' State guided by an enlightened Marxist theory; or that

market forces within capitalist society will always maximise the common good; then in either case we may stand in one spot all day, watching the blazing socialist sun move across blue heavens, or the ball of the Gross National Product roll down the affluent hill, gathering new blessings on its way. We need not recite this alphabet once again.

This alphabet, however, is not some special code, understood only by logicians. It is a common alphabet, to be mastered at the entry to all disciplines. Nor is it a severe lesson, to be administered periodically to "empiricists" (and only to them). To be sure, there are such empiricists who require this correction. But the lesson has two edges to its blade. Self-generating hypotheses, subject to no empirical control, will deliver us into the bondage of contingency as swiftly – if not more swiftly – than will surrender to the "obvious" and manifest. Indeed, each error generates and reproduces the other; and both may often be found, contained within the same mind. What has, it seems, to be recited afresh is the arduous nature of the engagement between thought and its objective materials: the "dialogue" (whether as *praxis* or in more self-conscious intellectual disciplines) out of which all knowledge is won. (Thompson 1978: 228–29)

I would like to argue that there are three things wrong with our current dominant organizing myth. First, the unit of analysis (the presumed arena of social action) is wrong. Modern states are not the primordial frameworks within which historical development has occurred. They may be more usefully conceived as one set of social institutions within the capitalist world-economy, this latter being the framework within which, and of which, we can analyze the structures, *conjonctures*, and events.

Secondly, the cast of characters have been doubly misstated. On the one had, our concepts of bourgeois and proletarian have been incredibly reified. They are defined in terms of a particular variant found in western Europe in the nineteenth century, whereas these concepts are relational and not formal or characterological. On the other hand, it is far from clear (at least it should not be an *a priori* assumption) that aristocrat and bourgeois are two contrasting, or even separate, roles. The same is true of the tandem, proletarian and peasant.

Finally, and above all, the basic tale is wrong. I wish to propose an alternate Fable for Our Time. Once upon a time, there were landowners (or aristocrats) who squeezed surplus out of peasants in various ways. But for a series of reasons (which we may debate) this system ran into serious trouble in Europe somewhere around

1250 or 1300. The bargaining power of the peasantry in the following two centuries rose significantly; partly because of peasant political action (revolts), partly because of a demographic downturn
(which enhanced the rarity value of skilled workers), partly because
of the internecine destruction of the nobility (itself the result of
economic squeeze). This was the so-called crisis of feudalism, also
known as the crisis of seigniorial revenues.

As the nobility grew politically weaker and the peasantry corres-
pondingly stronger, it was reasonable for the nobility to fear that
things were heading in the direction of a "paradise of kulaks." A
strategy to turn the tide was needed. This strategy was in fact
found. (Or if that sounds too voluntaristic, such a strategy
emerged.) It was the transformation of the feudal system into a
capitalist world-economy, the adoption of a different mode of production wherein the extraction of the surplus from the direct producers would be more indirect and less visible than in the old.

This strategy involved the "reconversion" of feudal landlords
into capitalist entrepreneurs, first of all in agriculture but also in
industry, commerce, and finance. Far from the bourgeoisie having
overthrown the aristocracy, we have instead the aristocracy becoming the bourgeoisie.

Of course, they coopted some commoners along the way, and on
the other hand many individual aristocrats were unable to make the
conversion. It was after all harder work (and strange work) to
exercise business acumen and hire thugs for the necessary exercise
of suppression than to engage oneself in the acrobatics of sword-
play. Furthermore, the coopted commoners showed an eagerness
to *"vivre noblement"* which was no doubt pathetic, but also useful
in reducing the likelihood of true conflict. Nonetheless there were
always some noblemen who were resistant to bourgeoisification and
some aspiring commoners who were impatient for aristocratization.
This accounts for many of the persistent intra-upper stratum struggles over the next few centuries; but essentially the conversion was
not only politically and socially successful, but economically successful as well.

The creation of the capitalist world-economy dramatically reversed the trend in the allocation of real revenue, away from direct
producers and in favor of the upper strata. The processes of capitalist development involved a reallocation and relocation of the work
force over a period of time. This is poorly represented, however,
by the image of the dispossessed rural peasant becoming property-
less urban proletarian. In fact, in most cases, the pattern of work-

ers' households *to this day* is far more complex than that, and most households in the modern world utilize a wide range of modes of obtaining incomes such that most of them over their lifetimes are neither "peasant" nor "proletarian" (in the classical image) but a mixture. Nor is this accidental or archaic; it has rather been central to the exploitation of this work force.

However, as time went on, the work force began to see through the "veil" of market transactions and to demand in various ways their "rights." The *jacqueries* of an earlier period blended into protests against the increasing "commercialization" of the world. This seemed archaic, a demand for previous "protections" of a feudal order; it was in fact an inchoate but clear opposition to the dispossessions of a capitalist order.

The upper strata had a simple answer to such protest – the traditional answer of superior force. But the use of overt force would tear the "veil" of impersonal market structures, thereby threatening to undermine one of the fundamental elements in the success of capitalism as a social system. A subtler mode of social control was needed. This subtler mode involved two elements: (a) the rule of law in the core countries, combined with some social welfare for the working classes – in short, political liberalism; (b) compensation for the loss of global surplus through redistribution in the core by the constant creation of new peripheries containing politically weaker working classes who could be maximally exploited – in short, the expansion of the world-economy and "imperialism."

This is not the place to review either the mechanisms which have permitted this historical system a certain moving equilibrium over time or the internal problems (or "contradictions"), both economic and political, that have led to the rise of a network of self-conscious antisystemic movements over a long period of time, and have brought this historical system to its present very long "structural crisis."

I will restrict myself to the two elements of this meta-history that treat directly the "historical disparities of development." Firstly, the operation of the system over historic time has led to the increasing polarization of the distribution of surplus, *provided* one measures this polarization within the real social entity, the capitalist world-economy *as a whole*, and not within individual nation-states. Secondly, it is the success of capitalism, and not its failure, that will bring about its demise. Capitalism has functioned (that is, it has permitted the unending accumulation of capital), not because it was the domain of unbridled free enterprise, free trade, and the free flow of the factors of production but because, at all times up to now, it was a system of partial free enterprise, partial free trade, and the partially free flow of the factors of production. It is the constant political intrusions into the market, the pervasive monopolies and oligopolies, the frequent restrictions on the flow of the factors of production (labor, commodities, and capital), the continuing existence of non-wage labor – all within a system in which no ultimate political authority could control the "anarchy" of production (production for profit) – that has permitted this unending accumulation of capital and its disproportionate concentration in a few hands and a few centers, that is, that has permitted polarization.

Nonetheless, the short-run and medium-run interests of some capitalists are regularly pushing towards the extension of the law of value into more and more arenas, the ever greater destruction of barriers to the free flow of the factors of production. In this fashion, capitalism undoes its own economic motors, and politically destroys its "protecting strata" (as Schumpeter insisted so convincingly).

You may say now that this is merely a new myth, one which may suit my theology better than yours, but in itself not provable and hence uninteresting. This is, however, to mistake the relationship between heuristic theory and complex reality. For it is metahistory which determines our collection of data (or to put it more strongly, our creation of data). It is our metahistory which channels our formulation of the hypotheses which "fail to be disproved." It is our metahistory which, above all, legitimates our analyses of the data. It is our grand interpretation of history which renders our smaller interpretations credible. The justification, therefore, of our metahistory comes neither from the data it generates nor from the null hypotheses it supports nor from the analyses it provokes. Its justification derives from its ability to respond comprehensively to the existing, continuing real social puzzles that people encounter and of which they have become conscious. It is in fact precisely the reality of the ever-increasing historical disparities of development that has called into question the old organizing myths which have not been able to account adequately for these disparties, and which has therefore been pushing world scholarship to the construction of an alternative methistory.

Far from simplifying our scientific tasks, the construction of a new metahistory in broad outline involves an enormous agenda of detailed work. It is almost as though the historical social sciences had to start from scratch again after 150 years of collective effort. Not quite, to be sure, since a very great deal of good (therefore useful) work has been done, but almost, nonetheless – because the data bases of the existing literature are grossly distorted. We need, first of all, a new cartography and a new statistics.

Maps are a neglected tool of the historical social sciences. Most of what they have to say seems so obvious. We use them to verify transfers of state territories at the moment of wars or of peace treaties. Sometimes, imaginatively, we use them to trace voting patterns or distributions of religious groups. Maps of course depend on boundaries, and the primordial boundaries of our maps are those of states. Even when we draw "functional" maps we tend to draw them within state boundaries.

As a consequence, we have no maps that would illustrate some of the most elementary processes of the world-economy over time. Take an obvious phenomenon like rural migration to urban-industrial centers. Start with an area like northern France which has had "industry" of one sort or another since the beginning of modern times (and earlier). Suppose we put forward the simple hypothesis that there was always migrant labor but, as the world-economy expanded and transportation improved, the radius of the circle of points of origin expanded (thus more frequently crossing state boundaries as time went on). This could be demonstrated on a map. But we would have to create this map now for the frist time. If then we drew parallel maps (or rather time-series of maps) for other "industrial centers" we might even be able to make more general assertions of similarities and dissimilarities.

Take a second elementary process. It is argued that the world-economy expands over time. This can be drawn on maps too, but never has been. We would of course have to decide on operational criteria for participation in the world social economy. We would have to be able to date "incorporation" into the world-economy. But it is surely not technically impossible, once the effort is serious-ly undertaken. Once we had such a time-series of maps, we could then also draw the contemporaneous boundaries of other historical systems, what I have termed the "external arena" of the world-economy. A set of maps from 1500 forward would show a clear pattern: the expansion of the world-economy and the gradual squeezing-out of other social economies. But what would a set of maps running from AD 500 to AD 1500 show, *drawn in this way*? I'm not sure we know.

Even more than a new cartography we need a new statistics.

Statistics (or at least historical statistics), as is obvious from the name, has been the compilation of numbers concerning states. This was its social origin and it has been very faithful to the task. We can express in quantitative form a good deal of things about the processes within a single state. We can make comparsions between states. We know about interstate flows, recorded as borders are traversed. But the lacunae are immense.

Suppose we wished to test the following proposition. There were three zones of consumption of cereal production in early modern Europe: one within 1 km of the point of production (and seldom passing through the "market"), one within 50 km, and one beyond 50 km. Let us hypothesize that between 1600 and 1700, total grain production in the European world-economy was stable (more or less), but the distribution in terms of percentages destined for different zones of consumption varied. Acquiring the statistical base to look seriously at this proposition would encounter enormous practical hurdles. The point is, however, that the present mode of *organizing* the data – that is, within state boundaries – does not permit us even to approach the issue.

Or take another question. There is today a renewed interest in so-called Kondratieff cycles. Once again there is collection of various time-series data. But most of these data continue to be collected within state boundaries. Suppose, however, that the waves exist within the world-economy as a whole but as the result of differing patterns in different zones. It would be perfectly possible to come up with negative results about the existence of Kondratieffs when reality was positive.

I could go on, but I believe I have sufficiently illustrated the point – the need for a new cartography and a new statistics, which would render possible (and in turn validate) the elaboration of an alternative metahistory. Let me draw one last implication of our work. All scientific activity is a matter of locating similarities and dissimilarities. But where is the emphasis? It depends on what we are comparing. We have for the last 150 years been comparing states – with each other, with themselves over time. We have sought to explain the dissimilarities. We ask questions such as: why was England the first country to have an industrial revolution? Why didn't Italy have a bourgeois revolution of the French variety? The search for dissimilarities among the states has masked, however, the continuity of the historical system in which they have found themselves. Our analyses would be more fruitful if we first (or at least also) made more *systematic* comparisons of longer-range entities, of historical system – of the capitalist world-economy as a whole with feudal Europe, with the Chinese world-empire (each taken as a historical system with both structure and organic development). It is not that this wasn't begun in the nineteenth century. But the constraints of our metahistory cut such efforts short. They were relegated to the musings of "philosophers." They should be brought back to the center of scientific attention. For we are living in the midst of a concrete transition from one kind of world-system, one specific historical system, to another. We are morally responsible for providing historical depth to contemporary practical decisions. To do this, I suggest, we need to revise our metahistory.

5

Societal Development, or Development of the World-System?

The theme of this German Sociological Congress is "Sociology and Societal Development." This title includes two of the most common, most ambiguous, and most deceptive words in the sociological lexicon – society (*Gesellschaft*) and development (*Entwicklung*). That is why I have entitled my talk in the form of a question, Societal Development or Development of the World-System?

Society of course is an old term. The *Oxford English Dictionary* (*OED*) gives 12 principal meanings to it, of which two seem most relevant to our present discussion. One is "the aggregate of persons living together in a more or less ordered community." The second, not very different, is "a collection of individuals comprising a community or living under the same organisation of government." The *OED* has the merit of being a historical dictionary and therefore indicating first usages. The first usages listed for these two senses are 1639 and 1577 respectively – hence, at the beginning of the modern world.

Looking in German dictionaries, I find the *Grosse Duden* (1977) offers the following relevant definition: "Gesamtheit der Mens-

This paper was prepared for the 22nd German Sociological Congress, 9–12 October, 1984 in Dortmund. This explains the frequent reference to definitions in German dictionaries. Of course, in 1990, the separate existence of the German Democratic Republic came to an end. This actually reinforces the point I had been making in the talk. The text is therefore unchanged despite the fact that some sentences may seem outdated.

chen, die unter bestimmten politischen, wirtschaftlichen und sozialen Verhältnissen zusammen leben," followed immediately by these examples: "die bürgerliche, sozialistische Klassenlose Gesellschaft."[1] The *Wörterbuch der deutschen Gegenwartssprache* (1967), published in the GDR, gives a rather similar definition: "Gesamtheit der unter gleichartigen sozialen und ökonomischen sowie auch politischen Verhältnissen lebenden Menschen," and it follows this by various examples including: "die Entwicklung der (menschlichen) Gesellschaft . . . ; die neue sozialistische, kommunistische Gesellschaft; die Klassenlose Gesellschaft . . . ; die bürgerliche, kapitalistische Gesellschaft." It precedes this definition with a notation that reads: "ohne Plural."[2]

Now, if one regards these definitions closely, which are probably typical of what one would find in most dictionaries in most languages, one notes a curious anomaly. Each of the definitions refers to a political component which seems to imply that each society exists within a specific set of political boundaries, yet the examples also suggest that a society is a type of state defined in terms of less specific, more abstract phenomena, with the last-mentioned dictionary specifically adding "no plural." In these examples, "society" is modified by an adjective, and the combined phrase describes the kind of structure which a "society" in the other usage, that of a politically bounded entity, is said to have. This latter usage of society can then take a plural, whereas the former cannot.

Perhaps you see no anomaly here. Yet I would like to start by endorsing the opening remark of one of the first serious attempts in modern social science to treat this matter. It is a German attempt, Lorenz von Stein's largely forgotten work on *Der Begriff der Gesellschaft und die soziale Geschichte der Französischen Revolution bis zum Jahre 1830.*[3] Stein says in the Introduction that "Der

---

[1] The English translation is: "the aggregate of persons living together under particular political, economic and social conditions" . . . "the bourgeois, socialist classless society."

[2] The English translation is: "the aggregate of persons living together under homogeneous social and economic as well as political conditions" . . . "the development of (human) society . . . ; the new socialist, communist society; the classless society . . . ; the bourgeois capitalist society" . . . "no plural."

[3] In the published English version we have two problems. One is the title which is rendered as *The History of the Social Movement in France, 1789–1850.* This omits from the title the fact that Stein was concerned with the *concept* of society. The passage is rendered as: "Society is one of the

Begriff der Gesellschaft gehört ... zu den schwierigsten in der ganzen Staatswissenschaft" (1959: vol. 1, 12).

Why does Stein talk of *Gesellschaft* as a concept in *Staatswissenschaft*? To be sure, one answer is that *Staatswissenschaft* was the term then in use in Germany that included the domain of what today in Germany is called *Sozialwissenschaften*, although the boundaries of the two are not identical. The use of the term *Staatswissenschaften* in nineteenth-century Germany, but not in England or France, is itself a significant phenomenon, reflecting an understanding of the social sciences from the vantage point of what I would call a semiperipheral state, but one outside the cultural circle of the hegemonic power. Yet this is not the whole answer. *Gesellschaft* is a concept of *Staatswissenschaft*, and "the most difficult one," because, as is clear from Stein's work itself, the concept "society" has its meaning for us primarily (even only) in the classic antinomy, society/state. And this antinomy in turn has its origin in the attempt of the modern world to come to grips with the ideological implications of the French Revolution.

Monarchs had been ousted before 1792, and/or forced by rebellions to change the constitutional structures of their regime. But the legitimation of such changes had previously been sought in the existence of some illegitimate act or acts of the monarch. The French Revolution was not justified on this basis, or at least came not to be so justified. Instead, the revolutionaries asserted with some vigor a new moral or structural basis on which to assign legitimacy, the concept of the popular will. As we know, this theoretical construct swept the world in the two centuries that have followed the French Revolution, and there are few today who contest it, despite all the attempts of conservative theorists from Burke and de Maistre on to disparage the doctrine, and despite the numerous instances in which popular sovereignty has been de facto ignored.

There are two problems with a theory that sovereignty resides in the people. First of all, we must know who and where are the people, that is who are and ought to be the "citizens" of a "state." I remind you that the central term of honorific address in the

most difficult concepts in political theory" (1964: 43). This translates the untranslatable *"Staatswissenschaft"* into an imperfect equivalent, "political theory." It so happens that the point I am making, the a priori definitional link between "society" and "state," comes out even more clearly in the German version.

heyday of the French Revolution was *"Citoyen."* But it is the "state" which decides who are the "citizens," and in particular decides who are the full-fledged members of the polity. Even today, nowhere is every resident of a state a citizen of that state, or a voter in that state. The second problem is how one knows what the popular will is. This is of course even more difficult than the first problem. I do not believe it is very much of an exaggeration to say that a very large part of the historical and social scientific enterprise in the nineteenth and twentieth centuries has been one vast attempt to solve these two problems, and that the key conceptual tool that has been used is the idea that there exists something called a "society" that is locked into a complicated, partially symbiotic, partially antagonistic relationship with something called the "state." If, however, you feel (as I do) that after 150 or so years we have not resolved these problems very well, perhaps the reason is that we have not given ourselves very adequate conceptual tools. Of course, if this is so, one would have to anaylze why this has occurred, and I will come to this matter.

Let us now look briefly at the other term of our title, which is "development." Development too has many, many meanings. The one in the *OED* most relevant to its usage here is as follows: "the growth or unfolding of what is in the germ ... of races of plants and animals." The *OED* traces this usage only to 1871, to a work of social science in fact, Tylor's *Primitive Culture*, volume I. Tylor is cited as saying: "Its various grades may be regarded as stages of development or evolution, each the outcome of previous history." Development, the *OED* adds, is "the same as evolution."

We get something similar in the German dictionaries. The *Grosse Duden* seems to aviod almost all usages in our sense until it comes to the compound *"Entwicklungsgesetz"* which it tells us refers to *"Wirtschaft und Gesellschaft."*[4] The GDR dictionary similarly treats the matter indirectly, through an example, "die kulturelle, gesell-schaftliche, geschichtliche, politische, ökonomische, soziale Entwicklung unseres Volkes."[5]

The English definitions make it abundantly clear how tied this usage in social science is to the doctrine of biological evolution which emerged in the latter half of the nineteenth century. This is

---

[4] The English translation is: "theory of evolution" ... "economy and society."
[5] The English translation is: "the cultural, societal, historical, political, economic, social development of our nation."

of course true of German as well. Duden's *Das Fremdwörterbuch* defines the *"Entwicklungsgesetz,"* a direct borrowing from English, as follows: "Theorie der Entwicklung aller Lebewesen aus niedrigen, primitiven Organismen."[6]

If we now combine the two terms, as you have done in the title of this congress (not at all in an unusual fashion), and talk of "Societal Development," we seem to be dealing with how some entity (an entity that is not the state, but also is not divorced from the state, and usually one sharing more or less the same boundaries as the state) has evolved over time from some lower to some higher or more "complex" state of being.

Where then is the "germ" from which one can trace this evolution, and how far back can one trace it? Let me mention briefly two possible examples of a "society" and ask some naive questions about them. On example I will take is German society. The second example is Puerto Rican society. I do not plan to review the abundant literature of scholarly and public debate on these two instances. This would be a monumental task in the case of the German example, and not such a small one in the case of the Puerto Rican example. I merely want to show that there are some very elementary problems in using the concept "society" in either instance. I know that these two cases have their peculiarities, and that some may say they are somehow not "typical" or "representative." But one of the realities of history is that every example is specific and particular, and I frankly am skeptical that there are any representative "instances" anywhere.

Let me ask the simple question, where is German society? Is it within the present boundaries of the Federal Republic? The official answer seems to be that today there are *"zwei deutsche Staaten"* (two German States) but only *"ein Volk"* (one nation). So the one "nation" or "people" seems to be defined, at least by some, as including both those persons found in the Federal Republic and those in the GDR.

What then about Austria? Are Austrians part of German "society," of the German "people"? Austria was only briefly, from 1938 to 1945, formally incorporated into the German state. Nevertheless, in the middle of the nineteenth century, Austria's incorporation into a then only potential German state was widely discussed

---

[6] The English translation is: "theory of evolution" ... "the theory of the development of all living beings from lower primitive organisms."

as a distinct possibility. There seems to exist a long nationalist tradition, or at least one long nationalist tradition, that would define Austria as part of German society.

Despite this, the official answer to my question, "Is Austria part of German society?" today seems to be no – but only today. That is, because of the efforts of the present-day Federal Republic to dissociate itself morally from the Third Reich, itself associated with *Anschluss*, any suggestion that Austria is not and will not always be a separate state (and therefore nation? therefore "society"?) is distinctly frowned upon, both in the Federal Republic and in Austria. But if a "society" is something which "develops" out of a "germ," how is it possible that a mere political event, the outcome of the Second World War, or further back the outcome of the Austro-Prussian War of 1866, could affect the definition of the social space of German society? After all, a "society" is supposed to be different from a state, a sort of underlying and developing reality, at least in part against and in spite of the state? If, however, every time we change state boundaries we change the boundaries of "society," how can we argue that the legitimacy of a government provided by a "society" is different from the legitimacy of a government provided by a state? The concept of "society" was supposed to give us something solid on which to build. If it turns out to be mere putty, which we can reshape at will, it will do us precious little good – little analytical good, little political good, little moral good.

If the German case is one in which there are today two, perhaps three sovereign "German" states, the Puerto Rican case seems virtually the opposite. As against a society with several states, here may be a society without any state. Ever since the sixteenth century there has been an administrative entity called Puerto Rico, but at no point in time has there ever been a sovereign state, a fully recognized member of the interstate system. To be sure, the United Nations does debate from time to time whether there ever will be one in the future, and so of course do the inhabitants of Puerto Rico.

If there is no state at all, how do we define the "society"? Where is it located? Who are its members? How did it come into existence? These, as you may immediately intuit, are political questions that have given rise to much passion. Recently, this intellectual controversy has been reopened in an unusual way by José Luis González who in 1980 published a book entitled *El país de cuatros pisos*. González is a man of letters who considers himself a Puerto

Rican nationalist. The book, however, is a polemic against certain Puerto Rican *independistas*, and in particular against Pedro Albizu Campos, not because they stood for independence, but because they based their claims on a totally wrong analysis of what is Puerto Rican "society."

González starts, in the best tradition of Max Weber, with an observed anomaly. Of all Spain's colonies in the Western Hemisphere, Puerto Rico alone has never obtained an independent status. How come? His answer revolves around his belief that Puerto Rican "society" precisely did *not* evolve out of some "germ." He suggests an alternative analogy: Puerto Rican "society" is a house of four stories, each story being added at specific historical moments. The first story is that created in the sixteenth to eighteenth centuries, mixing the three historical "races": the Taina (or indigenous Carib Indians), the Africans (brought over as slaves), and the Spanish settlers. Since the Taina were largely wiped out and the Spaniards were few in number and often only temporary residents, the Africans came to predominate. "Hence my conviction, expressed on various occasions and disconcerting or irritating to some people, that the first Puerto Ricans were in fact Black Puerto Ricans." (González 1980: 20).

It was only in 1815 that this ethnic mix changed in Puerto Rico. In 1815, the *Real Cédula de Gracias* opened the island to refugees from the various other Hispano-American colonies that were in the midst of wars of independence – and not only to Spaniards loyal to the Crown, but to English, French, Dutch, and Irish persons as well. Note well the date: 1815. It is the year of Napoleon's definitive exile, the founding of the Holy Alliance, the enthronement of British hegemony in the world-system. In addition, in the course of the late nineteenth century, Puerto Rico was the recipient of a recorded further wave of immigration, coming primarily from Corsica, Majorca, and Catalonia. Hence, by the end of the century, says González, a second story had been erected by these White settlers of the nineteenth century, and they constituted in Puerto Rico a "privileged minority" (González 1980: 24). Thus, continues González, it is not true, as Albizu Campos and others had claimed, that when American colonization began in 1898, Puerto Rico had a homogeneous "national culture." Quite the contrary, it was a "people divided."

González uses this fact to explain the differential response of Puerto Ricans to US colonization, which created the third story. To simplify his argument, he argues that the *hacendados* at first welcomed the Americans since they thought that the US intended to incoporate them eventually as part of the US bourgeoisie. When it became clear within ten years that this was not to be, the "privileged minority" turned to nationalism. Meanwhile, the Puerto Rican working class had initially also greeted favorably the US invasion, but for opposite reasons. They saw it as opening the door to "squaring their accounts" (González 1980: 33) with the landowning classes, who "were seen by the Puerto Rican masses for what they in fact were: foreigners and exploiters" (González 1980: 35).

And then there is the fourth story, that constructed not as a result of the initial cultural "Northamericanization" but rather as the result of the economic transformations beginning in the 1940s. It led initially to a "modernization-within-dependency" (González 1980: 41) of Puerto Rican society, but then subsequently to the "spectacular and irreparable breakdown" (González 1980: 40) of this fourth story in the 1970s. González does not discuss directly the further complication, that since the 1940s there has also been a massive migration of Puerto Ricans to the continental United States, and that today a substantial proportion of all Puerto Ricans were born and live outside Puerto Rico. Are these latter still part of Puerto Rican "society," and if so for how long will this be true?

I cite González not to debate the future of Puerto Rico, nor merely to remind us of the profound social divisions in our so-called societies, which are to be sure class divisions, but ones often (even usually) overlain with and linked to ethnic divisions. Rather, I cite the Puerto Rican case, as I did the German case, to underline the changing and debatable definitions of the boundaries of a "society" and to the close link such changing definitions have with historical events which are not products primarily of some "development" *intrinsic* to the "society."

What is fundamentally wrong with the concept of society is that it reifies and therefore crystallizes social phenomena whose real significance lies not in their solidity but precisely in their fluidity and malleability. The concept "society" implies we have before us to analyze something that is a tangible reality, albeit to be sure a "developing" one. In fact what we have before us is primarily a rhetorical construct, and therefore, as Lorenz von Stein says, a "difficult concept" of *Staatswissenschaft* (that is, in this case, of political philosophy). We do not, however, have an analytical tool for the summation or dissection of our social processes.

One of the underlying elements of world social science for the last 150 years has been a particular reading of modern European history. This reading of history is not limited to professional historians and social scientists. It constitutes a deep layer of our common culture, taught via the secondary school system to all, and simply assumed as a basic structuring of our comprehension of the social world. It has not been the subject of major controversy. Rather it has been the *common* property of the two principal *Weltanschauungen* of the last century, liberalism and Marxism, which otherwise have stood in stark opposition one to the other.

This reading of history takes the form of an historical myth which comprises two main statements. The first statement is that, out of a European medieval feudal world where seigniors ruled over peasants, there arose (emerged, was created) a new social stratum, the urban bourgeoisie, who first economically undermined and then politically overthrew the old system (the ancien régime). The result was a market-dominated capitalist economy combined with a representative political system based on individual rights. Both the liberals and Marxists described European history in this way; they also both applauded this historical process as "progressive."

The second statement in this historical myth is most clearly captured in the book by Karl Bücher, *Die Entstehung der Volkswirtschaft*, in which Bücher distinguishes three successive stages of European economic history – *geschlossene Hauswirtschaft, Stadtwirtschaft*, and *Volkswirtschaft*.[7] The key element here, the one in which Bücher represents the liberal-Marxist consensus, is the perception of modern history as the story of widening economic circles, in which the major jump was to go from a "local" economy to a "national" economy, a national economy located of course in a national state. Bücher underlines the connection insisting that "die Volkswirtschraft das Produkt einer jahrtausendelangen historischen Entwicklung ist, das nicht älter ist als der moderne Staat" (Bücher 1913: 90)[8]. Note incidentally once again the term "development." Bücher brings out explicitly the spatial implications that are implicit in the generic, descriptive categories found in the works of many other major figures of nineteenth-century social science: Comte and Durkheim, Maine and Spencer, Tönnies and Weber.

I think both of these statements comprising the dominant histor-

[7] The published English-language translation once again changes the title. It becomes *Industrial Evolution*. The three stages are translated as independent economy, town economy and national economy.

[8] The English translation reads: "National economy is the product of a development extending over thousands of years, and is not older than the modern State" (Bücher 1901: 88).

ical myth of modern European history are great distortions of what really happened. I will not discuss here why I believe the concept of the rise of a bourgeoisie, which somehow overthrew an aristocracy, is more or less the opposite of what really happened, which is that the aristocracy reconverted itself into a bourgeoisie in order to salvage its collective privilege. I have argued this case elsewhere. I prefer to concentrate my attention on the second myth, that of the widening circles.

If the essential movement of modern European history was from town economy to national economy, from the local arena to the national state, where does the "world" come into the picture? The answer is essentially as an epiphenomenon. National states are seen as spending a portion of their time and energy (a relatively small portion for the most part) on *inter*-national activities – international trade, international diplomacy. These so-called international relations are somehow "external" to this state, this nation, this "society." At the very most, some might concede that this situation has been evolving in the direction of the "internationalization" of the economy and of the political and cultural arenas, but only very recently (since 1945, or even since only the 1970s). So, we are told, there may now be, "for the very first time," something we can call world production or a world culture.

This imagery, which frankly seems to me more and more bizarre the more I study the real world, is the heart of the operational meaning of the concept, the "development of society." Allow me to present to you another imagery, another way of summarizing social reality, an alternative conceptual frame-work, which I hope can be said to capture more fully and more usefully the real social world in which we are living.

The transition from feudalism to capitalism involved first of all (first logically and first temporally) the creation of a world-economy. That is to say, a social division of labor was brought into being through the transformation of long-distance trade from a trade in "luxuries" to a trade in "essentials or "bulk goods," which tied together processes that were widely dispersed into long commodity chains. The commodity chains consisted of particular linked production processes whose linkage made possible the accumulation of significant amounts of surplus-value and its relative concentration in the hands of a few.

Such commodity chains were already there in the sixteenth century and predated anything that could meaningfully be called "national economies." These chains in turn could only be secured by the construction of an interstate system coordinate with the boundaries of the real social division of labor, the capitalist world-economy. As the capitalist world-economy expanded from its original European base to include the entire globe, so did the boundaries of the interstate system. The sovereign states were institutions that were then created within this (expanding) interstate system, were defined by it, and derived their legitimacy from the combination of juridical self-assertion and recognition by others that is the essence of what we mean by "sovereignty." That it is not enough merely to proclaim sovereignty in order to exercise it is illustrated well by the current examples of the "independent" Bantustans in South Africa and the Turkish state in northern Cyprus. These entities are not sovereign states because the other members of the club of sovereign states (in each case with one single exception, which is insufficient) do not recognize them as sovereign states. How many recognitions, and whose, it takes to legitimate a claim to sovereignty is unclear. That there is a threshold somewhere becomes evident when we observe how firmly Morocco stands opposed to the wish of the majority (a bare majority, to be sure) of members of the Organization of African Unity (OAU) to admit the Sahraoui Arab Democratic Republic to full status in this regional interstate structure. Clearly, Morocco feels that a recognition by the OAU would create pressure on the great powers, and the claim might thereby pass the threshold.

It has been the world-system then and not the separate "societies" that has been "developing." That is, once created, the capitalist world-economy first become consolidated and then over time the hold of its basic structures on the social processes located within it was deepened and widened. The whole imagery of going from acorn to oak, from germ to fulfillment, if plausible at all, makes sense only if it is applied to the singular capitalist world-economy as a historical system.

It is within that developing framework that many of the institutions we often describe quite mistakenly as "primordial" came into existence. The sovereignty of jurisdictions became ever more institutionalized, as (and to the degree that) some kind of social allegiance evolved to the entities defined by the jurisdictions. Hence, slowly, and more or less coordinate with the evolving boundaries of each state, a corresponding nationalist sentiment took root. The modern world-system has developed from one in which these "nationalisms" were weak or non-existent to one in which they were salient, well ensconced, and pervasive.

Nor were the nations the only new social groupings. The social classes, as we have come to know them, were also created in the course of this development, both objectively and subjectively. The pathways of both proletarianization and bourgeoisification have been long and sinuous, but above all they have been the outcome of world-scale processes. Even our present household structures – yes, even they – are constructed entities, meeting simultaneously the double need of a structure to socialize the labor force and one to give this labor force partial shelter against the harsh effects of the work-system.

In all of this description, the imagery I am employing is not of a small core adding on outer layers but of a thin outer framework gradually filling in a dense inner network. To contrast *Gemeinschaft* and *Gesellschaft* in the way conventionally done not only by German but by all of world sociology is to miss the whole point. It is the modern world-system (that is, the capitalist world-economy whose political framework is the interstate system composed of sovereign states) which is the *Gesellschaft* within which our contractual obligations are located. To legitimate its structures, this *Gesellschaft* has not only destroyed the multiple *Gemeinschaften* that historically existed (which is the point normally stressed) but has created a network of new *Gemeinschaften* (and most notably, the nations, that is, the so-called societies). Our language thus is topsy-turvy.

I am tempted to say we are really going not from *Gemeinschaft* to *Gesellschaft* but from *Gesellschaft* to *Gemeinschaft*, but that is not quite right either. Rather it is that our only *Gesellschaft*, the capitalist world-economy (and even it is only a partially-contractualized structure) has been creating our multiple, meaningful *Gemeinschaften*. Far from *Gemeinschaften* dying out, they have never been stronger, more complex, more overlapping and competing, more determinative of our lives. And yet never have they been less legitimate. Nor have they ever been more irrational, substantively irrational, and this is precisely because they have emerged out of a *gesellschaftliche* process. Our *Gemeinschaften* are, if you will, our loves that dare not speak their names.

Of course this is an impossible situation and we find ourselves amidst a worldwide cultural rebellion against these pressures all around us, one which is taking the widest of forms – the religious fundamentalisms, the hedonisms of withdrawal and the hedonisms of total self-interestedness, the multiple "countercultures," the Green movements, and not least the seething of really serious and really powerful anti-racist and anti-sexist movements. I do not

mean to imply that these diverse group are at all the same. Far
from it. But they are the common consequence of the relentless
spread of the ever more formally rational and ever more substantively irrational historical social system in which we all find
ourselves collectively trapped. They represent screams of pain
against the irrationality that oppresses in the name of a universal,
rationalizing logic. Had we really been moving from *Gemeinschaft*
to *Gesellschaft*, all this would not be occurring. We should instead
be bathing in the rational waters of an Enlightenment world.

At one level, there is much hope. Our historical system, as all
historical systems, is full of contradictions, of processes which force
us to go in one direction to pursue our short-run interests and in
another to pursue our middle-run interests. These contradictions
are built into the economic and political structures of our system
and are playing themselves out. Once again, I do not wish to repeat
here analyses I have made elsewhere about what I call "the crisis of
transition" (Wallerstein 1982), a long process taking perhaps 150
years, which has already begun and which will result in the demise
of our present system and its replacement by something else, without, however, any guarantee that this something else will be substantively better. No guarantee, but a meaningful possibility. That
is to say, we are before a historical, collective choice, the kind that
comes rarely and is not the lot of every generation of mankind.

I would prefer to develop here the question of the possible role
of the historical social sciences in this collective choice, which is of
course a moral choice, hence a political choice. I have argued that
the basic concept of "society" and the basic historical myths of
what I have called the liberal-Marxist consensus of the nineteenth
century, which combined to form the framework of social science as
the principal ideological expression of the world-system, are fundamentally offbase. Of course, this was no accident. The concept of
society and the historical myths were part of the machinery that
made the modern world-system operate so well in its heyday. In a
period of relative systemic equilibrium, the consciousness of the
intellectuals is perhaps the finest-tuned reflection of the underlying
material processes.

However, we are no longer in a time of relative systemic equilibrium. It is not that the machine has been working poorly, but
rather that it has been working only too well. The capitalist world-
economy has showed itself over 400 years magnificently adept at
solving its short-run and middle-run problems. Furthermore, it
shows every sign of being able to do more of the same in the

present and near future. But the solutions themselves have created changes in the underlying structure, which are eliminating over time this very ability to make the constant necessary adjustments. The system is eliminating its degrees of freedom. I am unable here to argue this case. I simply assert it, and use it to explain the fact that, amid the constant hosannas to the efficiency of capitalist civilization, we see everywhere the signs of malaise and cultural pessimism. The consensus has therefore begun to break down. And this is what is reflected in the myriad of antisystemic movements that have began to develop momentum and get out of hand.

Among the intellectuals, this malaise is reflected in the growing questioning of fundamental premises. Today we have physical scientists who are doubting the whole philosophical description of science as the "disenchantment of the world," one that goes from Bacon to Newton to Einstein, and are asking us to understand that science is rather the "reenchantment of the world" (Prigogine and Stengers 1979). And I am coming before you to express what many have come to feel, that it is futile to analyze the processes of the *societal development* of our multiple (national) "societies" as if they were autonomous, internally evolving structures, when they are and have been in fact primarily structures created by, and taking form in response to, world-scale processes. It is this world-scale structure and the processes of its development that provide the true subject of our collective enquiry.

If I am anywhere near right, it has consequences for us. It means of course that we must collectively rethink our premises, and therefore our theories. But it has an even more painful side. It means we must reinterpret the meaning of our entire stock of slowly accumulated "empirical data," a stock whose constant growth is making our libraries and our archives bulge, and which serves as the historically created and distorted basis of almost all our current work.

But why will we do this? And in whose name, in whose interest? One answer that has been given for at least 75 years now has been "in the name of the movement, or the party, or the people." I do not reject that answer because of some belief in the separation of science and values. But that answer is no answer, for two reasons. First, the movement is not singular. Perhaps at one time, the family of antisystemic movements could lay claim to a semblance of unicity, but surely no longer. And in terms of world-scale processes, there is not merely a multiplicity of movements, but even of types of movements. Secondly, the collectivity of movements is undergoing a collective crisis concerning the efficacy of the strategy of change which emerged out of the nineteenth-century debates. I refer to the strategy of achieving transformation through the acquisition of state power. The fact is that the antisystemic movements have themselves been the product of the capitalist world-system. As a consequence, they have by their actions not merely undermined the world-system (their ostensible objective, partially achieved) but they have also sustained this same system, most particularly by taking state power and operating within an interstate system which is the political superstructure of the capitalist world-economy. And this has created inbuilt limits on the ability of these movements to mobilize effectively in the future. Thus it is that, while the world-system is in crisis, so are its antisystemic movements, and so I may add are the analytic self-reflective structures of this system, that is, the sciences.

The crisis of the movements has its locus in their collective increasing inability to transform their growing political strength into processes that could truly transform the existing world-system. One of their present constraints, though surely not the only one, has been the ways in which their own analyses have incorporated large segments of the ideology of the existing world-system. What the historical social sciences can contribute in this crisis of transition is therefore an involvement that is simultaneously engaged with the movements and disengaged from them. If science cannot offer praxis, it can offer the insights that come from distance, provided it is not neutral. But scientists are never neutral, and hence the science they produce is never neutral. The commitment of which I am speaking is of course the commitment to substantive rationality. It is a commitment in the face of a situation where collective choice is being made possible by the decline of the historical social system in which we are living, but where the choice is made difficult by the absence of a clear-cut alternative social force standing for a wise choice.

In this situation, in purely intellectual terms, it means we have to rethink our conceptual apparatus, to rid it of the nineteenth century's ideological patina. We will have to be radically agnostic in our empirical and theoretical work, while trying to create new heuristic frameworks which will speak to the absence, not the presence, of substantive rationality.

You will forgive me if, before a congress of German sociologists, I invoke Max Weber. We all know his passionate address to the students in 1919, "Politics as a Vocation." There is a deep pessimism in that talk:

Not summer's bloom lies ahead of us, but rather a polar night of icy darkness and hardness, no matter which group may triumph externally now. Where there is nothing, not only the Kaiser but also the proletarian has lost his rights. When this night shall have slowly receded, who of those for whom spring apparently has bloomed so luxuriously will be alive? (Gerth and Mills 1946: 128)

We must wonder if the polar night which did indeed come as Weber predicted is yet behind us or whether still worse is to come. Whether the one or the other, the only possible conclusion we should draw is the one that Weber did draw:

Politics is a strong and slow boring of hard boards. It takes both passion and perspective. Certainly all historical experience confirms the truth – that man would not have attained the possible unless time and again he had reached out for the impossible. (Gerth and Mills 1946: 128)

I have said that our concepts can be traced to the intellectual conundra bred by the French Revolution. So can our ideals and our solutions. The famous trinity, "liberté, égalité, fraternité," is not a description of reality; it has not infused the structures of the capitalist world-economy, in France or anywhere else. This phrase was in fact not really the slogan of the so-called bourgeois revolution but rather the ideological expression of the first serious antisystemic movement in the history of the modern world that was able to shape and inspire its successors. Liberty, equality, and fraternity is a slogan directed not against feudalism but against capitalism. They are the images of a social order different from ours, one that might one day be constructed. For this we need passion and perspective. It scarcely will be easy. It cannot be done without a fundamental reassessment of strategy on the part of the antisystemic movements, another subject I have not been able to discuss here. (See, however, Wallerstein 1984, part II.) But it will also not be done unless those who say that they strive to understand social reality, that is, we, the historical social scientists, will be ready to repeat, in science as in politics, Weber's final plea, "in spite of all!"

6

The Myrdal Legacy: Racism and Underdevelopment as Dilemmas

Ignorance is seldom random but instead highly opportunistic.
Gunnar Myrdal, *Economic Theory and Under-developed Regions*

Introduction

The Myrdal legacy is the set of Myrdal questions, not the set of Myrdal answers. Answers to questions abound in the historical social sciences, but few worry about which questions to ask. Myrdal said so himself. Theory, he asserted, is "no more than a correlated set of questions to the social reality under study" (Myrdal 1968: 25).

Gunnar Myrdal spent a large part of his intellectual life doing research on, developing theory about, and offering practical solutions for two enormously big parts of contemporary social reality, racism and underdevelopment. He studied racism in the specific context of United States history, and and he entitled his book *An American Dilemma*. But of course we know that racism is not an exclusively United States dilemma; it is a dilemma of our world-system. I do not know if Myrdal believed, when he turned his attention after the Second World War to the problem of the economic development of so-called underdeveloped countries, that he was moving to another, different arena of public policy. I in any case do not think he was. I believe rather that racism and underdevelopment constitute in fact but a single dilemma.

The dictionary definition of dilemma insists that it involves an obligatory choice between equally unpleasant alternatives. I am not sure Myrdal intended to convey the connotation of equally unpleasant alternatives. He probably was using the term in the looser, more popular sense of a situation in which the actor is under contradictory pressures but for which a political solution exists, involving a difficult but not impossible choice. I think the belief in the existence of middle-run political solutions to knotty social problems was central to Myrdal's ethos. For example, he closes *An American Dilemma* with this peroration:

> The rationalism and moralism which is the driving force behind social study, whether we admit it or not, is the faith that institutions can be improved and strengthened and that people are good enough to live a happier life. With all we know today, there should be the possibility to build a nation and a world where people's great propensities for sympathy and cooperation would not be so thwarted.
>
> To find the practical formulas for this never-ending reconstruction of society is the supreme task of social science. The world catastrophe places tremendous difficulties in our way and may shake our confidence to the depths. Yet we have today in social science a greater trust in the improvability of man and society than we have ever had since the Enlightenment. (Myrdal 1944: 1024)

Myrdal did not limit himself to doing the research that might lead to these "practical formulas." He also purported, in all of his work, to address himself to the still broader issue of the theoretical and methodological implications of what he saw as the necessary relationship between the scientist and the objects of scientific enquiry. He called this the issue of "value in social theory" or "objectivity in social research," the titles of two of his books (Myrdal 1958; 1969) and the subject as well of appendices, or special chapters, in almost all the others. Myrdal strongly rejected the two major formulae for eliminating so-called bias in social science. He said that biases can be erased neither "simply by 'keeping to the facts' and by refined methods of statistical treatment of the data" nor by "the scientists stopping short of drawing practical conclusions" (Myrdal 1944: 1041). Quite the contrary:

> Social science is essentially a "political" science; ... practical conclusions should not be avoided, but rather be considered as a main task in social research; ... explicit value premises should be found and stated; ... by this technique, we can expect both to mitigate biases and to lay a rational basis for the statement of the theoretical problems and the practical conclusions. (Myrdal 1944: 1045)

Furthermore, for Myrdal, not only is it a positive thing to assert explicit value premises, but it is a seriously negative thing to fail to do so:

> The practice of expressing political attitudes only through the medium of purportedly objective arguments and scientific theories is probably in the long run highly injurious to the actual policy that one wishes to support. Quasi-scientific rationalization of a political endeavour may be an effective propaganda weapon; yet its effect at the crucial time, when the ideal has acquired enough political backing to be transformed into practical action, is in a democratic setting almost always inhibitory and disintegrating. I make an exception for completely conservative strivings which seek nothing more than the preservation of the status quo; from such a political standpoint doctrinaire thinking may be less dangerous. (Myrdal 1954: xii)

Well, what value premises then? Myrdal is quite clear on his own premises: "the desirability of political democracy and of equality of opportunity" (Myrdal 1957: vii). I am perfectly happy to make these premises mine and to take the discussion from there. And what then are the dilemmas? And whose dilemmas are they? It is clear what is the thrust of Myrdal's position. On the one hand, persons, nations, perhaps the entire world-system make valuations – a word on which Myrdal insists – concerning what he calls the "general plane." The so-called "American Creed," a centerpiece of his analysis of the United States, is one such set of valuations on the general plane. However, Myrdal also tells us that the American Creed is a "humanistic liberalism developing out of the epoch of Enlightenment" (Myrdal 1944: 8). It thus seems clear that the humanistic liberalism to which he is referring is far more widely held than only in the US. Europe too has been heir to the Enlightenment, and so today is much of the rest of the world. That is, Myrdal was implicitly saying that his own value premises – "the desirability of political democracy and of equality of opportunity" – are those of much of the world, so long, that is, as people are expressing their valuations on a "general plane."

But against this "general plane" of valuations, Myrdal sees various "specific planes of individual and group living [where] all sorts of miscellaneous wants, impulses, and habits dominate [people's] outlook" (Myrdal 1944:lxxi). It is the conflict between the two sets of valuations – those at the general and those at the specific planes – that constitutes the "dilemma(s)." Myrdal of course is basically restating Rousseau's concept of the conflict between the general and the particular wills. He is reminding us of the clash between universalism and particularism. And, most importantly, he is asking us to see this conflict in valuations not simply as "hypocrisy;" he is asking us to see commitment to the valuations on the general plane as more than mere "lip-service;" (Myrdal 1944: 21). He is telling us that we live morally amidst genuine dilemmas.

Whose dilemmas are they? They are the dilemmas of course of all those who are heirs to the Enlightenment, who believe in political democracy and equality of opportunity. These are our friends, our neighbors, our leaders, ourselves. And these are of course very much the social scientists as a collective community.

I propose to discuss the Myrdal question in two parts. First, what are the origins of racism and underdevelopment? How are they linked? Why have these "dilemmas" remained "unsolved?" Secondly, how have the historical social sciences approached these issues in the past? What is the source and nature of the sea-change which is occurring today in the theory and methodology of the historical social sciences? What will be the consequences of this transformation of the historical social sciences for the "dilemmas" of racism and underdevelopment?

I

Whence racism and underdevelopment? Both racism and underdevelopment are phenomena of the modern world. Racism is not xenophobia, which has of course existed throughout history, and underdevelopment is not poverty and/or a low level of technology, which have also existed throughout history. Rather, racism and underdevelopment, as we know them, are specific manifestations of a basic process by which our own historical system has been organized: a process of keeping people out while keeping people in.

Let me explain. Capitalism, which is the defining characteristic of the modern world-system, is an inegalitarian system by definition. I know this is a favorite theme of critics of capitalism, but it is as much a favorite theme of defenders of capitalism. The way the defenders express this reality is to say that appropriate reward for effort and enterprise motivates innovation and growth. Everyone is said to benefit thereby. But reward, if it is to have any meaning whatsoever, means having something more than what those who are not rewarded have. The critics express this reality differently. They say that some who control accumulated wealth exploit others who do not, and thereby appropriate disproportionately current accumulation. This debate is familiar to everyone and I do not propose here to discuss it once again. I merely wish to underline the point that both sides quite clearly accept the premise that capitalism involves unequal distribution of material goods. They differ of course on the the evaluation of this reality, the degree to which it has been historically inevitable, and the nature of the social and political consequences, but they agree on the basic description.

And yet, "on the general plane," as Myrdal would say, everyone (or virtually everyone) denounces racism and underdevelopment, and considers them illegitimate, unfortunate, and eliminable. That is, almost all people, almost all ideological schools of thought have for some time been proclaiming the universalist ideal of a world without racism and without poverty; but all have nonetheless continued to support and to maintain institutions which have directly and indirectly perpetuated, indeed increased, these presumably unwanted realities.

How has this been possible? Let me develop my seemingly paradoxical formulation in which I suggested that one of the basic formulae on which our own historical system, the capitalist world-economy, has been organized is that of keeping people out while keeping people in. It is less paradoxical than it sounds, and it is in fact the key to our understanding how the system functions. It is also a differentia specifica of this historical system, distinguishing it from all those previously existing, which normally operated on the principle of including some and excluding others. The others who were excluded were those about whom one felt xenophobic. They were those one eliminated, by killing them if necessary and possible.

Consider what happens in our own system. In each state within the capitalist world-economy, there exists a range of occupations and positions which are remunerated unequally. Virtually all individuals are located in households which normally pool income from multiple sources (wages, market transactions, rents, transfer income, subsistence activities) to create a fund which they expend in order to reproduce their existence (and perhaps additionally to invest). These households have two obvious long-term characteristics. First, they can be located on an ordinal scale of long-term or life-time income. This might be called their "class" dimension. I am of course aware that class is not merely a categorization according to income, but whatever the definition of class, most analysts would argue that there is a direct correlation of class and level of total income, whether as consequence or as cause.

Secondly, however, all households can also be identified as having an "ethnic" dimension. Again I am aware of the multiple debates around the concept of "ethnic group." I am using the term "ethnic dimension" simply to refer to any form of social identity and identification socially framed by presumed "ascribed" characteristics (whether biological or cultural) such as race (or skin color), language, religion, country of ancestral origin, etc. The point is that, in any state today, there exist categorizations of residents along these "ethnic" dimensions. And these "ethnic" groups are always socially ranked along an ordinal scale. That is, in all states, one group tends to be the dominant one locally, although states vary enormously in terms of whether this dominant group is a quite large or a relatively small percentage of the total population. There are always some group or groups at the bottom of the scale.

The first question that then arises is what is the link between the "class" and the "ethnic" dimensions of the households. It would not be hard to demonstrate that, across the world-system, there is everywhere a positive correlation, imperfect but real, between the class and the ethnic rankings of households. In particular, the "lowest" class category and the "lowest" ethnic stratum overlap very heavily. It is this simple reality that is at the root of what we call racism.

The second question that arises is what is the link between the "class" and "ethnic" dimensions of households and their political rights. Again, as a general rule, it can be said that there is a correlation between "class" and "ethnic" ranking and access to political rights, even in so-called "liberal democratic" states. Those at the bottom tend to be excluded from political rights in one of two ways. They may be excluded from the category of "citizen" altogether, usually on the grounds that they are immigrants, or children of immigrants, or even fictive immigrants (as in South African legal theories of apartheid). Or they may be excluded not de jure but de facto, by the use of various forms of coercion, fraud, pressure, etc., to deny the lowest stratum access (or full access) to political rights. In all of this, I do not suggest that the rest of the population (those that are "higher-ranking" in the ordinal scales) have full rights or the same rights relative one to the other – the situation in fact varies considerably from country to country – but simply that there is an extra degree of political exclusion for those lowest on the class and ethnic dimensions, and particularly on those who are low on both dimensions, whom I shall designate as the "class-ethnic understratum."

This phenomenon is quite widespread, probably without exception. One is hard pressed to name a single state in the world today that does not have a "class-ethnic understratum." This being so, all the particularistic explanations which are put forward in the context of particular states lose their plausibility. We are pushed to asking not merely why there should be an understratum everywhere, but why this understratum should tend in most cases to have an ethnic dimension.

The answer to the question of why there exists an understratum is virtually self-evident. If one has an inegalitarian historical system, and the capitalist world-economy is an inegalitarian system, then it follows by definition that there must be understrata. That they are found in each and every state located within this system is not necessarily the logical consequence, but it is quite clearly the empirical reality. But why should such strata tend to have an ethnic dimension? This is so far from being logically self-evident that it can be analyzed by Gunnar Myrdal, and not by him alone, as the source of a moral "dilemma."

Another way to put this question is to ask what would be the consequence of a capitalist world-economy from which all racism, all ethnic consciousness had in fact disappeared? What would happen, that is, if we had as now unequal distribution of rewards according to occupational roles, but if simultaneously the *only* justification for the inequality were stated in "class" terms? There are after all only two possible "class" languages. There is the class language of the *ancien régime*, or of any system which has one version or another of caste stratification. People who receive higher rewards deserve them by virture of their nobler birth. This language has been decisively rejected as illegitimate within the capitalist world-economy. In a sense, this rejection is the great ideological legacy to the world-system of the French Revolution. It would take a brave soul to publicly defend today the desirability of unequal allocation of reward by virtue of birth within certain caste groups. The language of the legal equality of all persons is now a given of world political discourse.

There is a second possible class language, however, one less at odds with our Enlightenment heritage. It is the language of meritocracy, *la carrière ouverte aux talents*. This language is widely used today. The key slogan is equal opportunity, by which is meant the absence of legal obstacles to individual mobility between "class" categories. It is usually stated thus: a child born to a poor household should have an equal opportunity with anyone else to achieve a career rank in adult life that is high on the ordinal scale, providing of course that the child is "talented," whatever that might be taken to mean.

We know that there is a considerable amount of individual upward social mobility all the time within the framework of the capitalist world-economy. I say considerable, but it is doubtful than in any generation, in any individual country, it has ever been more that 5 percent of the population who have been upwardly mobile. Still 5 percent, generation after generation, could wipe out inequality. But we know that it has not been wiped out, even in the wealthiest countries, certainly not at all in the capitalist world-economy as a whole. It follows, both deductively and empirically, that there must be, and must always have been, an amount of downward social mobility as great, or almost as great, as the amount of upward social mobility. If so, whatever the change for particular individuals or households, the global or systemic distribution has changed comparatively little, at least in terms of the existence of ordinal class ranking in the various states.

As long as this reality were seen only through the prism of a class perspective, there would only be one moral conclusion to draw: income is allocated largely on the basis of a caste system, and the concept of equal opportunity is largely a sham. This goes so against the ideological truths that prevail today, so against the internalized sentiments not merely of defenders of the system but of the rebels as well that it would be horrendous to contemplate. If, however, we add the ethnic dimension, this horrendous phenomenon immediately becomes more plausible, more reasonable, more palatable, more acceptable. No doubt it causes some disquiet, which is why the Carnegie Corporation hired Gunnar Myradal to do "a comprehensive study of the Negro in America" (F. P. Keppel in Myrdal 1944: xlviii). But however disagreeable the findings of Myrdal to the Carnegie Corporation, or to the general population of the United States, or to anyone else, they pale in comparison with what might be thought about the finding that the underclass were treated like "Negroes" in the absence of an ethnic dimension, which turns out to be in fact an ethnic justification.

This is what racism is about. It provides the only acceptable legitimation of the reality of large-scale collective inequalities within the ideological constraints of the capitalist world-economy. It makes such inequalities legitimate because it provides theoretically for their transitory nature while in practice postponing real change for the Greek calends. The theoretical justification is subtle because it speaks simultaneously but differently to those who have the low status and those who do not. The hinge of the argument is that those who have low ethnic status (and consequently low occupational position for the most part) find themselves in this position because of an unfortunate, but theoretically eradicable, cultural heritage. They come from a group which is somehow less oriented to rational thinking, less disciplined in its work ethic, less desirous of educational and/or earned achievement. Because we no longer claim that these presumed differential aptitudes are genetic but merely cultural we congratulate ourselves on our having overcome the crudities of racism. But of course we have overcome only its most crude, least defensible form, the one form that is totally inconsistent with the Enlightenment heritage. We tend to forget that if a cultural heritage differs from a biological one in that it is historically changeable, it is also true that if the word "culture" means anything here it indicates a phenomenon that is slow to change, and slow to change precisely because it has become part of the superego of most members of the group in question.

The subtle double message that follows is this: the oppressed are told that their position in the social world can be transformed, provided that they are educated in the skills necessary to act in certain ways, said to be the ways that have accounted for the higher recompenses given to the higher-ranking groups. And the oppressors are told that they would benefit by an education in the presumed values of the state, the desirability of providing equality of opportunity for the oppressed. Thus both sides are exhorted to pursue their education, which is in some sense a prerequisite for abolishing the inequalities. In the present, there are always partial remedies, never definitive abolition of inequalities. The definitive abolition is always in the future.

In the meantime, the correlation of low class status and low ethnic status persists. If it is modified for one group, it reappears for another. It need not have anything to do with race per se. Pierre Vallières asserted that Québécois were "white niggers." And in the meantime this continued correlation maintains the sense of ethnic identity, a phenomenon if anything reinforced by whatever political ameliorations are introduced. Furthermore, it is this consciousness of ethnicity, even more than its reality, which contributes a crucial element for the operation of the system. For ethnic consciousness necessarily means ethnic socialization of the young by their elders. And ethnic socialization, if it is to serve the interests of the group, must include a large dose of realistic perception of social polarization. Thus, the child born into a household of low-ranking ethnicity is normally taught certain occupational expectations and the behavioral patterns that most accord with the realities the child will eventually face. This is of course true of the child born into a household of high-ranking ethnicity as well. It follows that although the mechanism of ethnic consciousness enables oppressed strata to struggle politically for their rights, it simultaneously (and in contradiction) reinforces their socialization into their oppressed roles.

Finally, we should not overlook the degree to which the ethnicization of the work force adds a degree of flexibility to the capitalist system that has been historically very helpful in maintaining its efficient functioning. For the capitalist world-economy operates by means of a cyclical rhythm of expansion and contraction and a constant albeit slow-moving relocation of the leading nodes of economic activity. Hence the quantitative demand for particular class-ethnic understrata is always varying. Today country X can use 5 million such workers but tomorrow it needs only 3 million. At the same time, however, country Y may be moving in an opposite direction. This can take the form of unemployment. It can also take the form of "upward" and "downward" mobility currents. Whenever this happens, one tends to see over a generation or two a redefinition of ethnic categories. Some new names appear, and old ones disappear. The categories seem to evolve to fit the quantity needed. At the end there is always some class-ethnic understratum (or I should say understrata), but they have been reshaped, sometimes extensively, to fit the evolution of the world-economy. It is precisely because "ethnicity" is so incredibly malleable in its specific manifestations, despite the fact that it is defined fictively as a community of unchanging past realities (and hence future probabilities), that it is so difficult to pin down in terms of persisting essences.

This then is how racism, which is nothing but this whole complex system, works to keep people in while keeping people out. It does this in two senses. One is obvious. It serves to minimize the political capacity of the understratum while keeping them in occupationally. But a second way is less obvious and probably more important. Racism keeps people in occupationally when their active current labor is required and enables the system to put them on hold at other times, but always to put them on hold in such a fashion that they can rapidly be brought back in actively when the market conjuncture changes. Furthermore, this understratum has internalized values such that it is willing, even eager, to be brought back in. Thus it can be rightly considered to be a "reserve army" in the literal sense of the term.

We can now see how the explanations of racism as a phenomenon within the separate states of the world-system and under-development as a phenomenon of the interstate system are congruent. In the first place, there is a worldwide allocation of economic activities (and hence of occupational roles) which is unequal and hierarchical. We speak of this today as the core–periphery axial division of labor in the world-economy. It surely has a "class" dimension. However, it even more obviously has an "ethnic" dimension. The biggest difference between racism and underdevelopment is in the views of the critical analysts. Whereas at the national level the class hierarchy seems clear and one often has to argue the case that it is correlated with an ethnic hierarchy, at the level of the world-system the situation is inverted. The ethnic hierarchy (here taking a "national" guise) is obvious, and one often has to argue the case that it is correlated with a class hierarchy. Nonetheless, today it is increasingly accepted that there does exist a class-ethnic (that is, nation-class) understratum at the world level, to which we refer by such locutions as the Third World.

The congruence of the state-level and world-level phenomena continues when one examines the ideological discussion. The "backwardness" of the Third World – we no longer dare use the word, backward, but we continue to think it in our private minds – is explained by a deep-seated cultural difference. The result is said to be the generally poor economic performance in the Third World, as well as prejudice against the Third World in the so-called de-veloped countries. The remedy is once again said to be education. The Third World must learn the skills, and, even more, absorb the underlying values, of the industrialized world, and they will then "catch up." The industrialized countries must learn to shelve their prejudices, and aid their brethren to catch up. Today we educate. Tomorrow we shall be equal. But tomorrow, for the dilemma of underdevelopment as for the dilemma of racism, remains a long time away.

Nationalist consciousness or Third World consciousness plays an analogous role on a world level to ethnic consciousness within a state. It organizes people to struggle against the inequalities; but since it also involves a training in the power realities of the world-system it simultaneously socializes peoples into their existing roles in the world-system.

Furthermore, just as the constantly evolving market situation of the world-economy requires constant relocations at the national level, so it does at the world level, too. We need today more or less of X or Y occupational/economic roles, and often we find it optimal that they be located in new sites. This requires ethnic redefinition. Yesterday, Greeks, Italians, and Spaniards were Mediterraneans. Today they are Europeans. Yesterday the Japanese led the Yellow Horde. Today, as the South African government so elegantly puts it, they are "honorary Whites." Who knows? Tomorrow Swedes may once again become what they were centuries ago, pale-skinned barbarians. World ethnicity, world-systemic racial categories are always there in our historical system, and always form a hierarchy, but the names of the categories are in regular flux.

Finally, there is the way in which whole peoples are kept in while they are kept out. This is of course true at the level of the relation of political capacity to market role. The underdeveloped countries play a crucial role in the productive processes of the world-system but they surely have little political power. This is true as well at the purely market level. In periods of world economic contraction, whole peoples can be pushed back into a forced autarky and left to survive as best they can, just as *gastarbeiter* can be sent home. But when the upturn comes, they can be pulled right back in. And furthermore they will often be more than happy to be thus pulled back in.

Why then have these "dilemmas" remained "unsolved"? Here I can be much briefer. Indeed there is little to say. The "dilemmas" remain "unsolved" because nobody is in the least bit interested in "solving" them. To solve them is to transform the existing system at its roots. There have in fact been three social approaches to the "dilemmas." The conservative approach has been that of denial. The "dilemmas" don't exist, or scarcely exist, or go away by themselves. A major part of Myrdal's scholarly work represented an attempt to pierce this conservative armor, to persuade the privileged of the world that the dilemmas were real and that there were massive inconsistencies between societal valuations and societal structures.

The liberal approach – I use the word liberal in its early nineteenth-century European and its contemporary United States usage; I could as well use the word reformist or Social Democrat – has been to urge legislation or policy changes in one form or another, in attempts to meliorate the inequalities. No doubt this attempt, viewed globally and over the whole space of the world-system, has had some impact. But after four centuries of such ameliorative politics – I date it at least from the defense by Las Casas of the fact that Native Americans have souls – after four centuries, how much melioration has there been? I do not think the global balance sheet is very impressive. Is there really less racism and less underdevelopment in the late twentieth-century capitalist world-economy than in its early days in the sixteenth century?

Has then the radical or revolutionary approach more to its credit? I am skeptical. The radicals, or revolutionaries, have for the most part defined racism and underdevelopment as secondary symptoms of some primary malady. They have concentrated their intellectual attention on what they conceived to be the primary symptoms, and their political attention on the intermediary strategy of obtaining state power. In the process they have no doubt made some telling political and intellectual blows against the system, but by relegating racism and underdevelopment to the category of secondary issues they have missed the historic boat, and acted to reinforce the system almost as much as they have acted to undermine it.

Racism and underdevelopment, I fear, are more than dilemmas. They are, in my view, constitutive of the capitalist world-economy as a historical system. They are the primary conditions and essential manifestations of the unequal distribution of surplus-value. They make possible the ceaseless accumulation of capital, the *raison d'être* of historical capitalism. They organize the process occupationally and legitimate it politically. It is impossible to conceptualize a capitalist world-economy which did not have them. Perhaps we should go back to the dictionary definition of dilemma. From the perspective of those who hold power in the capitalist world-economy, solving or not solving the "dilemmas" of racism or underdevelopment are "equally unpleasant alternatives." The system cannot operate without them, and in the long run the system cannot operate with them. It is more than a difficult choice; it is an impossible one.

II

I wish now to turn to the second half of the Myrdal legacy. The first half concerns the negative social realities constituted by racism and underdevelopment. The second half is concerned with the role of the social scientist in relation to these realities.

Gunnar Myrdal was trained as an economist. He was awarded the Nobel Prize for Economics. Yet all his life he considered himself a dissenter from what he called "conventional economic theory" because he considered that it "work[ed] with 'closed models' with too few variables" (Myrdal 1976: 83). Against this conventional economic theory he posed something called "institutional economics" based on a "holistic approach" that was made imperative methodologically because social systems work through "circular causation."

Myrdal was quite clearly exasperated by the conventional economists. In one of his last essays, "What is Political Economy?" (Myrdal 1981) he describes the historical process by which the adjective "political" had come to be dropped from "political economy" and how in the early nineteenth century economists had adopted the reigning moral philosophy of their time, utilitarianism. Subsequently, the neo-classical authors grounded this utilitarian moral philosophy in hedonistic associational psychology. They did this, he notes, at the very moment that the professional philosophers and psychologists had abandoned these theories. "The very apparent isolation of economic science from the other social sciences, and from philosophy as these disciplines developed, dates from that time" (Myrdal 1981: 42).

Myrdal has of course already treated this in his very first book in Swedish published in 1930. *Vetenskap och politik i nationalekonomien.* Although this book was translated into German in 1932 and into Italian in 1943, it was not translated into English until 1953. His comments at the end of his life on the impact of this book are poignant:

> By demonstrating the superficiality and logical inconsistency of this modern welfare theory [that is, the one developed by the first generation of neo-classical authors] almost 50 years ago ... I thought I had finally disposed of it. But it grows like a malignant tumor. Hundreds of books and articles are produced every year on welfare economics, reasoning in terms of individual or social "utility" or some substitute for that term. But if the approach is not entirely meaningless, it has a meaning only in terms of a forlorn hedonistic psychology, and a utilitarian moral philosophy built upon that psychology. I have always wondered why the psychologists and philosophers have left the economists alone and undisturbed in their futile exercise.

> The trend toward narrow professionalism in contemporary establishment economics in regard to training, reading, and indeed awareness of everything outside the narrow field they have staked out for their work, protects them form being disturbed by much knowledge about modern psychology and philosophy. And the relative neglect we can now find in the curricula at most universities of the study of the history of economic science helps them have an exaggerated belief in the newness of their own contributions to welfare economics. In particular, it protects them from grasping that what they are attempting is normative economic theory, but in disguise since they are not prepared to call themselves political economists. (Myrdal 1981: 43)

Myrdal is not, in my view, too harsh on establishment economics, but in his anxiety to gore the ox, he tends to ignore the fact that the folly of establishment economics is merely a *reductio ad absurdum* of a much more widespread malady, the narrow blinkers that all of the historical social sciences have put upon themselves.

You may have noticed that I have repeatedly used this somewhat unusual locution, the historical social sciences. Perhaps I should explain myself. History and the social sciences as we know them today are largely a product of nineteenth-century thought. To be sure, historiography has a much longer tradition, and the social sciences had many proto-practitioners before then, usually under the rubric of philosophy. However, the French Revolution produced an institutional shock to the world-system which resulted in a whole series of cultural transformations. One was the emergence of social science as a specialized activity. Specifically, what had been a single domain of intellectual discourse with rather vague boundaries became differentiated, primarily between 1848 and 1914, into a series of so-called disciplines, each with a name, often a neologism. The main names were history, geography, economics, sociology, political science, anthropology, and (let us not forget) Orientalism.

Neither Swedish universities nor any others had departments, or even chairs, in many of these fields in 1850. Yet by 1914, most universities had some of these fields as departments and, by 1960, almost all universities throughout the world had almost all of them. As of 1850, there were no scholarly associations, as we know them today, grouping scholars in these fields. How could there be, since the fields were not yet considered to be clearly circumscribed social realities? Yet by 1914, national associations bearing these names existed in Europe and North America, and again by the 1960s this was true throughout the world. International associations bearing these names are only a twentieth-century creation. The same thing can be said of scholarly journals. In short, a massive process of the institutionalization of separate so-called disciplines has taken place within the last century or so, but only since then.

If we ask ourselves not merely why the medieval university's faculty of philosophy became differentiated into the multiple "disciplines" we know today, but why this differentiation took the exact form it took, we can see that its ultimate form reflected the reigning ideology of the nineteenth-century world-system, classical liberalism in its British variant. The first premise was that the great achievement of the modern world was the proper separation of the three spheres of human activity: the public sphere of the exercise of power, the semi-public sphere of production, and the private sphere of everyday life. To confound these spheres was "medieval"; to separate them, divine. This was the origin of that threefold division of knowledge which is so fundamental to our contemporary epistemology: the political, the economic, and the socio-cultural arenas. Or in terms of contemporary university departments and professional associations: political science, economics, and sociology.

The second premise was that we live in a progressively evolutionary world. The primary lesson that had been learned from the French Revolution was that change was normal. The impact of the French Revolution and its Napoleonic extension was to undermine fatally the older discourse about the social world, one now seen to be incompatible with the functioning of an industrializing, capitalist world, a world, dedicated to and believing in progress. Hence we have a history which is worth knowing primarily in its illustration not of moral virtue nor of golden ages but of the slow but steady achievement of perfection – in short, the Whig interpretation of history. Since of course what was past was less good, somehow less pure than what is present and new, history cannot tell us much about the present and had best be kept separate, and distant, from the study of the present. History furthermore was thought only really to exist when it culminated in our present. History was about us, not them. Consequently, as late as the 1960s, an eminent historian like H. R. Trevor-Roper could assert that there is no such thing as African history.

The third premise was the utilitarian view of human psychology, itself transmuted, as Myrdal noted, from natural law theories, which assumed the existence of a "human nature" (curiously enough discovered to emulate the social habits of successful entrepreneurs). This premise permitted us to assume that there were laws of human/social action that were at once universal and knowable. And it thereby allowed the adoption of the Newtonian model of science by those fashioning our views of the more complex world of social reality.

The fourth premise was the self-evident superiority of Western civilization. To be sure, this premise existed long before the nineteenth century. It was inherent in the Christian world-view, and to be fair it was paralleled by comparable (albeit reversed) assumptions in other civilizational zones. But in the nineteenth century this world-view seemed to have the empirical justification of the military and technological power of "Europe" which permitted it truly to rule the world.

It is therefore not hard to see why we ended up with the disciplinary divisions we did, as of say 1914. Economics, sociology, and political science represented the separate study of the three presumably separate spheres of contemporary life, each searching for the universal laws believed to govern its sphere. History became the study of Europe's past, particularly its political past. The exotic peoples in the process of being conquered in Africa, Asia, the Americas, Oceania required dedicated specialists to study them. Since these peoples were "primitive" and had no documents, they had to be studied *in situ*, and since they were "primitive" and had not yet learned to differentiate their spheres of human activity, they had to be studied ethnographically, that is, by describing the linked set of their presumably unchanging patterns. This was ethnographic study as opposed to either the universalizing study of the European present or the historical (that is, evolutionary) study of the European past. Finally, Orientalism emerged as the study of that segment of the world of exotica which had a so-called "high" civilization, that is, had writing: the worlds of China, India, Islam, etc. They were studied not ethnographically but philologically in order to understand the specific codes of the civilized elites of each of these other civilizations, their religions (which were termed "world" religions, unlike narrow tribal beliefs), their complex languages, their art forms. But once again, they were studied not in a universalistic mode (as was Europe's present) or historically (as was Europe's past) but as remnants of previously unchanging particularities, that is, as precious, if decaying, dollhouses.

All these disciplinary divisions seem so obvious to us today that we seldom note how peculiar they are. Spatial relations, for example, could not be easily accounted for in the reigning model but were obviously somehow there. This was handled by creating a special discipline, geography, and then relegating it to a sort of pariah status in the intellectual hierarchy.

All alternative groupings were squashed. The one major alternative was developed in late nineteenth-century Germany, the creation of a field called *Staatswissenschaft*, the structure of which represented a basic challenge to the tri-modal differentiation of the economic, the political, and the social, as well as the binary distinction between the universal present and the historical past. The story of the institutional elimination of *Staatswissenschaft*, accomplished more or less by the 1920s, has never really been told. I personally think we have to see the *Methodenstreit*, which originated in the German-speaking world, as a major factor in the institutional destruction of *Staatswissenschaft*. I believe that the way the *Methodenstreit* accomplished this elimination was by constituting itself as an enormous diversion from the real issues.

The heart of the *Methodenstreit* was the assertion of a particular antinomy as central to epistemological issues: that between nomothetic and idiographic knowledge, presented as the only two possible (and/or desirable) but mutually exclusive ways of knowing. The two sides pictured the debate as one between the existence of universal laws that were to be the objective of research (hence the term, social *science*) and their nonexistence explained by the uniqueness of each specific human/social phenomenon. It was easy to fit the new so-called disciplines into this matrix. Economics, sociology, and political science came to be the nomothetic disciplines, knowable by studying the European present which incarnated universal achievement. The idiographic disciplines were then history (the uniquely evolving European past) and anthropology plus Orientalism (each describing unique unchanging non-European past/presents). There was therefore no room for any intellectual categorization, such as *Staatswissenschaft*, which cast a skeptical eye on both nomothetic and idiographic claims.

The fake ferocity of the *Methodenstreit* not only eliminated the alternatives like *Staatswissenschaft* but also reinforced the compartmentalization of the historical social sciences, one set of which was nomothetic (and scientific) while a second set was idiographic (and hence, in the jargon, humanistic). We consequently had not only a division into "disciplines" but also a grouping of these "disciplines" into two separate "faculties" – the social sciences and the humanities – an additional institutionalization that was achieved, perhaps a bit imperfectly, virtually everywhere.

The institutionalization of these categories had a further implication for our collective research. The numbers of scholars expanded steadily and enormously. Training programs were created and the increased valuation of rules of precision in research became a natural corollary. But how does one become precise in nomothetic and in idiographic research?

The path to precision of a universalizing science is quantification as a necessary step in the search for formulae which are linked in theorems. This puts a clear constraint on actual empirical research. From the initial requirement that research be as quantitative as possible, it is not far to go to a derived requirement that empirical enquiry should be conducted in loci for which quantifiable data exist, and the "harder" (that is, the more elaborate and more carefully compiled) the better. It should take no great stretch of the imagination to see that, since most quantitative data that exist in the world are and have been collected by governments – the term statistics is derived literally from the term state – the more "advanced" the state, the more recent the occurrence, and the more narrowly defined the phenomenon, the "harder" the data. Thus we are pushed further and further into the immediate present, in particular, that of certain countries, and into smaller and smaller scope, a push that is reinforced by the natural differentiation occurring as the result of the expansion of the number of researchers. This narrowing of empirical focus seldom raised intellectual issues for the practitioners of this research since, if human nature is considered to be universal, what we learn about how it operates in, say, Stockholm in 1988 is universally applicable, provided only we have followed the exigencies of precision in our techniques.

The path to precision of idiographic knowledge is of course different. When Ranke exhorted us all to study history *wie es eigentlich gewesen ist*, his target was a mode of historiography which had dealt in heroic mythology. But how were we to know what had *really* happened? Ranke and the others had a basically ingenious answer: locate what people had written down at the time of the occurrence. The concept of "archives" was no small intellectual breakthrough. But who kept archives? The answer is of course that basically they were kept by the same people as those who kept statistics: primarily officials of the states, who, however, kept (and keep) both archives and statistics only concerning those matters they deem important. It is no accident that the use of archives pushed us first of all to diplomatic history and secondly to political history in general. Using archives is of course time-consuming work. In addition, later scholars using the same archives as earlier scholars were pushed to produce greater and greater detail. The precision and the time it requires, combined with the expansion of the size of the research community, have led scholars to define more and more narrowly the subject matters of their investigations.

Hence the logic of the *Methodenstreit* and its methodological implications, turned the worldwide enterprise of the historical social sciences from its grand beginnings to the study of the ever smaller in scale both in time and in scope, in both nomothetic and idiographic empirical research. In the process scholars who objected to such a perverted outcome were ignored, as Myrdal was to complain of the ignoring of so-called "institutional economics" by the "malignant tumor" of nomothetic and universalizing economics, and major intellectual questions were ignored because they couldn't be handled within the framework of either half of the *Methodenstreit* antinomy.

We were therefore unable to explain racism and its persistence. We could not explain underdevelopment and its persistence. We could not even explain how and why the states came into existence, nor why we have assumed implicitly that every state has a "society" and every "society" a state. And a world of knowledge that cannot explain such central phenomena is bound to run into great difficulties. The real world is bound to catch up with it. The First World War and the Russian Revolution were shock enough. Fascism and Nazism were even more unsettling. I believe the Bandung phenomenon was still more unnerving. No doubt the historical social sciences "handled" each of these successive shocks by some adjustment to their theorizing and their practices. But it was a little like adding on additional epicycles to the Ptolemaic model. The whole analysis was becoming too cumbersome. When the world cultural revolution of 1968 came, it was all a bit too much, and the edifice shook and today continues to crumble.

Politically, 1968 represented in my view not merely an antisystemic revolutionary moment (that is, a worldwide upsurge against the capitalist world-economy as a historical system) but also, and as importantly, a revolution against the historic antisystemic movements themselves. These movements in their three major variants had, in the period from 1945 to 1968, been able at last to achieve power more or less: the Social-Democrats (interpreted a bit loosely) in the West, the Communists in the East, and the national liberation movements in the South. The upsurge of 1968 was to a significant degree a critique of these movements for their failure to be truly antisystemic.

As a revolutionary moment, 1968 has passed, and passed definitively. But so did 1848 as a revolutionary moment. However, 1968, like 1848 before it, has left enormous legacies. Among them is its impact on the universities and the world of intellectual discourse. What 1968 did was to break the total control over the world university system by the heirs of nineteenth-century thought and restore the university to its role as an arena of intellectual debate. In the process, the *Methodenstreit* ceased to be the only possible framework for epistemological debate. The previously uncrossable border between historical or humanistic studies and contemporary or social scientific studies ceased to be gospel. Perhaps most radically of all, that arena of tacit consensus within which the very real struggles between nineteenth-century liberalism and nineteenth-century Marxism occurred, a tacit consensus that had framed our conceptual understandings in the historical social sciences, was at last under challenge.

The result has been disorder. Rehashed versions of early nineteenth-century conservatism have rushed to fill the breach. While noisy and aggressive, thus far they have been weak on intellectual substance, gaining credit primarily out of the discredit of the liberal-Marxist arena of consensus. On the other hand, new subject matters have appeared in the universities which derive directly from the 1968 world revolution: in particular, women's studies, and multiple versions of what generically might be called "ethnic" studies. They have shown great vitality, but they are still largely in the phase of consciousness raising, and have not yet developed the strength fundamentally to reshape the agenda of the university system. Some of us have been putting forth a "world-systems perspective" as a challenge to the conceptual frameworks and methodological biases of the historical social sciences. I must confess, however, that, whatever the reputation of the world-systems perspective, it too has failed thus far to have a major impact on the university agenda.

In short, we are in the midst of great confusion. There is in fact today no longer any clear university agenda and I insist that this is the first time this has been true in at least 100 years. This is because the world of scholarship – itself for the first time ensconced in a *worldwide* university community – is in the midst of a great sea-change, whose outcome is still unclear.

The evidence for this sea-change is everywhere. I have been noting what has been happening in what I call the historical social sciences. But we should not miss what has been happening in the physical sciences and in mathematics. Prigogine (along with many others) argues that Newtonian linear dynamics and equilibrium analysis are very special cases of a more general process in which nonlinear dynamics and far-from-equilibrium analyses play the central role. He has called for restoring the "arrow of time" even to physics, and has argued that the aim of science is not to simplify but to explain complexity. Mandelbrot similarly argues that Euclidian geometry is a very special case of a more general process, in which the real world must be measured primarily in fractal dimensions (that is, dimensions that are for the most part not integers). Chaos, catastrophe, and bifurcation have become the code words of a movement that is revising all of modern science from top to bottom.

At the moment that the physical scientists are in the process of rejecting the Newtonian premises on which neo-classical economics is based, will the neo-classical economists be the last defenders of an increasingly irrelevant and, in the current intellectual scene, increasing antiscientific mode of theorization? Will Nobel Prizes for Economics continue to be given to persons who offer proofs for theorems whose disproof gains Nobel Prizes in Physics and Chemistry?

Conclusions

What conclusions then shall we draw from the Myrdal legacy? I draw the following:

First, the dilemmas to which Myrdal devoted his intellectual life are even more pervasive and knotty than he thought. He seemed to believe that, somewhat like a psychoanalyst, once he revealed the underlying mechanisms and hidden rationalizations of existing contradictions between social values and social realities, society as patient would readjust its mode of functioning. The dilemmas of racism and underdevelopment are not, however, so tractable. They constitute rather the very tissue of our present historical system. They are not curable maladies, but defining characteristics. Their manifestations may change, but their reality is constant.

Secondly, the issue of value in social theory is quite as central as Myrdal believed. And he has not been ignored in this respect as much as he seemed to fear. He was indeed a great prophet whom we ignore today at our moral and intellectual peril. The sea-change of which I spoke has unleashed the force of all those who understand that the nineteenth-century pretense of excluding value from social research was just that, a pretense. And the position that Myrdal espoused has now acquired tremendous support from an unlikely quarter, the natural scientists, who are saying that the "arrow of time" and the inescapable impact of the researcher on the object of study are phenomena not only true of the historical social sciences but of physics and mathematics as well. Prigogine has called this development the "reenchantment of the world."

Thirdly, Myrdal was quite on the mark in his methodological concerns. As we know, his central organizing metaphor was that of "circular and cumulative causation," based on the recognition that there is "no . . . tendency towards automatic self-stabilisation in the social system" (Myrdal 1957: 13). But what needs to be underlined is that, in the far-from-equilibrium situations where bifurcations occur, these bifurcations are stochastic in character, processes whose outcome cannot be predicted, and where relatively small fluctuations have very large and irreversible consequences.

Fourthly, the logic of Myrdal's position, as evidenced in the intellectual "disorder" of the past two decades, indicates that we are in urgent need of a restructuring of the world university system. We need it in order to permit us to weather the sea-change and to revamp our theorizing and our methodologies in such a way as to enable us to cope with the social and intellectual bifurcations that are upon us. I therefore call for the abolition of the departments of economics, of sociology, of anthropology, of political science, of geography, of history, and their merger into a single department of the historical social sciences. I make this call of course symbolically. For while the so-called disciplines can no longer plausibly defend their legitimacy intellectually as separate disciplines, they are organizationally well fortified in their trench-like structures. No doubt were this call heeded, there would emerge over the next 50 years many new subdisciplines, with their specific intellectual definitions and perhaps their specific training programs for apprentice scholars. But the essential prerequisite of such a complex redefinition is the creation of a single intellectual arena, based on a single debate about appropriate heuristic theorizations, in the holistic study of a singular intellectual phenomenon, the modes of functioning of historical social systems – the one in which we live, the ones that have existed at prior moments in historical time, and the ones that are possible.

Fifthly, this restructuring of the historical social sciences cannot be conceived as somehow isolated, either from the rest of the intellectual world or from the social world of which it is both a reflection and an integral motor. In the mid-nineteenth century the social sciences emerged in tandem with and in tension with the social movements. They reciprocally determined each other. So will they now. When Myrdal asked when and how his dilemmas would be resolved, he came up with the only possible answer: "When power has been assembled by those who have grievances, then is the time when ideals and the social conscience can become effective" (Myrdal 1957: 70). The social movements create the intellectual issues that the historical social sciences seek to answer. The historical social sciences, in theorizing these issues, create both the tools for, and the barriers to, their solutions.

I thus will end with this thought of Gunnar Myrdal. The "logical crux of all science" he said, is that:

> it assumes in all its endeavours an *a priori* but its ambitions must constantly be to find an empirical base for this *a priori*.
>
> We are thus constantly attempting what in its perfection is impossible, and we are never achieving more than makeshifts: these, however, can be better or worse. In our present situation the task is not, as is sometimes assumed, the relatively easy one of filling "empty boxes" of theory with a content of empirical knowledge about reality. For our theoretical boxes are empty primarily because they are not built in such a way that they can hold reality. We need new theories which, however abstract, are more realistic in the sense that they are in a higher degree adequate to the facts.
>
> Meanwhile, I believe it to be a disciplining force in our dispersed efforts ... that a clear concept of the ideal is constantly kept in mind and given a directing role in all our research. To begin with, we need to free ourselves from the impediment of biased and inadequate predilections and unreal and irrelevant theoretical approaches which in our academic tradition we are carrying with us as a heavy ballast. (1957: 163–64)

Let us all join Gunnar Myrdal in his call to go "Against the Stream" (1972). And let us remember, as he said in his Nobel speech, that "when politicians and experts become timid about giving due importance to moral commitments, realism is absent" (Myrdal 1975: 420).

7

Development: Lodestar or Illusion?

There is perhaps no social objective that can find as nearly unanimous acceptance today as that of economic development. I doubt that there has been a single government anywhere in the last 30 years that has not asserted it was pursuing this objective, at least for its own country. Everywhere in the world today, what divides left and right, however defined, is not whether or not to develop, but which policies are presumed to offer most hope that this objective will be achieved. We are told that socialism is the road to development. We are told that *laissez-faire* is the road to development. We are told that a break with tradition is the road to development. We are told that a revitalized tradition is the road to development. We are told that industrialization is the road to development. We are told that increased agricultural productivity is the road to development. We are told that delinking is the road to development. We are told that an increased opening to the world market (export-oriented growth) is the road to development. Above all, we are told that development is possible, if only we do the right thing.

But what is this right thing? There is of course no shortage of people who will respond to this query, and respond vigorously, even passionately. If there are protracted revolutionary movements in the world, the underlying drive is to end an oppressive situation. But the other drive that sustains the revolutionaries is the expectation that their victory at the state level will open the door at last to the real development of their country.

At the same time, there has been considerable disillusionment of late with the fruits of past development policies. In China they talk about the ways in which the Cultural Revolution is said to have blocked for a decade, and so set back, development. In the Soviet Union, they talk about the ways in which bureaucratic rigidities and political errors have damaged the economy, and they call for a *perestroika*. In Africa, they debate what explains the serious worsening of their economic situation since independence and following a "decade," in fact several decades, of efforts to develop. In the United States and Western Europe, they talk about how too large or too inappropriate government involvement in the economic process has hampered initiative and therefore has created a less desirable economic situation that these countries presumably enjoyed previously, or would presumably otherwise enjoy. In all of this grumbling, virtually no one in China or the Soviet Union or Africa or the US or Western Europe has challenged either the desirability or the viability of development as an objective. The critics or reformers or whatever they call themselves have merely argued that new and different policies must be adopted to replace those which they assert have failed.

We think of economic development as a post-1945 concept. And it is certainly true that most of our current language, as used by politicians and intellectuals, is a product of the geopolitics of the post-1945 era in the world-system. And it is certainly also true that since 1945 the concept as doctrine has been applied more widely and with greater social legitimation than ever before. But of course the basic idea has much older roots. It seems in fact that its history is concurrent with the history of the capitalist world-economy itself. Full-fledged intellectual debates about how countries might be developed were occurring at least as early as the seventeenth century. What else, after all, was at issue in the proposed policies we group together today under the heading of mercantilism?

I should like therefore to review what we know of the history of this capitalist world-economy in order to address five questions:

1 Development is the development of what?
2 Who or what has in fact developed?
3 What is the demand behind the demand for development?
4 How can such development occur?
5 What are the political implications of the answers to the first four questions?

Then, and only then, will I come to the question in my title: is development a lodestar or an illusion?

I

Development is a word that has two different connotations. One is the reference to the processes of a biological organism. From little acorns do giant oaks grow. All organic phenomena have lives or natural histories. Somehow they begin; then they grow or develop; eventually they die. But, since they also reproduce, the death of a single organism is never the death of the species.

The presumed socio-economic analogy is clear. Nations or states or societies somehow (and somewhere) begin; then they grow or develop. The rest of the analogy, however, is rarely pursued. There are few discussions of the likelihood that these entities will eventually die, or that the species will survive via a process of reproduction. We might wonder why the analogy is not pursued to its fullest, and why all our attention is concentrated on what are taken to be the normalities or abnormalities of the middle segment of the sequence, the presumed growth process.

One reason may be that development has a second connotation, more arithmetic than biological. Development often means simply "more." In this case, we are making an analogy not to an organic cycle but to a linear, or at least monotonic, projection. And of course linear projections go to infinity. Now, infinity is far away. But it is there, and it is always possible to imagine more of something. This is clearly very encouraging as a social possibility. Whatever we now have some of, we might have more of tomorrow.

Of course, infinity is also quite terrifying. Infinity is in a very real sense a void. Endlessness is not everyone's cup of tea. There is an entire literature of clinical psychology about the ways in which human beings need to bound their universes, to create an environment of manageable scale, one which therefore offers a reasonable possibility that it is somewhat controllable. Durkheim's discussion of anomie is another version of the same argument.

Here, however, we come immediately upon a social relativity. In a set of groups who are located on a scale in terms of quantity of possessions, and who are all seeking more, those groups at the top end of the scale have only the void before them, whereas groups who are at the bottom are bounded by groups above them. So while some may face the uncharted prospects of seeming endlessness, others are clearly facing primarily the more manageable project of "catching up" to those who already have more.

There is a further element in the picture, as we all know. There are good times and there are bad times, periods of boom and periods of bust or at least of stagnation. The social interpretation of good and bad times tends to be quite straightforwardly relational. Good times are those moments in which we think we have more than previously. Bad times are those in which we think or fear we have less. If then we distinguish between groups at the high end of the scale of possessions and those at the low end, economic expansion and contraction present different pictures. Those at the high end to be sure have the comfort of being at the high end. They may, however, in times of expansion fear the void and in times of contraction fear that they will no longer be at the high end. Those at the low end start from the base knowledge of their relatively low level of material reward. Expansion then may open up the optimistic hope of immediate absolute improvement and relative middle-term catching up. Contraction offers on the other hand the gloom of decline from an already low level.

It seems to me therefore not hard to understand why people feel so passionately about development and oscillate so rapidly among alternative schemata for realizing development. Develpoment as the achievement of "more" is the Promethean myth. It is the realization of all our libidinal desires. It is pleasure and power combined, or rather fused. The desire lies within all of us. What the capitalist world-economy as a historical system has done is to make these desires for the first time socially legitimate "Accumulate, accumulate!" is the leitmotif of capitalism. And in fact, the scientific-technological output of this capitalist system has created some widely visible spectacles of significant accumulation, and an impressive consumption level for about 10–20 percent of the world's population. In short, the realization of the dream of endless accumulation has come to be not merely legitimate but to seem in some sense plausible.

At the same time, as living beings, we are all too conscious of the problem of death and suffering. We are all aware that if some consume much, most do not. We are all equally aware that consumption is a present-oriented activity, and that in the future we shall not be there to consume. Those who consume well tend to draw the organismic implication that not only they as individuals but the groups of which they are a part will one day "decline." In short, they are faced with "civilization and its discontents."

II

However, although the controversies concerning development have deep resonances in the collective social psychologies (or mentalities) bred by historical capitalism, the basic issue is not psychological but social. The fact is that historical capitalism has been up to now a system of very differential rewards, in both class and geographic terms. As an empirical fact, this seems to me uncontestable, whether or not we think it theoretically inevitable or historically enduring.

Yet it is also the case that if we look at the various geographical-juridical zones that are today sovereign or potentially sovereign states, some are uncontestably better off than they were at previous moments in the history of the capitalist world-economy, whether the comparison is made between a given state today and that same state (more or less) 50 or 100 or 300 years ago, or the comparison is made between a given state's ordinal ranking in GNP per capita and the ordinal interstate rank level of the same state 50 or 100 or 300 years ago. This is usually what we mean when we mean when we say that a given state, say the US or Sweden, has "developed." It is "better off" materially, and (many would argue) politically (expansion of civil rights, etc.).

Who then has really developed in this sense? At one level the answer is easy. What we mean by the locutions, "developed" and "underdeveloped" countries, as they have come to be used in the last 30 years, is precisely the list of those who have "developed" (or not) in either or both senses I spelled out above over the past 50–300 years. Generally speaking, we think of the countries of Western Europe plus Japan as the members of the list of "developed" countries. We think of the so-called Third World as constituting the list of underdeveloped countries. The socialist countries present the most controversial category in terms of either comparison: where they are today in relation to where they were; are where they stand in an ordinal ranking today compared to formerly. Analysts do not agree on what the basic economic measurements show and/or on whether these measurements are valid indicators for the socialist countries.

What then do we know of the pattern of "national development" within the frame-work of the capitalist world-economy prior to 1945? I believe there are a number of things we can say today with some clarity.

One, a capitalist world-economy began to form centered on the European continent in the sixteenth century. From the beginning, this involved the establishment of integrated production processes we may call commodity chains. These commodity chains almost all tended to traverse the existing political boundaries. The total surplus extracted in these commodity chains was at no point in time distributed evenly in terms of the geographical location of the creation of the surplus, but was always concentrated to a disproportionate degree in some zones rather than in others. We mean by "peripheries" those zones that lost out in the distribution of surplus to "core" zones. Whereas, at the beginning of the historical process, there seemed little difference in the economic wealth of the different geographical areas, a mere one century's flow of surplus was enough to create a visible distinction between core and periphery in terms of three criteria: the accumulation of capital, the social organization of local production processes, the political organization of the state structures in creation.

Thus, by 1600 we could already say three things about the emergent peripheral zones (such as east-central Europe and Hispanic America) compared with the emergent core zones in northwest Europe. The per capita consumption was lower. The local production processes used labor that was more coerced and received less real income. (This was of course a major reason why per capita consumption was lower.) The state structures were less centralized internally and weaker externally. It is crucial to note that while all three statements were true by 1600, none had been true as of 1450. The three empirical truths were the consequence of the operation of the capitalist world-economy.

Two, the mode of obtaining a larger proportion of the surplus was the relative monopolization of some segment of the commodity chain. The monopolization could occur because of some technological or organizational advantage which some segment of the producers had or because of some politically enforced restriction of the market. Whatever the source of monopolistic advantage was, it was inherently vulnerable. Others could over time try to "copy" in one way or another the technological or organizational advantage or try to undermine the politically enforced restrictions of the market. This of course was the constant desire of producers who received less than others of the overall created surplus.

The vulnerability of historically temporary monopolizations was real. The advantages were constantly under attack – within states and between states. The eighteenth century concern with the "wealth of nations" was simply one ideological expression of the interest that producers had in maintaining or creating their own monopolistic advantages and undermining those of others. What we call mercantilism was simply one organized method of this struggle, in which producers whose abilities to corner surplus were somewhere in the middle rank sought to use the state structures in which they were influential to undermine economically stronger rivals, located in other state structures.

The recurring problem of "overproduction" relative to any existing market, which regularly led to stagnations in the world economy, was similarly the result of new producers jumping on a bandwagon of highly profitable goods and undermining monopolistic advantage by the expansion of total production. Whereas mercantilist policies sought to overturn existing advantage through political mechanisms, entry into production undermined advantage via the market. The net result could be the same, and neither method excluded the other.

When one kind of monopoly in the commodity chains was undermined, producers sought to create other new kinds of monopolistic advantages, since this was the only viable mechanism of cornering a large (as well as disproportionate) share of the capital accumulated through marker-oriented production. What we call technological advances simply reflect this search for new monopolistic advantages. Often entirely new commodity chains were established. Certainly old ones were constantly reorganized.

Since locational rent is a relatively rare (and in the long run economically minor) phenomenon, the only reason why some geographic areas have been better off than others in terms of capital accumulation, the only reason, that is, why some are more central and others more peripheral at any given time, is their immediate past history within the operation of the world-economy. That a given geographical zone occupies a given role is far from immutable. Indeed, every time a major monopoly has been undermined, the pattern of geographical locations of advantage has been subject to reorganization. In our discussion, we tend to ignore the relationships involved and instead summarize such phenomena in terms of juridical units we call states. Hence we observe interstate "mobility." Some states "rise." Of course, this means, this must mean, that other states "decline." It must mean this, as long as surplus is accumulated unevenly and we therefore can rank geographical-juridical zones ordinally.

Three, the frontiers of this capitalist world-economy which was originally located in Europe were expanded over the subsequent three centuries. The explanation of why these frontiers expanded lies in processes internal to its changing structure. The fundamental process may be described as a sequence. The exhaustion of "leading" monopolies led to periodic economic stagnations in the world-economy (so-called Kondratieff B-phases). Each economic stagnation led to a whole series of changes designed to restore the overall rate of profit in the world-economy as a whole and to ensure its continued uneven distribution: reduction of costs of production by reduction of wage costs (both by the further mechanization of production and by site relocation); creation of new monopolized leading products via innovation; expansion of effective demand by further proletarianization of segments of the work force.

The last change, however, entailed on balance a rise in real income for those segments, and hence was in partial contradiction with the objective of increasing the global rate of profit. It is at this point that expansion of the boundaries of the world-economy comes into play, as a mode of incorporating new low-cost labor which would in effect compensate for the increases in real wages elsewhere and thereby keep down the global average. Of course, global averages were of no concern to individual capitalists. The uneven distribution of profit remained crucial. But the path to this objective lay in part through expansion of the reach of the capitalist world-economy.

The fact that the dominant forces in the capitalist world-economy sought at various moments to expand its boundaries did not mean necessarily that they could. Peoples everywhere offered resistances, of varying efficacy, to the process of incorporation into the world-economy, especially given the fact that incorporation was so unattractive a proposition in terms both of immediate material interests and the cultural values of those being incorporated. Here, however, the capitalist world-economy benefited from the advantages of its internal mechanisms. The constant reward for innovation had the effect among other things, of technological advances in armaments and therefore a steadily growing disparity in the control of military force between the core states of the capitalist world-economy and those political structures outside the world-economy. Conquest, even the conquest of bureaucratically organized world-empires or at least their piecemeal dismemberment, became more and more possible.

It is quite clear now what the process of incorporation involved when it occurred. On the one hand, it meant the transformation of a certain number of production processes in these areas such that they were integrated into the commodity chains of the world-economy. Initially the incorporated zones fit in at one of three points in the chain: production of a raw material – a cash-crop (including food-crops) or mineral product – involved in some manufacturing process in core areas; production of additional food crops to feed the work force in peripheral zones producing the raw materials; use of local surplus to sustain a work force that would migrate for specified periods to work in the production of raw materials or of the food-crops needed to sustain the producers of raw materials.

The second transformation that occurred in the incorporation process was the reconstruction of existing political structures into states operating within the interstate system of the capitalist world-economy. This involved sometimes the fusion of several, and sometimes the remoulding of existing political structures, sometimes their dismemberment, sometimes the creation of entirely new and quite arbitrarily delimited structures. Whatever the case, the crucial element was that the resulting "states" (sometimes they were those non-sovereign "states" called "colonies") had to operate within the rules of the interstate system. They had to maintain a certain degree of effective internal control which would permit the flows necessary to the operation of the commodity chains. But they could not be so strong *vis-à-vis* the states in the core zone of the world-economy that they could effectively threaten the interests of the major existing monopolizers.

The multiple expansions of the capitalist world-economy occurred sporadically but continually from the seventeenth through the nineteenth centuries. By the late nineteenth century, there were no areas left on the globe outside the operations of its interstate system. If there were still geographical zones not involved in any of the commodity chains that made up the functioning of the capitalist world-economy, they were not many, and by and large the remaining few non-involved loci came to be involved by the time of the Second World War.

The fourth observation has to do with overall growth in the forces of production and levels of wealth. Though it is logically irrefutable that, in an ordinal ranking, if some rise others must fall, it might still be possible that either or both of the following could be also and simultaneously true: (a) all or most states have "risen" on some absolute measurement of "development;" (b) the dispersion of the absolute measures has diminished. Indeed, the main argument of liberal developmentalists has been that this could be true, and many of them would argue further that it has been in fact historically true.

I think it is unquestionable that for 10–20 percent of the world's population at the top in terms of income, the absolute level of consumable wealth has risen over the past 400 years, and risen considerably. Furthermore, since this 10–20 percent of whom I speak are unevenly distributed across the globe, it is certain that for a majority of the population of the core zones the statement is true. If therefore we utilize state-level measures like GNP per capita we wil find such an increase, even when we control for price inflation.

The question is not whether the extraordinary expansion in accumulated physical plant and real wealth due to the transformation of the forces of production has occurred or not. Of course it has. Nor is it whether this expansion has not benefited the world's so-called middle strata, or cadres. Of course it has. The question is primarily whether it has meant any rise in real well-being for the large majority of the world's population. Certainly, up to 1945, when this majority was still largely rural, it is quite dubious that it did. If anything, in terms of absolute income, these populations were probably worse off than their ancestors had been. The gap between their incomes and those of the top tenth or top seventh of world's population had certainly grown enormously over the previous four centuries.

We thus come to the point in time with which we began the discussion – 1945. The transformation of the capitalist world-economy since 1945 has been remarkable in two regards. The absolute expansion of the world-economy – in population, in value produced, in accumulated wealth – has probably been as great as in the entire period of 1500–1945. The political strength of anti-systemic forces has been incredibly greater than before 1945. These two facts, taken together, provide the explanation of why "development" has become so central an ideological theme and field of combat since then. When the United Nations proclaimed the 1970s the "Decade of Development," the combination of material growth and growth in antisystemic forces was thought by many to herald a fundamental transformation of the pre-1945 structure of the world-economy. The heralded transformation did not occur. And today, less than 20 years later, the debate largely centers around why it has not occurred.

What then did occur since 1945 so far as the structure of the capitalist world-economy is concerned? Two things, mainly. The absolute development of the forces of production has meant a massive reduction of the percentage of the world population engaged in producing primary goods, including food goods. The absolute growth of the manufacturing sectors and the absolute and relative growth of the tertiary sectors have led to a runaway "urbanization" of the world which is still going on at a reckless pace. In the process we have gone a considerable distance towards exhausting the pools of low-cost labor which have hitherto existed. The boundary limits are being reached. Virtually all households are at least semi-proletarianized. And economic stagnations continue to have the consequence of transforming segments of these semi-proletarianized households into proletarianized ones. Both leading and lagging profit margins must as a consequence now decline.

Of course, efforts may be made by firms and state agencies to try to fight back by constantly attempting to "marginalize" some formerly proletarianized households. And there is much evidence that this occurs. Indeed, a good deal of the neo-liberal governmental policies undertaken in many countries during the 1980s represented attempts to do just this. For example, the frequent proposals in the US and Western Europe to allow individuals to opt out of collective social insurance schemes would, if adopted, have this effect. The resistance has been great. And I think the evidence of the next 30 years will show conclusively that it is politically more difficult for capital to "marginalize" proletarianized populations than it is for segments of the working class to "proletarianize" themselves. Thus, the net movement will in all likelihood remain in the direction of full proletarianization of households, which means higher-cost wage-labor. If this is true, then capital is faced with an increasing squeeze.

The second main transformation of the post-1945 period has been the remarkable series of triumphs of all the branches of the worldwide family of antisystemic movements. One manifestation has been the creation of a series of countries we call "socialist countries," meaning that they claim the heritage in one way or another to the Third International. To be sure, some of these triumphs were due primarily to the military prowess of the USSR, but a significant number were the result of internal revolutionary forces – notably China, Korea, Vietnam, Yugoslavia, Albania, and (with a somewhat special history) Cuba.

A second manifestation of this was the triumph of national liberation movements in a number of countries of the Third World. In many cases this too was the outcome of a significant popular struggle. The process of course varied considerably from country to country, but a minimal list of countries where a significant popular struggle took place might include India and Indonesia, Ghana and Algeria, Angola and Mozambique, Nicaragua and Zimbabwe.

A third manifestation of this has been the coming to power after 1945 of labor and/or social democratic parties in the Western world and the institutionalization of a "welfare state" in most of these countries.

I am not arguing that the coming to power of Marxist-Leninist parties in the socialist bloc, of national liberation movements in the Third World, and of social democratic parties in the OECD countries were the same thing. But there were nonetheless three elements they shared in common. First, each was the result of the upsurge of popular forces in their countries, forces which saw their victories as in some sense being antisystemic. (You and I may or may not agree with this conceptualization; I merely at this point suggest that it was a widespread self-image.) Secondly, each involved parties or movements that had been in political opposition (and frequently illegality) assuming governmental office. Thirdly, and most relevant to our present discussion, in each case the groups in power set themselves the double policy objective of economic growth and greater internal equality.

I said they shared three things in common. In fact, of late, there is a fourth. Each type of movement in power has come under internal criticism from within their countries, and often even from within the movements in power, for their failures to achieve, or to achieve to a sufficient degree, these goals – economic growth and greater internal equality. This is the source of the disillusionment to which I referred at the outset.

III

This then brings us to the third question that I said I would address: what is the demand for development about? The twin goals indicate the double answer. On the one hand, development was supposed to mean greater internal equality, that is, fundamental social (or socialist) transformation. On the other hand, development was supposed to mean economic growth which involved "catching up" with the leader. For everyone this meant catching up, somewhere down the line, with the United States. This was the objective even for the USSR, as was made notorious in prediction that the USSR would "overtake" the US by the year 2000.

But social transformation and catching up are seriously different objectives. They are not necessarily correlative with each other. They may even be in contradiction with each other. This latter, it seems to me, is the heart of what Mao Zedong was arguing in the 1960s. In any case, it should be clear by now that we have to analyze these objectives separately and cannot continue blithely to assume their pairing, which developmentalists, both liberal and Marxist, as well as many of their conservative opponents, have for the most part done for the past 150 years.

I say that both liberals and Marxists have blithely assumed that growth leading to catching up and an increase in egalitarian distribution are parallel vectors, if not obverse sides of the same coin, over the long run. What I really mean is that the ideological statements of both groups have asserted this. The question remains, however, as to which of the two objectives, derived from the two different connotations of the concept of development, has been the driving force of the political thrust towards development. To put it bluntly, which of the two objectives did people, do people really care about? To which did they give priority?

The answer has to be that the states have always given their priority to catching up and that the movements have been split on this issue. Indeed the split goes back to the very beginning of their individual and collective histories. The movements brought together under one organizational roof those who wished to have more, to catch up to (and implicitly to surpass) some others, and those who have searched for equality. The ideological belief that the two objectives were correlative served initially as organizational cement. This cement often took the form of the assertion that it was through economic growth (the end of scarcity) that equality would be made possible. However, the coming to power to the movements has forced them to operationalize their priorities, which has unglued, at least partially, the ideological coating. Hence the disillusionment, or at least the confusion and discontent.

This was scarcely a problem before 1945, for two reasons. One, the capitalist world-economy was still in secular expansion. As long as that was true, the prospects of a growing pie were there to ensure that everyone could hope for more. Those who could hope for more in a near future usually supported the system outright. Those whose hopes for more seemed more distant usually formed the social base of the antisystemic movements, one of whose principal attractions was that they seemed to offer a political route to speeding up the realization of the hope for more.

Secondly, as long as the capitalist world-economy was in secular expansion, the antisystemic movements remained politically weak. Though the movements claimed to represent the popular classes and hence the overwhelming majority of the population, their support was always being eroded at both ends of their sociological spectrum. On the one hand, at the top end, for those popular strata that were relatively better off, the lure of individual mobility, perfectly rational in a system in secular expansion, undid their sense of collective solidarity in the struggle. And at the low end, those strata that were worst off (the semi-proletarianized households) were often defeated, hard to organize, or simply scrambling for subsistence. Some too were rendered docile by the prospect of full-time employment, which constituted significant upward mobility, not of course into the bourgeoisie but into the proletariat. This was plausible only for a few, but it was never certain which few this was. And hence it seemed a plausible prospect of many. This double "defection" is of course the explanation of why the traditional nineteenth-century scenario of a workers' revolution has never really occurred thus far.

Paradoxically, the political weakness of the antisystemic movements prior to 1945 was their strength. Because they could never be in power, they could maintain untouched their unifying if contradictory ideology and hence they could survive, and survive quite well, as movements. It was the weakening of the political carapace of capitalism which, by allowing the antisystemic movements to arrive at state power in large numbers, exposed the deep internal cleavage of these movements, the rift between those who sought upward mobility and those who sought equality.

So the answer to the question, what is the demand for development about? is that there is no single coherent answer to that question to be gained through historical analysis. The slogan has masked a contradiction that is deep and enduring. What has happened since 1945, and especially since the 1970s, is that this contradiction is now a glaring one, and we are collectively being required to make political choices that are quite difficult and quite large.

IV

Before, however, we can deal with the political choices, we must clear up one more historical question, how in fact "national development" did occur, where it occurred, or at least where it is claimed that it has occurred – more or less in the OECD countries.

The usual picture that has been painted is that, between say 1750 and 1950, a number of countries have successively "developed" or "industrialized," the latter term usually taken as a synonym or indicator of development. The tale is usually told this way. First, England developed, then perhaps some other Western countries, finally the whole list (plus Japan). This version of historical events takes us down to, say, 1950. At that juncture, the more conservative and more radical versions differ. The more conservative scenario is that the process is still continuing since 1950, with some countries like the Republic of Korea demonstrating this fact. The more radical version is that while such development did occur in the nineteenth century, the conditions are now entirely different and the obstacles to national "capitalist" development far greater. Hence today the only alternative is said to be a radically new path of total rupture with the system.

But before examining the export-oriented model vs. the delinking model, let us first ask whether this scenario in fact reflects accurately what occurred? There is another way of reading world history for the period 1750–1950. Instead of seeing it as the story of a succession of successful national development efforts, we could see it as the story of the secular expansion of the world-economy as a whole. I remind you of two aspects of this structure we discussed: the polarization of zones which has been accentuated over time, and the constant expansion of the outer boundaries of the system. What has been happening seems to me quite simple. The increase of the geographical scope of operations led to an increase in the populations included in the world-economy. They were added in order to create low-cost, surplus-creating but not surplus-retaining segments of the worldwide commodity chains. As such segments grew absolutely, it had to mean that there was parallel growth of other segments of these commodity chains. And if the first segments were low on the retention of surplus, that of course meant that the others were higher. If core zones had not grown in size (and therefore in geography) at the same time as peripheral zones, the system would no longer have been a capitalist one.

The fact that, in 1950, many more geographical loci seemed to be "developed" than in 1750 was not the consequence of the fact that a dozen or two dozen states had "developed" their "national" economies. It was that a dozen or two came to enclose the principal fruits of the expansion and development of the capitalist world-economy as a whole. The OECD states did not "achieve" their "national development," they had it "thrust upon them." What developed was the capitalist world-economy. It was as though there were an expanding inkspill of accumulated surplus which spread to the near parts of the blotter. That it was registered in the national accounts of one country rather than another was not necessarily or primarily the result of the policies of that country.

The situation has indeed changed today. The geography of the whole system can no longer expand. Ergo the geographic reach of the core can no longer expand. It there is to be any significant change in which geographical areas are core-like, this is *more than ever* a zero-sum game. If a new area comes in, an old area must go out. This was always partially true, but only partially, because of the overall expansion of the system. Now it is entirely true. If in the next 30 years China or India or Brazil were in a true sense to "catch up," a significant segment of the world's population elsewhere in this world-system would have to decline as a locus of capital accumulation. This will be true whether China or India or Brazil "catches up" via delinking or via export-orientation or by any other method. This will be true as long as states, separate states, are each searching for ways to develop themselves. Catching up implies competition, and competition means that one country's development will be at someone else's expense ultimately.

V

We therefore arrive at the issue everyone really cares about: what shall be done? What political implications shall we draw from this analysis? The first one I draw is the most radical. National development may well be a pernicious policy objective. This is for two reasons. For most states, it is unrealizable, whatever the method adopted. And for those few states which may still realize it, that is, transmute radically the location of world-scale production and thereby their location on the interstate ordinal scale, their benefits will perforce be at the expense of some other zone. This has always been true up to a point. It is more true than ever today.

I hear the shouts of all those who are suffering by the current unequal allocation of the world's created surplus. What then shall we do? Surely you do not expect us to do nothing. And my answer is: surely not.

At this point I must make an assumption. The assumption is that the objective is truly an egalitarian, democratic world, and not simply a reversal of fortunes inside our present inegalitarian, un-democratic world-system. If this is the objective, what is the route? In the late nineteenth and early twentieth centuries the dominant view was that the route was via nationally organized working class movements. In the period since 1945 this view has evolved de facto into a somewhat different one: that the route is via popularly organized national movements.

But will popularly organized national movements in fact achieve greater equality and democracy? I have become increasingly skep-tical of this, as have many others. I think popularly organized national movements have found themselves in a dilemma for which there is no easy solution and which has contributed strongly to the sense of impasse and frustration that has been growing of late.

The great argument in favor of state-organized attempts to retain surplus created within the frontiers is that the state is the only agency potentially capable of going against the strong currents of unequal exchange flows structurally central to the functioning of the capitalist world-economy. This is a very strong argument and has secured wide support. The great negative, however, of that argu-ment is that the state as an agency requires decision-making actors, those who occupy the key political and bureaucratic posts. And these persons have a direct interest as a subgroup in the choice of priority between an emphasis on growth/catching up and equality. It is clear that economic self-interest pushes them towards the growth and "catching-up" goal, and the consequences for the popular strata tend to be in the middle run usually at best no change for the better, sometimes even a worsening of their condi-tion. As long as solutions are framed and sought at the national level, the dilemma will remain, and states governed by erstwhile antisystemic movements will remain repressive of their own popular strata and at best only partial winners of the catching-up game, to the primary benefit of the cadres.

Is not another strategy available for the movements? I am not referring to a world-level strategy, if by that one means a strategy that requires implementation by a world-level movement. Such an alternative is unrealisitic, at least at present. World revolution or even coordinated worldwide political struggle remains a rhetorical flourish for the most part. I am thinking rather of attacking the flows of surplus at another point, at the point of their production. Suppose that antisystemic movements concentrated their energies everywhere – in the OECD countries, in the Third World coun-tries, and yes, in the socialist countries as well, on efforts aimed at retaining most of the surplus created. One obvious way would be to seek to increase the price of labor or the price of sale by the direct producers. These prices, like most prices, are controlled by market considerations, but market considerations *within parameters established by political struggle.* These parameters are subject to change, and change constantly. This is exactly what capitalists know. They spend a considerable amount of their worldwide political energy on the politics of pricing.

The OPEC oil price rise of the 1970s was a marvelous instance of this. It was clearly a consciously political struggle, and the OPEC countries initially did very well for themselves. No doubt you may retort, look at what happened in the 1980s. Without going into the details of the anti-OPEC counteroffensive which did over a decade force OPEC to retreat, the retreat illuminates all the pitfalls of national-level development strategies. When the OPEC countries retained after 1973 a larger percentage of the flow of surplus, it was the states who retained this. It was then up to the states to redistribute this – to the cadres, to the creation of infrastructure, to the workers, etc. The pressures were obvious and so were the vulnerabilities.

If the start of the process had been a rise in the price of labor on OPEC oil fields, the impact might have been less dramatic, but it might also have been considerably more difficult to reverse. If the struggle had been a workers' struggle within the OPEC states and not an OPEC state struggle against the world powers-that-be, the politics would have been quite different. A steady politically induced rise in surplus retention would be unlikely to lead to serious losses in the world market. That is, if tomorrow, in all the NICs (Newly Industrializing Countries), textile workers were paid 20 percent more, the choice facing the purchasers of such textiles might only be to turn to other equally expensive zones. They might do this in part. Or they might look for new NICs. The battle would have its ups and downs. But, and this is the crucial point, in a world-economy that is in the process of exhausting its reserve labor forces, such a battle would have far more ups than downs.

In a sense what I am calling for is a return of the pendulum. The first great strategy in the fight against inequality involved the so-called class struggle. In the nineteenth century this struggle was fought both in the workplace (via the construction of trade unions) and in the political arena (via the construction of socialist parties). Capitalists fought back in two main ways. They used the state to repress such movements. And they recruited new workers from the national and worldwide pool of reserve (semi-proletarianized) households.

Since the distribution of proletarian and semi-proletarian households was not random but stratified nationally, ethnically, racially, it was clear that a political strategy that focused on proletarian households missed a good half of the battle. Thus we got the swing, ever more sharply in the twentieth century, to what might be called an "anti-imperialist" focus. The struggle now emphasized *national* liberation and national development of the national economy, and within the OECD states the emphasis shifted to the anti-racist struggle, an equivalent shift in emphasis.

Meanwhile, however, the inexorable drive of capitalism for the accumulation of capital has been undermining its ability to command access to a de facto unlimited reserve labor force. This has now become quite limited. The strategy of capitalists has thus shifted. The OPEC-type battle in fact serves them quite well. None of the Seven Sisters (the major oil trans-national corporations) suffered from the OPEC price rise. Quite the contrary! As long as the focus is on national distribution of the accumulated surplus-value, capitalists can relocate the locus of their capital without necessarily losing long-run control over it.

On the other hand, capitalists are now vulnerable to the original strategy of a "class" struggle as they were not before because of the fact that the world-economy has reached its geographic limits. But this then requires a reorganization of the emphasis of the movements. The movements cannot afford their close links to the states, even to the regimes they have struggled to bring to power. Their concern must be how at each point on very long commodity chains a greater percentage of the suplus can be retained. Such a strategy would tend over time to "overload" the system, reducing global rates of profit significantly and evening out distribution. Such a strategy might also be able to mobilize the efforts of all the many varieties of new social movements, all of which are oriented in one way or another more to equality than to growth.

This is not a new Fabian strategy. We will not inch our way to world equality. Rather it is premised on the belief that global rates of profit are quite open to political attack at a local level. And, as the local victories cumulate, a significant cave-in of political support for the system will occur. For it will force the greedy to fall out among themselves, and to try to eat into the portion of the surplus they apportion to their agents and intermediaries. But that of course would be collectively suicidal, since an underfed "army" tends to refuse to fight, and without an "army" to protect the capitalists (that is, an extensive political and ideological apparatus), the capitalist world-economy has no secure way to survive.

VI

Well, then – Development: lodestar or illusion? I hope by now my answer is obvious. National development is today an illusion, whatever the method advocated and used. If all our energies are turned in that direction, then capitalism may have the 200 extra years Schumpeter hoped it could create for itself. And with the 200 extra years, the privileged strata of the world may be able to manage a transition to a completely different but similarly inegalitarian world-system.

But development can be a lodestar. We can try to force the pace of the secular trends of the capitalist world-economy, exactly what capitalists fear most. The local and localized demands for greater participation and higher real income, that is, worldwide unruliness by producers in the loci of production (using this term in its broadest sense) is politically mobilizing and economically redistributive. It also disarms the tenants of the status quo of some of their best weapons: the political divisions between proletarian and semi-proletarian households (nationally and worldwide); and the appeal to sacrifice (of the surplus each produces) on behalf of the state.

This strategy is less obvious than one thinks. None of the traditional or erstwhile antisystemic movements – the Social-Democrats in the West, the Communist parties of the world, the national liberation movements – are preaching it, even secondarily, in any serious way. And almost none of the newer antisystemic movements that have arisen in the last 20–30 years are doing so either, or at least they are not doing so with the kind of conscious intent to overload the system I am advocating. The movements still have too much faith in equality via growth; what they need to seriously envisage is growth through equality. But it cannot be an egalitarianism that turns its back on individual realization and social variation. Equality is not in competition with liberty. They are intimately linked. When an attempt is made to keep these objectives separate – as happened in the Cultural Revolution – it fails to achieve either.

The weakness of the capitalist world-economy is in its self-fulfillment. As it becomes more and more commodified, it undermines its ability to maldistribute surplus and hence to concentrate its accumulation. But it is far from enough to say more commodification is the route to the undoing of the system. For, left to themselves, the dominant forces will seek to slow down the pace. The efforts of national development have been traditionally seen as something that has speeded up the pace. I suggest that they should be seen instead as substitutes for other policies that would have speeded up the pace far more and far faster.

An emphasis on surplus retention by the producers, that is, an emphasis on greater equality and democratic participation, far from being utopian, could be devastatingly effective. The great barrier to that today is less the large-scale capitalists than the antisystemic movements themselves. They must become aware of their historic ambivalence about the two meanings of development – more, and more equal. And they must opt for the latter. In such an option, the state is not irrelevant. There are many ways in which the state apparatuses can abet this program. But if the state apparatuses are the motor, then development will be an illusion and not a lodestar.

Part III

Concepts of Time and Space

8

A Comment on Epistemology: What is Africa?

In the beginning were the words, and the words were with the gods, and the words were the gods. There were many peoples and each had its gods. This is still true, except that the "Western" religious tradition developed an important variation on the theme. First, the multiplicity of gods was replaced in this tradition by a singular god, who thereupon had to be the god of all the world. The only version still extant of this first phase of the shift to monotheism is Judaism. Judaism managed to combine the idea of one god for all with the idea of a "chosen people." This combination restrained the universalism of Jewish monotheism, but is also restrained the intrusiveness.

Jewish monotheism was succeeded by two other versions, Christianity and Islam, which eliminated the "chosen people" idea. However, the logic of this elimination was that there was no longer any restraint on universalist claims. This meant inevitably that these religions had to become proselytizing religions. Both did in fact proselytize, with some considerable success in each case, but of course less than total success. The African continent's religious pattern in the twentieth century is good evidence of this relative but not total success. As we know, the emergence of the capitalist world-economy, originally located in a Christian zone of the world, was accompanied by a process of "secularization." In this process, Christian proselytization for its universal god was to some extent replaced by, to some extent overlain by, a more secular form of universalism, incarnated in the concepts of scientific truth and technological progress. Marxism derived from this latter tradition and was one major variant of this assertion of the reality of universal truth.

The African continent was thus confronted in the process of its incorporation into the capitalist world-economy by an intrusive ideology which not only rejected the worth of the gods who had been Africa's but also was pervasive in that it took on multiple clothings: Christianity, science, democracy, Marxism. This experience was not of course unique to the African continent, nor was the reaction of Africa unique. Cultural resistance everywhere to this intrusive, insistent, newly dominant ideology took ambiguous forms. On the one hand, many Africans accepted, seemed to accept, the new universalism, seeking to learn its secrets, seeking to tame this god, seeking to gain its favor. On the other hand, many Africans (often the same ones) rebelled against it. There is nothing surprising in this. It has long been commonplace to observe such an ambiguous reaction. The situation is such that we can speak of a double bind, in which there was no reaction that could remove the pressure and the oppression.

In the course of the last 100 years, the concept of Africa has emerged. It is a European word, and its definition was first given by Europeans. But those so defined have struggled in recent years to take control of the defining process, or to take more control of this process, which is inherently a process that is both continuous and always reciprocal (that is, never one-sided). For example, the political decision taken in 1958 at the first Conference of Independent African States in Accra states "north of the Sahara" within the definition of Africa has had important and thus far lasting effects.

Nonetheless, as long as we live in a singular, hierarchical world-system, the capitalist world-economy, posing the question of whether a set of ideas, or a way of thinking, is universal (European) or African returns us only to the double bind which the system itself has created. If we are to get out of this double bind, we must take advantage of the contradictions of the system itself to go beyond it.

We must start with the classic question of Jean Genêt in *Les nègres* (Genêt 1960). "Mais, qu'est-ce que c'est donc un noir? et d'abord, c'est de quelle couleur?" What Genêt is trying to make us realize is that the definition of the universal is a particular definition of a particular system – the modern world-system – and that, within that system, the definition of the particular has no particularities but is a universal of that system. As long as that system is functioning reasonably well, the debate about the relationship of the universal and the particular is not only vain and unresolvable but also the very process of the debate tends to reinforce the structure of cultural hierarchy and oppression internal to that system.

It is only when the system itself comes into systemic crisis that, at the level of idea-systems as well as at that of social movements, we have real options and therefore the possibility of real debates. But we are in such a systemic crisis now. And we are in such a debate. However, it is well to be clear what the debate is about. It is not about whether there is, has been, or could be a "specifically African" set of ideas or concepts or world-views that could substitute for, supplement, or rebut a Western set, either in the study of Africa or of anything else. To pose the question that way is to place us back into the double bind, to play the game in terms of the rules of an oppressive system now in crisis.

The debate is rather about two things. What is science, and what is scientific knowledge? Not in Africa, but everywhere. It is a question as much for North America or Western Europe as for Africa. The second question is what systemic options do we have. If the modern world-system is in crisis, what alternatives present themselves? If it were true that "progress" is inevitable, then the question would be meaningless. But if rather we accept that systemic transitions can go in various directions, then and only then do we have an epistemological question: how can we know the range of options, and what kinds of scientific endeavors will further one or another option?

The contribution of Africans (I am not sure if one can call it the contribution of Africa) could be that the weight and constraints of the existing idea-systems tend to rest less heavily on them than on Europeans, and the movements that emerge there – in the larger political arena, and in the academy – will hopefully reflect this. It may be therefore that more coherent insights into options will arise there. But they will only arise if they are not placed in the old cul-de-sac of universalism vs. particularism.

9

Does India Exist?

My query, "does India exist?" is absurd. In the contemporary world, there is a political entity named India; hence India obviously exists. But it is not absurd, if the query is taken to be ontological, analogous to the ancient theological query, "does God exist?" If India exists, how do we know it exists? and who created India, and when?

Let us start by a counterfactual proposition. Suppose in the period 1750–1850, what had happened was that the British colonized primarily the old Mughal Empire, calling it Hindustan, and the French had simultaneously colonized the southern (largely Dravidian) zones of the present-day Republic of India, giving it the name of Dravidia. Would we today think that Madras was "historically" part of India? Would we even use the word "India"? I do not think so. Instead, probably, scholars from around the world would have written learned tomes, demonstrating that from time immemorial "Hindustan" and "Dravidia" were two different cultures, peoples, civilizations, nations, or whatever. There might be in this case some "Hindustan" irredentists who occasionally laid claim to "Dravidia" in the name of "India," but most sensible people would have called them "irresponsible extremists."

My question then is, how could what historically happened between AD 1750 and 1850 have affected what historically happened between say the sixth century BC and 1750, presently conventional dates for "pre-modern India?" It can do so because what happened in the distant past is always a function of what happened in the near past. The present determines the past, and not vice versa as our logico-deductive analytical frameworks try to force us to think.

I wish to make three points. Each will be made about India. They would equally be true if I substituted Pakistan, or England, or Brazil, or China for India. What I have to say about India is not specific to its history. It is generic about all currently existing sovereign states, members of the United Nations.

The first proposition is that India is an invention of the modern world-system. The operation of the capitalist world-economy is premised on the existence of a political superstructure of sovereign states linked together in and legitimated by an interstate system. Since such a structure did not always exist, it was one that had to be built. The process of building it has been a continuous one in several ways. The structure was first created in only one segment of the globe, primarily Europe, more or less in the period 1497–1648. It was then sporadically expanded to include a larger and larger geographic zone. This process, which we may call the "incorporation" of new zones into the capitalist world-economy, involved reshaping political boundaries and structures in the zones being incorporated and creating therein "sovereign states, members of the interstate system," or at least what we might think of as "candidate sovereign states" – the colonies.

The process was continuous in a second sense. The framework of the system has been continuously strengthened over the past 500 years. The interstate system has been increasingly clearly defined and its powers specified and enhanced. In addition, the "stateness" of the "sovereign states" has been increasingly clearly defined and their powers specified and enhanced. Hence we have been moving in the direction of ever "stronger" state structures that are constrained by an ever "stronger" interstate system.

Within such an optic, we could say that the "sovereign state" of India was created in part by the British in the period 1750–1850. But it was not created by the British alone. Other "great powers" (such as France) also had something to do with this, insofar as they recognized its juridical reality and insofar as they were not strong enough to alter the boundary lines that emerged. But most of all, the populations resident during this period on the Indian subcontinent had a very great deal to do with the creation of "India." The existing political structures, of varying military and social strengths, of varying political objectives, resisted and collaborated in the process in various ways. The British did not meet a tabula rasa but vital structures which they combated. The actual history is complex.

The point is that the outcome was the result of this history in all its complex specificity. The point also is that the outcome in terms of boundaries was not at all foreordained, but that whatever would have been the outcome would have become the entity we know as India. Had Nepal been absorbed into "India" in that period, we would no more talk of a Nepalese people/nation/culture today than we speak of a Hyderabad people/nation/culture.

As is well known, when India became a fully sovereign state in 1948, the erstwhile colony was divided in two, and there came into existence Pakistan. Subsequently Pakistan was divided, and there came into existence Bangladesh. None of this was foreordained in 1750–1850. *A fortiori*, it was not foreordained by the history of the pre-1750 period. The freshness of these divisions leads some still to proclaim their "illegitimacy." But legitimacy is a function, among other things, of duration. As the years go by, the realities of the "past" become more and more unquestionable – until of course the day that they are suddenly, dramatically, and above all successfully challenged, which can always happen.

My second proposition is that India's pre-modern history is an invention of modern India. I am not saying it didn't really happen. I presume, given all the inbuilt control mechanisms of world historiography, there are few (or no) statements found in the textbooks which do not have some evidentiary basis. But the grouping of these statements in an interpretative narrative is not a self-producing phenomenon. "Facts" do not add up to "history." The historian invents history, in the same way that an artist invents his painting. The artist uses the colors on his palette and his vision of the world to present his "message." So does the historian. He has a large leeway, as does the artist. The leeway is not total. It is socially constrained. A narrative that reflects some bizarre psychopathology of the individual author will simply not be read, or more importantly, not taught, not believed, not used.

The historian's narrative of past events "interprets" these events in terms of long-term continuities and medium-term "conjunctural" (or cyclical) shifting patterns. We are therefore told that something called India has a "culture," or is the product of a culture. What does this mean? It means that India is said to have or to reflect a certain world-view (or a specific combination of world-views), to have a distinguishable artistic style, to be part of a specific linguistic tradition, to have been the locus of specific religious movements, etc.

But what in turn do such statements mean? They do not mean

(were never intended to mean) that every individual resident in this geographic zone, now and from time immemorial, shared these cultural traits. Rather, they are supposed to represent some statistical parameter over some usually unspecified period of time. But which parameter? the mean, the median, the mode? Just to pose the issue this way is to invite ridicule. But it also points up the arbitrariness of all statements about India's (or anyone else's) "culture." India's culture is what we collectively say it is. And we can disagree. We can also change our mind. If 50 years from now we define India's historical culture differently from the way in which we define it today, India's culture will have in fact changed *in the past*.

So how did we come to invent India's current version of its historical culture? In broad brush strokes, the answer is simple. The British specifically, and the Europeans generally, made statements about what they believed it to be, or wanted it to be. Indians, living their "culture," heard these statements, accepted a few of them, rejected many of them, and verbalized an alternative version, or several versions. The single greatest influence on the version that prevailed in the period 1850–1950 was probably that of the Indian nationalist movement. Today the government of independent India authorizes textbooks for schools, and the Indian government has replaced the Indian nationalist movement as the shaper of India's history. India's poets, historians, and sociologists try to get into the act, and no doubt have some influence. So do the millions of scheduled castes when they decide to convert to Buddhism or to Islam, or not to convert. If enough of them convert, the continuity of Indian Buddhism will suddenly reemerge as an interpretative strand of Indian history.

My third proposition is that India currently exists, but no one knows if, 200 years from now, it will still exist. Perhaps India will have been divided into five separate states. Perhaps India will have reabsorbed Pakistan and Bangladesh. Perhaps the whole system of sovereign states within an interstate system will have disappeared. Any of these occurrences, if they occur, will transform the past. India may come to seem a transitory and unimportant concept. Or it may be deeply reinforced as an enduring "civilization."

There is no question that, at the present time, nationalism in general, certainly including in India, is a remarkably strong world cultural force. It seems stronger today than any other mode of social expression or collective mentality, although in the last ten years or so, religious consciousness has once again surfaced as a serious competitor to nationalist consciousness as a motivating force in many parts of the world. But nationalism, in historical terms, is a very new concept. It is clearly a product, and indeed a late product, of the modern world-system. It would be hard to argue that it existed before the nineteenth century. Perhaps in the twenty-first century, it will have spent itself. It is hard to predict with any confidence. This should make us hesitate at least in asserting the long-lasting quality of Indianness as a social reality.

Let me ask one final question. As I said at the outset, what I have been saying about India, I could equally well say about Pakistan or England or Brazil or China. Is there then nothing special about India, nothing specific to the Indian case? Of course there is. India as a concrete entity is different in multitudinous and important ways from every other state or nation or people or civilization. The real social world is a complex entity composed of incredibly complex groups and individuals. Everything is specific.

We have, however, two choices about specificity. Either we surrender intellectually to it, in which case the world is a "blooming, buzzing confusion." Or we try to explain it. Specificity is not just there. India (that is, the India we think we observe today) is not just there. It is the result of a long historical process, one which it shares in detail only at certain elementary (albeit crucial) levels with other presumably comparable entities.

I am not here to deny in any way the historical specificity of India. Indeed, the whole objective, as I see it, of sociological analysis is to end up with a historical interpretation of the concrete. What I am here to assert is that what is included in the description of the historical specificity of India is an ever-changing, very fluid phenomenon. The historical ground on which we stand is about as stable as that covering a fault in the earth. The possibility of an earthquake hangs over us as an ever-present threat. Hence India exists, at least at this instant at which I write.

10

The Inventions of TimeSpace Realities: Towards an Understanding of our Historical Systems

Few things seem as self-evident to us as time and space. A significant proportion of the education of children under the age of six is devoted to teaching them the concepts and terminology of time and space. They learn about time and space in the same way they learn about the family, the larger social structure, the gods, language, comportment, their bodies, that is, through the teaching and example of parents, elders, and peers. They normally learn all these things in the form of an orthodoxy. There are some "truths" about each of these subjects which are external, objective, eternal. Children are expected to memorize and internalize these truths.

In our modern world, as we grow up, the education to which we are all constantly submitted, evolves. In one field after another, the orthodoxy is relaxed, and we are introduced to the idea that our knowledge, our truths are in fact social creations. They are but one way of perceiving the world among multiple alternative ways. Of course our educators usually still insist that the way they teach is the best way, but there are few persons who, at age 18, fail to realize that the ways they have learned are not the only possible ways. Indeed, a good deal of our later education consists of discussing how we are supposed to react to and handle ourselves in what is sometimes referred to as a "multicultural" reality.

Thus as adults we all tend today to know, even to keep in the forefront of our minds, that there are many gods, many societies, many sets of familial customs and values, and of course many languages, many different modes of social behavior, many sexualities. In this litany, which any one of us can recite, the most striking gap seems to be about time and space. Few of us would say there are many kinds of time or many kinds of space. For some reason, our education in the realities of social relativism, in the social origins of our organizing concepts, tends to stop short of time and space. Time and space are, for most of us, just there – enduring, objective, external, unmodifiable. Time and tide wait for no man, we are told. But is it true?

In 1958, Fernand Braudel published a famous essay on "History and the Social Sciences: The *Longue Durée*" (Braudel 1969). In it, he argued that time was a social creation and that the historian could not allow himself to be imprisoned by the utilization of only one variety of time. Braudel distinguished three principal categories of social time, which he defined doubly: in length of time-span and in the object of measurement.

In terms of length of time-span, he called his times short-term, medium-term, and long-term. Of course, such language does not get us very far. The terms constitute an ordinal listing, but they provide us in themselves with neither orders of chronometrical magnitude nor ways of relating any specific time-usage to one of these categories.

Braudel of course did not stop there. He immediately gave his three time-spans substantive names. I will give the names first in French, because they pose some problems of translation. Short-term time, he said, is the time of *l'histoire événementielle*, a term Braudel picked up from Paul Lacombe and François Simiand, who had invented it at the turn of the twentieth century. Middle-term time is the time of what he called *l'histoire conjoncturelle*. And long-term time, the *longue durée* as we have come to call it even in English, is the time of *l'histoire structurelle*.

L'histoire événementielle is usually translated as the "history of events." It might perhaps better capture the spirit of the term to translate it as "episodic history." *L'histoire conjoncturelle* is often mistranslated "conjunctural history." The term "*conjoncture*" in fact does not refer to a conjuncture but rather to either phase (the rising or the declining phase) of a cyclical process, one half, so to speak, of a bell-shaped curve on a chart. I think it would be more fruitful to translate it therefore as "cyclical history," although that term too is ambiguous in English, since the cycle referred to is not that of the entirety of human history, as when we say that Toynbee has a cyclical concept of history in that each civilization repeats some basic pattern. Braudel's cycles are cycles *within* something.

That something is what *l'histoire structurelle* refers to. It may be translated, as it usually is, as "structural history," but here too, a confusion immediately arises. We are used to thinking of "structures" as the antinomy of that which is "historical," as in the structuralist anthropology of Lévi-Strauss. Braudel himself is aware of this possible confusion. He in fact therefore added a fourth time, the *very* long-term, which he says is that of Lévi-Strauss's structures. He also calls it the *too* long-term, and says of it that "if it exists, [it] can only be the time period of the sages" (Braudel 1972a: 35).

To understand Braudel's categories, one has to see that he is fighting a war on two fronts, against the two nominally antithetical positions which have dominated social thought since at least the middle of the nineteenth century, idiographic and nomothetic epistemologies.

On the one side stand the traditional historians, the idiographers, for whom time contains a series of events, which occur on specific dates. The dates in question are primarily the dates of political occurrences. The time is just there, in the calendar. It marks the moments when battles were fought, treaties were signed, monarchs ascended the throne, and legal changes were instituted. Dating such events gives us a chronology and thereby a narrative, a story, a history that is unique and explicable only in its own terms. The facts are out there, waiting as it were to be uncovered by the historians who seek the primary data, which are the only true data, in the archives that have preserved these data for us.

No doubt, says Braudel, these "events" probably occurred. But two things must be noted. First, some events are recorded at the time and others are not. Some occurrences are discerned later by historians as events and others are not. There is no a priori reason to assume that an occurrence of 1450, recorded in 1452, and discerned as an event by a historian in 1952 is, in terms of the truths of today, more or less important than another occurrence of 1450, unrecorded or undiscerned. And secondly, even if we have recorded and discerned as events the more significant rather than the less significant occurrences, do these in any sense matter? Braudel (1966 [1949]) in a famous *boutade* in *The Mediterranean*, said that "events are dust."

In place of the events that are dust, Braudel urged us to focus our attention on two objects of analysis, two kinds of time he considered more real. There are the enduring structures (primarily economic and social) that determine over the *longue durée* our collective behavior – our social ecology, our civilizational patterns, our modes of production. And there are the cyclical rhythms of the functioning of these structures – the expansions and contractions of the economy, the alternation of emphasis in political and cultural phenomena that regularly occur. Underneath the ephemeral happenings of the immediate public arenas lie the enduring continuities of patterns (including the pendular patterns) that change slowly.

But having adjured us to remember that fundamental historical change is slow, he hastened to remind us that nonetheless history is indeed the story of social change. And thus he came to the other front against which he waged his intellectual struggle. In the search for universal eternal patterns of human behavior he sensed great danger. In such efforts, historical time becomes in fact irrelevant:

> The mammoth architecture of this ideal city remains motionless. History is absent from it. World-time, historical time, is there, but, like Aeolus's winds, imprisoned in a goatskin. Sociologists are not opponents of history but of historical time – the reality which still remains powerful, even when one tries to divide it up and diversify it. The historian never escapes from this constraint, but sociologists almost invariably escape; they flee either to the perpetually fixed moment, which is, as it were, suspended above time, or to recurrent phenomena that belong to no single age; so they proceed according to attitudes of mind that are at opposite poles, confining themselves to the strictest concentration on the event or to the very long-term. (Braudel 1972a: 37–38)

There in a nutshell it is. The two antithetical poles, idiographic history and nomothetic social science, are in fact only a single intellectual position, since they are but two modes of trying to escape from the constraints of historical reality.

And what is this historical reality? It is the reality of enduring but not eternal sets of structures (what I would call historical systems), which have their patterned modes of operation (what I would call their cyclical rhythms), but also have a continuous slow process of transformation (what I would call their secular trends). Events are dust not only because they are ephemeral but also because they are dust in our eyes. But the motionless ideal city is similarly an illusion that can blind us. Beware, Braudel cries out, the endless morphologies that universalistic social science creates. As he said of one such effort by Georges Gurvitch – even Georges Gurvitch who for Braudel represented a "welcoming, almost fraternal brand of sociology":

> How could the historian let himself be persuaded by this? With this range of colours it would be impossible to reconstitute the single white light that he must have.... It is a way of rewriting the same equations without altering them. (Braudel 1972a: 37)

In this analysis of the varieties of social time, in this impassioned plea of Braudel that our collective attention ought to turn from the episodic and the eternal to structural and cyclical time, curiously, there is no mention of space. This is all the more curious since, in his major works, space was central to his analyses. Braudel even called himself sometimes a geohistorian and considered himself a disciple of Vidal de la Blache as well as of Lucien Febvre.

What I would like to do is to take Braudel's four times – episodic time, cyclical time, structural time, and the time of the sages – and argue that each of these times has a space. And I would further like to argue that time and space are not two separate categories but one, which I shall call TimeSpace.

We have already noted that Braudel distinguished his four "times" in two ways: by length of time-span and by substantive object described. The spatial parallel to length of time-span might be breadth of space-scope. But this makes little sense. In any case, as we have noted, it is hard to find a precise quantitative measurement of the lengths of time-span. How long are events? An instant, a day, a year, a decade? How long is the life of a structure? 500 years? A millenium? We might have even greater difficulty with breadth of space-scope.

I would suggest that we instead turn to the substantive objects that are being described. Here I think we can find some plausible spatial counterparts to the categories of social time. Episodic time is served by immediate geopolitical space, which is, of course, every bit as controversial and as constructed a phenomenon. Take, for example, a presumed event of 1987–88, what some newspapers refer to as "Palestinian unrest in Israel." We have, to be sure, a difficult time dating it. Did it begin in late 1987, or in 1948, or in 1917? But we have just as difficult a time locating it geopolitically.

Is this unrest occurring in Israel, or in Palestine, or in Gaza and the West Bank, or in the territories occupied by Israel, or in Gaza, Judea, and Samaria? Or is it occurring in that larger space we term the Middle East? I do not propose to answer these questions, since (as is obvious) there is no correct answer. Any answer implies a political and a historical judgment, and that is precisely what the unrest is about. Still, we could not have discourse about this unrest without attributing to it some immediate geopolitical space.

But perhaps you will think that the space is only unclear because I am talking of a current situation about which passions ride high. It turns out that the boundaries of space are not much clearer if we take an episode from earlier centuries. In the sixteenth century the Burgundian Netherlands, part of the realms of the King of Spain, rebelled. The history books call this an event, "the Revolt of the Netherlands," and they date it as going from 1566 or 1568 to 1648. Curious event, be it said in passing, to have lasted 80 years.

I remind you of two sub-events in this lengthy event. The first sub-event took place in 1579. There was a truce in the conflict which resulted in the division of the area into two parts along a line more or less the same as the current frontier between the Nether-lands and Belgium. The area north of that line was in the hands of the forces that led that revolt and was at that point in time called the United Provinces. South of the line a regime loyal to Spain continued to rule, and the area was called the Spanish Netherlands. The temporary truce-line became a long-term reality. These two areas are still politically separate today. One would have thought that the contemporary Belgians, the heirs of those who sided with the King of Spain, would accordingly hesitate to identify themselves with the Revolt of the Netherlands.

Here I intrude the second sub-event. Early in the conflict, one of the councilors of the King of Spain, the Comte d'Egmont, scion of one of the great aristocratic families of the Burgundian region (more precisely of Flanders, which is part of contemporary Bel-gium), urged prudence and conciliation upon the king. He was eventually accused of tacit support of the revolt and executed. In some sense, therefore, he was a martyr of the revolution. It was thus with some surprise that I discovered some years ago a statue of him not in Amsterdam but in Brussels, a statue celebrating his opposition to foreign despotism. I enquired of a Belgian friend what he had been taught, when he was in school, about the role of the Comte d'Egmont, and how Belgians today perceived the Revolt of the Netherlands. Did they just celebrate its early phase, when Flanders and Brabant were regions of rebellion as well, or the whole of it? Was it, I wanted to know, their heritage too, and not only the heritage of the Dutch? Thereupon my second jolt. My friend replied that he did not know, since he was from Liège and, as I must surely be aware, Liège, although part of contemporary Belgium, had not been part of the Burgundian Netherlands. Thus it became clear to me that the space in which the Revolt of the Netherlands had occurred was as fuzzy as the time in which it had occurred, and that clearly the debate about the time and the space were linked.

Let us turn to cyclical time, the times of the alternating rhythms. I believe that to cyclical time corresponds what I shall call "ideological space." Let me illustrate with a spatial category which everyone today uses. It is East-West. If I use the term, we all know it refers to contemporary division of the world that is political, military, cultural, and above all ideological. We know that there has been a so-called cold war between East and West, and that currently many consider this cold war to have ended.

But of course, this particular usage of East and West does not go back further than 1945. It would not make much sense with reference to 1935 or 1925, and would make no sense whatsoever with reference to 1915. To be sure, there have been other East-Wests in our historical parlance. There were Greece and Persia, Rome and Byzantium, Europe and the Orient. And I suppose one could argue that there are analogies among all these usages conceptually. But it is clear that the post-1945 use of East-West is tied to a particular cyclical phase of the history of the modern world. And it is not at all clear that it is surviving the end of this politico-economic cycle.

Furthermore, I point out that East-West is not a categorization of space that is uncontested. There were dissenters about the utility of the distinction from the outset. In the 1950s these dissenters grew politically stronger in the world-system and by the 1960s they proclaimed a rival spatial division as more meaningful, that which we have come to call North-South. Once again, I do not wish to debate the merits of the conceptual importance of East-West versus that of North-South, or to propose, as some do, that they are equally important, or to come out in favor of a "three worlds" theory. And I surely do not wish to enter into the thorny issue of which countries fit into which box (and when). I merely wish to underline that East-West and North-South are obviously socially created geographic categories of fundamental importance to our understanding of the contemporary world. But they are also, as we readily admit, categories that are linked with a given time period. This time period is too long to be called the time-span of an event. These categories are much larger than that. They are linked with, are explained by, and in turn explain, major economic, political, and social thrusts that are in some sense "medium-term" in time-span.

It should now be clear that to structural (long-term) time corresponds structural (large-scale) space. Furthermore, this structural space need not be constant over chronological time. Allow me to illustrate this matter very simply by taking the historical system about which I have been writing, the capitalist world-economy. Like all other historical systems, the capitalist world-economy has a temporal beginning and it will have a temporal end. Of course, these temporal boundaries are by no means self-evident. I for example have argued in my writings that the capitalist world-economy came into existence in the long sixteenth century (see Wallerstein 1974; 1980c; 1989b; 1983). Others would date it later. A few would date it earlier. And of course not everyone agrees that such a historical system has ever existed at all. Furthermore, it is clear that no one during the long sixteenth century (or virtually no one) yet conceived of this historical system as a system. Indeed, it was not until sometime in the nineteenth century that anyone began seriously to analyze this historical system at all. And it is only in the past 20 years that the concept, the "capitalist world-economy," has taken root in world scholarship, and even now only among some scholars. But of course it is easy to explain why recognition of the structural time involved in this system lagged far behind the unfolding of the historical reality.

But what is the structural space of this capitalist world-economy? The first thing to say is that its outer boundaries have evolved. The second thing to say is that there is great debate about when and how. I myself believe that in the long sixteenth century the capitalist world-economy included geographically much of Europe and parts of the Americas, but that at that time it included neither Russia nor the Ottoman Empire nor the Indian subcontinent nor western Africa. I believe that these latter zones were all incorporated into this world-system in the course of its second great expansion, which ran approximately from 1750 to 1850. But others, using the same basic model, would argue that these areas were already "inside" the world-system in the sixteenth and seventeenth centuries (for Russia, see Nolte 1982; for India, see Chaudhuri 1981). This is in part an empirical debate. But it is even more a theoretical debate about the nature of structural space.

A similar structural debate exists about the post-1945 boundaries of the capitalist world-economy. Most people placed the former so-called socialist bloc of countries "outside" the system. They felt these countries had in some sense "withdrawn" from the system. A few, including me, thought this was an incorrect way to conceptualize what was occurring historically even then. (For some of the debate about this question, see Chase-Dunn 1982). Once again it is a matter of how we conceptualize and therefore how we measure structural space.

Some of the concepts of structural space relating to the world-economy have become common parlance. The conceptual pair, core-periphery, although invented in its current usage only in the 1920s and diffused even among a minority of scholars only since circa 1950, is now to be found in encyclopedias (as for example *The New Palgrave* published only in 1987). Core-periphery refer to spatial concentrations of economic activities to be found within the capitalist world-economy. But are such "spatial" concentrations to be described at the level of state boundaries? That is, can we designate various states as core states and others as peripheral states? This is a very knotty question, and a quite contentious one. Some insist that the spatial units thus described must be smaller than states. But of course, as we descend in space-scope for the purpose of locating core and periphery, we edge ourselves towards an asymptote where, once we arrive at the level of individual enterprises, we have lost almost all significant spatial reference. Of course, we can instead move in the other direction, towards zones larger than states. In this case, North-South becomes a metaphor for core-periphery, and becomes not ideological space which is medium-term, but structural space which is long-term, existing therefore not in cyclical time but in structural time.

This opens up many other questions. Can, over a period of time, spatial locations (in the sense of immediate geopolitical space) change their location in ideological space, thereby maintaining as opposed to undermining structural space? Of course. We call this the "rise and decline of nations," and of course it can be analyzed utilizing the concepts of structural space. Yesterday, Japan was a locus of cheap labor. Today it is a so-called core state. Tomorrow, it may be the hegemonic world power. In this process, ideological space changes. The West is perhaps replaced as a category by the OECD, which includes Japan. But structural space endures. The same structural categories persist despite the geopolitical relocations.

Furthermore, core and periphery are not the totality of possible concepts. There is the controversial concept of the semiperiphery as a continuing ongoing location in the structural space of the capitalist world-economy (see Arrighi and Drangel 1986). There is also the concept of the "external arena," which is a spatial concept inherently linked to the process of "incorporation" of zones into the capitalist world-economy (see Hopkins and Wallerstein 1987). Once again, I am not arguing the virtues of the particular concepts, merely illustrating that such concepts exist.

Finally, what corresponds to the time of the sages may be called eternal space, and is to be found in the generalizations of nomothetic social science which are said to hold true "across time and space." As time becomes irrelevant in such a formulation, so of course does space. If incest is a universal taboo, inherent in the nature (the biological nature?) of human socializing, then it matters not at all whether we study it here or there, now or then. And indeed so I was told as a student. In this view, if we wish to know more, scientifically, about complex (therefore complicated and messy) phenomena like the history of humanity, we shall ultimately find it in the truths of simpler, purer, intellectual worlds – in biology, ultimately in physics. As a first step, the Royal Geographical Society might consider renaming itself the Royal Meteorological Society.

Braudel said of the very long-term, the too long-term, *if* it exists, it must be the time of the sages. In this spirit, *if* eternal space exists (and the word from our friends, the cosmologists, these days leads us to realize what a slight reed the universe constitutes if one wants to think of some things as eternal and unchanging) – if eternal space exists, it must be where the sages preach.

Where are we then? The TimeSpace of our nomothetic social scientists seems an irrelevant illusion. The TimeSpace of our idiographic historians – events in immediate geopolitical space – seems a series of self-interested inventions about which there will never be agreement as long as political discord exists in the world. In neither case is TimeSpace taken seriously as a basic ingredient of our geohistorical world. But since these two groups have together dominated our social analyses for two centuries now, no wonder we have never been taught to think seriously about time or space. No wonder we tend to think of them as somehow just there.

It is, I think, incumbent upon us to become far more careful, far more self-aware in our utilization of TimeSpace realities. There is first of all the purely linguistic problem. The domination of the idiographer-nomothetist condominium over world social thought for the past two centuries has rendered all our vocabulary incredibly confusing, in all the major scholarly languages. Words such as time and space – just like words such as state or family – seem to have a clear meaning. But they have this clear meaning only if you accept the premises of the idiographers and the nomothetists. If you do not, it might be better to use totally different words for the different kinds of time and space, the different kinds of states and families, as in fact we find people often did in many of the so-called pre-modern languages. This would, however, be now perhaps too much of a cultural wrench, and besides not everyone would agree that this should be done. Thus some of us insist, as I have been doing, on creating linguistically clumsy locutions such as "ideological space" or "structural TimeSpace." If therefore others persist in talking merely of "space" or of "time," there is a problem of the congruence of terminology, and an inevitable need for conceptual translation. But in conceptual as in linguistic translation, *traduttore traditore*.

The linguistic problem is small, however, beside the more fundamental intellectual problem – how we perceive our world, to what end we utilize our efforts at knowledge, how we organize our scientific activity. The idiographic-nomothetic joint vision was part and parcel of the scientism and optimism which has formed the ideological glue of our present historical system, the capitalist world-economy. This ideology reached its mature version in the eighteenth-century Enlightenment and its religious commitment to the inevitability of human progress. By the nineteenth century, Enlightenment ideas were the unanalyzed assumptions not merely of intellectuals but of popular thought as well. In this atmosphere, it was perfectly understandable that the epistemological debates of the newly emerged social sciences, including both history and geography, should have been limited to what appeared to be the only two plausible alternatives: the exclusive reality of the seemingly concrete, scientific datum (away with all philosophical guesswork!) or the exclusive reality of the universally true scientific theorem (away with the messy unclarity of unanalyzed complexity!).

But, as Braudel reminded Gurvitch, we are constrained by reality and the nineteenth-century world moved on into a twentieth century that has conspired to belie Enlightenment premises and expectations. Slowly, but quite unremittingly, the complexities of the social world have forced themselves upon us, and the plausibility of the ideographic-nomothetic condominium has paled, or at least has been shaken. We must therefore reconstruct the very ways in which we think. We must reexamine the most obvious of our concepts, and hence first of all (or maybe it is last of all) both time and space.

There is one last TimeSpace to consider. It is the time of which the theologians speak, *kairos* as opposed to *chronos*, the "right time" as opposed to "formal time," which Paul Tillich (1948: 33) argued was the distinction between "qualitative" and "quantitative" time. You may perhaps wonder whether historical social scientists should have any concern with theological TimeSpace. In fact, however, the chronosophies of mankind have such theological concepts deeply embedded within them. They merely dress them up in secular clothing. I suggest to you that the intermeshed concepts of "crisis" and "transition" – two of the commonest words in our social scientific vocabulary – are nothing but avatars of *kairos*.

But when and where do crises and transitions occur? We invoke the terms too readily. Crises and transitions are not related to cyclical-ideological TimeSpace, despite our propensity to label each downturn in a cycle as a crisis and each upturn in a cycle as a transition to a new order. Cyclical-ideological TimeSpace is fundamentally repetitive, albeit in the form of a spiral. We have tended to cry crisis and transition, somewhat like the little boy who cries wolf. And our words have regularly been belied by subsequent reappraisals of how little has changed.

But real change, fundamental change, structural change, does of course occur. Structural TimeSpace is concerned with actual geohistorical social systems. Insofar as they are systems, they persist via the cyclical processes that govern them. Thus, as long as they persist, they have some features that are unchanging; otherwise, we could not call them systems. But insofar as they are historical, they are constantly changing. They are never the same from one instant to the next. They are changing in every detail, including of course their spatial parameters. This tension between the cyclical rhythms and the secular trends is the defining characteristic of a geohistorical social system. That is, they all have contradictions which implies that they must all at some point come to an end.

It is when their demise is in sight that a system is in crisis, and must therefore be in transition to something else. This is the "right time" and of course the "right place" to which the concept of *kairos* refers. The theologians are reminding us of something fundamental, of the existence of fundamental moral choice which comes rarely but, when it comes, comes unavoidably.

People resist fundamental moral choice. They always have; they always will. For choice is not easy, and it is for the most part not really possible. It is in fact true that almost all that we do is determined, by which we mean that we are constrained, even into the inner recesses of our mind, by our social biographies. And it is perfectly possible for the analyst to explain and therefore forecast probable social behavior, ultimately in intimate detail.

But the determination of our action is the result of the effective functioning of an ongoing geohistorical social system. Suppose, however, that the system is no longer ongoing. Suppose that the contradictions of the system are so fully developed that we find ourselves in a systemic crisis, and therefore in a transition. Is the outcome of the crisis, of this transition, determined? Many of us would like to think so. In ancient times, we shifted the responsibility of the fundamental moral choices to the gods, and entrusted ourselves to their good humor. Modern secularists were shamed into abandoning the gods. But, unwilling to make the choices, they entrusted themselves to the avatar of the gods, History with a capital H, which guaranteed Progress with a capital P. The transition would always and necessarily be from the less good to the better, from the savage towards the civilized, from slavery towards freedom, from exploitation towards equality.

Unfortunately, *kairos* is the TimeSpace of human choice. It is the rare moment when free will is possible. It is the TimeSpace where, in Prigogine's language, "cascading bifurcations" ensure the "transition to chaos," and out of this chaos, a new but not easily predictable order will emerge:

> The "historical" path along which the system evolves as the control parameter grows is characterized by a succession of stable regions, where deterministic laws dominate, and of instable ones, near the bifurcation points, where the system can "choose" between or among more than one possible future. (Prigogine and Stengers 1984: 169–70)

Human beings therefore, faced with *kairos*, faced with what I shall term transformational TimeSpace, cannot avoid moral choice. It is thrust upon them, at the "right" time and place, at a moment of qualitative time and space whose length and breadth are of uncertain measurement and unpredictable locus. But despite all these uncontrollable elements, we can be certain that there is a *kairos*, a TimeSpace at which transformation does occur, a TimeSpace in which we all exercise our free will for good or ill. And when it comes, we choose our new order.

In offering this small model of five kinds of TimeSpace – episodic geopolitical TimeSpace, cyclico-ideological TimeSpace, structural TimeSpace, eternal TimeSpace, and transformational TimeSpace – I have not been offering you a child's coloring book in which one will find the instructions for which crayon to use. I have rather suggested that we start down a very difficult, very unsettling road of questioning one of the bedrocks of our intelligence, our certainties about time and space. At the end of the road lies not simplicity but complexity. But our geohistorical social systems are complex; indeed they are the most complex structures of the universe. If we are to have some hope (it cannot be more than that) of fashioning them or reconstructing them or building them in ways that are humanly satisfying, then we must understand them in their complexity. And, as a first step, we must see how we have been shaping the categories of TimeSpace to read this reality, we must ask *cui bono*, and we must struggle for more adequate categories.

Part IV
Revisiting Marx

11

Marx and Underdevelopment

Karl Marx in his life work was caught up in the basic epistemological tension of any and all attempts to analyze large-scale, long-term processes of social change: simultaneously to describe the characteristics and the principles of a "system" in its unique process of development.

This tension between a theory that is necessarily abstract and a history that is necessarily concrete cannot by definition be eliminated. Just like most other thinkers facing and aware of this tension in their intellectual activity, Marx resorted to the tactic of alternating emphases in his writings. It is easy therefore to distort his interest, by pointing to only one end of this pendulum and presenting it as the "true Marx" in ways he would have rejected, and frequently did.

Because, however, this tension is ineradicable, it follows by definition that no thinker, however insightful, can ever state things in such a way that they are correct 100 years later. The very evolution of the 100 years creates additional empirical reality which means that the previous theoretical abstractions *must* be modified. And so it will go forever. Marx would have written the *Communist Manifesto* differently in 1948 than in 1848, and *Capital* differently in 1959 than in 1859. We must do the same.

"Marx and underdevelopment" is a curious theme in many ways, since Marx did not really know the concept of underdevelopment. It is a concept alien to his work as he usually expounded it. It is a concept which in many ways challenges Marx's ideas every bit as much as it challenges traditional bourgeois liberalism. For we must never forget that liberalism and Marxism are joint heirs to Enlightenment thought and its deep faith in inevitable progress.

Yet nonetheless underdevelopment is a concept that opens the door to analyses which alone will be able to confirm the essential thrust of Marx's insight into world-historical development, and most specifically into the historical processes of the capitalist mode of production. From the combination of abstract and concrete analyses that Marx and Engels undertook, the socialist movements, the "Marxists," drew in fact, it seems to me, three primary messages (at least until recently).

Message number one was the centrality of the proletariat to the economic and political processes of the capitalist world. The industrial proletariat, and only the industrial proletariat, produced the surplus-value, whose seizure (or accumulation) was the entire object of the capitalist enterprise (M-C-M), the accumulated capital then being used to renew the process ("expanded reproduction of capital") in order to accumulate still more capital.

Politically, it was the industrial proletariat, and it alone, which had "nothing to lose but its chains," and therefore alone had the self-interest and lucidity to perceive the contradictions of capitalism and to seek to transform the world into a Communist one. From this centrality of the proletariat a political lesson was drawn. The struggle for socialism/communism had to be led by an organized political party rooted in the proletariat and reflecting its interests.

Message number two was the priority of the most "advanced" countries (*"De te fabula narratur"*). Capitalism was a progressive development in the double sense of the word "progress." It represented an "advance" over prior forms of social organization. It was a process which developed out of them and only in due time (no "bold leaps").

This had a clear implication both for socio-historical analysis and for political action. For both it meant that Europocentrism was not merely legitimate; it was in some sense mandatory. For it was in western Europe that capitalism first developed; it was in western Europe that the proletariat first emerged; it was consequently in western Europe that successful socialist revolutions would first occur.

Message number three was the economic importance of the distinction, which was also a historical sequence, of merchant capital and industrial capital. These were two distinct forms of capitalism, one located in the sphere of circulation (and hence not involving productive labor) and one located in the sphere of production. It was only when industrial capital came to be (sequentially) dominant in a given zone that we could say "true" capitalism existed, and surplus-value was being extracted.

The political implication of this distinction was that the triumph of industrial over merchant capital in a given state was somehow progressive, and that it might be the duty of working class movements to support the struggle to achieve this triumph, even perhaps to substitute itself for any industrial bourgeoisie which failed to play its "historic" role.

And *yet*, even though these messages are clear and have determined a good deal of subsequent use of Marx's ideas, he himself offered us significant cautions about these notions. On message one, the proletariat as meaning primarily (if not exclusively) wage-earning urban industrial workers, let us look first at his famous discussions of the peasantry in *The Class Struggles in France* and *The Eighteenth Brumaire*.

> Thus it came about that the French peasant cedes to the capitalist, in the form of *interest* on the *mortgages* encumbering the soil and in the form of interest on the *advances made by the usurer without mortgages*, not only rent, not only the industrial profit, in a word, not only the *whole net profit,* but even *a part of the wages,* and therefore he has sunk to the level of the *Irish tenant farmer* – all under the pretence of being a *private proprietor....*
>
> The condition of the French peasants, when the republic had added new burdens to their old ones, is comprehensible. It can be seen that their exploitation differs only in *form* from the exploitation of the industrial proletariat. The exploiter is the same: *capital.* (Marx 1978: 121–22)

> The small holding of the peasant is now only the pretext that allows the capitalist to draw profits, interest and rent from the soil, while leaving it to the tiller of the soil himself to see how he can extract wages. (Marx 1979: 190)

There are two clear warnings in these passages. The first is the use of the term "wages" to describe the income retained by the peasant proprietor. The second is the statement that the latter's relationship to the capitalist "differs only in *form*" from that of the industrial proletariat. (Note in addition the use of the modifying adjective "industrial" for "proletarian," as though there were several varieties of proletarians.) We all know that for Marx to call something a difference in form means to indicate that this difference is secondary and minor and does not detract from the *essential* similarity of the two phenomena. As if further to underline this point, Marx speaks of the "wages" of the peasant proprietor, although no money passes in this case from any "employer" to him as an "employee."

As for the idea that surplus-value can only be extracted from a wage-earning employee, Marx specifically states the opposite, spelling out how surplus-value can be extracted not only when there is no real subsumption of labor but also when there is not even the formal subsumption of labor. See this passage from the *Resultate*:

> In India, for example, the capital of the *usurer* advances raw materials or tools or even both to the immediate producer in the form of money. The exorbitant interest which it attracts, the interest which, irrespective of its magnitude, it extorts from the primary producer, is just another name for surplus-value. It transforms its money into capital by extorting unpaid labour, surplus labour, from the immediate producer. But it does not intervene in the process of production itself, which proceeds in its traditional fashion, as it always had done. In part it thrives on the *withering* away of this mode of production, in part it is a means to make it *wither* away, to force it to *eke out* a vegetable existence in the most unfavourable conditions. But here we have *not yet* reached the stage of the formal subsumption of labour under capital. (Marx 1977: 1023)

Finally, there are his oft-noted discussions of slavery, where he clearly distinguishes between slavery within "the patriarchal system mainly for home use" and slavery within the "plantation system for the world-market." He talks once again explicitly of the creation therein of surplus-value, and he asserts:

> Where the capitalist outlook prevails, as on American plantations, this entire surplus-value is regarded as profit; where neither the capitalist mode of production itself exists, nor the corresponding outlook has been transferred from capitalist countries, it appears as rent. (Marx 1967: vol. III, 804)

Nor is slavery somehow marginal to the functioning of capitalism. Indeed, in a letter to P. V. Annenkov, 28 December 1846, he precisely criticizes Proudhon for implying this:

> Direct slavery is as much the pivot upon which our present-day industry turns as are machinery, credit, etc. Without slavery there

would be no cotton, without cotton there would be no modern industry. It is slavery which has given value to the colonies, it is the colonies which have created world trade, and world trade is the necessary condition for large-scale machine industry. (Marx and Engels 1982: 101–2)

Slavery and other non-wage relations of production are not marginal to capitalism because of the distinctive "process of circulation of industrial capital":

No matter whether commodities are the output of production based on slavery, or peasants (Chinese, Indian ryots), of communes (Dutch East Indies), of state enterprise (such as existed in former epochs of Russian history on the basis of serfdom) or of half-savage hunting tribes, etc. – as commodities and money they come face to face with the money and commodities in which the industrial capital presents itself and enter as much into its circuit as into that of the surplus-value borne in the commodity-capital, provided the surplus-value is spent as revenue; hence they enter into both branches of circulation of commodity-capital. The character of the process of production from which they originate is immaterial. They function as commodities in the market, and as commodities they enter into the circuit of industrial capital as well as into the circulation of the surplus-value incorporated in it. It is therefore the universal character of the origin of the commodities, the existence of the market as world-market, which distinguishes the process of circulation of industrial capital. (Marx 1976: vol. 2, 110)

Note once again that all these forms of production are considered to have created "surplus-value" once they enter into the "circuit" of capital. "The character of the process of production from which they originate is immaterial."

When we turn to message two, the question of the priority of what today we call the core areas of the world-economy, we find a similar prudence in the famous Preface to the first German edition of *Capital*. Let me cite it at some length:

The physicist either observes physical phenomena where they occur in their most typical form and most free from disturbing influence, or, wherever possible, he makes experiments under conditions that assure the occurrence of the phenomenon in its normality. In this work I have to examine the capitalist mode of production, and the conditions of production and exchange corresponding to that mode. Up to the present time, their classic ground is England. That is the

reason why England is used as the chief illustration in the development of my theoretical ideas. If, however, the German reader shrugs
his shoulders at the condition of the English industrial and agricultural labourers, or in optimist fashion comforts himself with the
thought that in Germany things are not nearly so bad, I must plainly
tell him, "*De te fabula narratur!*" Intrinsically, it is not a question of
the higher/lower degree of development of the social antagonisms
that result from the natural laws of capitalist production. It is a
question of these laws themselves, of the tendencies working with
iron necessity towards inevitable results. The country that is more
developed industrially only shows, to the less developed, the image
of its own future. But apart from this. Where capitalist production is
fully naturalized among the Germans (for instance, in the factories
proper) the condition of things is much worse than in England,
because the counterpoise of the Factory Acts is wanting. In all other
spheres, we, like all the rest of Continental Western Europe, suffer
not only from the development of capitalist production, but also
from the incompleteness of that development. Alongside of modern
evils, a whole series of inherited evils oppress us, arising from the
passive survival of antiquated modes of production, with their inevitable train of social and political anachronisms. We suffer not only
from the living, but from the dead. *Le mort saisit le vif!* (Marx 1967:
vol. I, 8–9)

Notice how "*De te fabula narratur*" is immediately qualified. It is
not that one country has a "higher" degree of development and the
other a "lower" one. We are talking of laws that cover both. Nor is
Germany in fact the same as England; it is *worse*. It suffers not
merely from "the development of capitalist production" but from
the "incompleteness of that development." And this present differential will determine the future. "*Le mort saisit le vif!*"

We get in fact a further kind of qualification in the comparisons
between England and France in *The Class Struggles in France*.
Marx is explaining why the French industrial bourgeoisie in 1848
did *not* rule the French state, as the English bourgeoisie ruled the
English state:

The industrial bourgeoisie can rule only where modern industry
shapes all property relations to suit itself, and industry can win this
power only where it has conquered the world market, for national
bounds are inadequate for its development. But French industry, to
a great extent, maintains its command even of the national market
only through a more or less modified system of prohibitive tariffs.
(Marx 1987: 56)

The situation, it seems, differs fundamentally between a country that has "conquered the world market" and the others. But can, logically or empirically, more than one country at a time "conquer the world market?" It seems doubtful, and Marx himself seems to opt for the single-country hypothesis:

> In France, the petty bourgeois does what normally the industrial bourgeois would have to do; the worker does what normally would be the task of the petty bourgeois; the task of the worker, who accomplishes that? No one. In France it is not accomplished; in France it is proclaimed. It is not accomplished anywhere within the national walls; the class war within French society turns into a world war, in which the nations confront one another. Accomplishment begins only when, through the world war, the proletariat is pushed to the fore in the nation which dominates the world market, to the forefront in England. The revolution, which finds here not its end, but its organizational beginning, is no short-lived revolution. The present generation is like the Jews whom Moses led through the wilderness. It has not only a new world to conquer, it must go under in order to make room for the men who are able to cope with a new world. (Marx 1978: 117)

In this wilderness through which we are wandering, there are two possible paths we can take. We can decide that it is only in the most "advanced" country that the transition to socialism can occur (or can first occur). We know this is one inference Marx at times drew. Or one can go another route. We can decide that the situation is so special in the country which dominates the world market that it tells us nothing of real politics elsewhere. De facto, most Marxist parties have gone this latter route, without in many (even most) cases being ready to admit this theoretically and therefore to deal with the necessary consequences of such an attack on the theoretical priority of the center.

Marx himself seems aware of the dilemma and tries to save the situation by the thesis of a revolutionary zigzag:

> Just as the period of crisis occurs later on the Continent than in England, so does that of prosperity. The original process always takes place in England; it is the demiurge of the bourgeois cosmos. On the continent, the different phases of the cycle through which bourgeois society is ever speeding anew occur in secondary and tertiary form. First, the Continent exported incomparably more to England than to any other country. This export to England, however, in turn depends on the position of England, particularly with

regard to the overseas market. Then England exports to the overseas lands incomparably more than the entire Continent, so that the quantity of Continental exports to these lands is always dependent on England's overseas exports at the time. While, therefore, the crises first produce revolutions on the Continent, the foundation for these is, nevertheless, always laid in England. Violent outbreaks must naturally occur rather in the extremities of the bourgeois body than in its heart, since the possibility of adjustment is greater here than there. On the other hand, the degree to which Continental revolutions react on England is at the same time the barometer which indicates how far these revolutions call in question the bourgeois conditions of life, or how far they only hit their political formations. (Marx 1987: 134–35)

In a letter to S. Meyer and A. Vogt in 1870, Marx suggested another, even more "Third-Worldist," version of this zigzag, where revolution in Ireland is considered to be the prerequisite for revolution in England.

Ireland is the bulwark of the English landed aristocracy. The exploitation of that country is not only one of the main sources of this aristocracy's material welfare; it is its *greatest moral strength*. It, in fact, represents the domination of England over Ireland. Ireland is therefore the *great means* by which the English aristocracy maintains its domination in England herself. If, on the other hand, the English army and police were to withdraw from Ireland tomorrow, *you would at once have an agrarian revolution there*. But the overthrow of the English aristocracy in Ireland involves as a necessary consequence *its overthrow in England*. And this would fulfill the preliminary condition for the *proletarian revolution* in England. The destruction of the English landed aristocracy in Ireland is an *infinitely easier* operation than in England herself, because in Ireland the land question has hitherto been the exclusive form of the social question, because it is a question of existence, of life and death, for the immense majority of the Irish people, and because *it is at the same time inseparable from the national question*. This quite apart from the Irish being more passionate and *revolutionary in character* than the English. (Marx and Engels 1942: 288–89)

One last caution of Marx should be noted. This has to do with message three on the merchant vs. industrial capital distinction so dear to those who believe that, in a capitalist world, the sphere of production has some kind of ontological distinctiveness from and primacy over the sphere of circulation. No doubt Marx utilized extensively this distinction, but when he came to discussing "spheres" of the circuit of capital, he could sound strangely "circulationist." Marx is always clearest when he engages in polemics. In 1846, he attacked Proudhon. In 1875, he attacked Lassalle. Over a period of 30 years, the complaint remained virtually the same. In a letter to Annenkov, he wrote about Proudhon:

> Mr. Proudhon is so far from the truth that he neglects to do what even profane economists do. In discussing the division of labour, he feels no need to refer to the world *market*. Well! Must not the division of labour in the fourteenth and fifteenth centuries, when there were as yet no colonies, when America was still non-existent for Europe, and when Eastern Asia existed only through the mediation of Constantinople, have been utterly different from the division of labour in the seventeenth century, when colonies were already developed? And that is not all. Is the whole internal organization of nations, are their international relations anything but the expression of a given division of labour? And must they not change as the division of labour changes? (Marx and Engels 1942: 98)

And against Lassalle's Gotha Program, he thunders:

> It is altogether self-evident that, to be able to fight at all, the working class must organize itself at home *as a class* and that its own country is the immediate area of its struggle. Insofar as its class struggle is national, not in substance, but, as the *Communist Manifesto* says, "in form." But the "framework of the present-day national state," for instance, the German Empire, is itself in its turn economically "within the framework" of the world market, politically "within the framework" of the system of states. Every businessman knows that German trade is at the same time foreign trade, and the greatness of Herr Bismarck consists, to be sure, precisely in his pursuing a kind of *international* policy. (Marx 1972: 390)

Once again we get the distinction of form and substance. The form of class struggle may be national, indeed "must" be national. But the economic substance is the world market, and the political substance the system of states. Both the "internal organization of nations" and their "international relations" *necessarily* change in function of changes in the "division of labor," which is located in the world market.

I remind you that I have not cited at length from Marx in order to discover the true Marx. There is no true Marx. There are two Marxes, at least two. There have to be, since he was caught in that inescapable epistemological dilemma of which I spoke. Rather, I have cited him at length to demonstrate that, at the minimum, we should remember his qualifications, his prudences, his ambiguities. I do this because I wish now to turn to the culs-de-sac into which much Marxist analysis and praxis has fallen, as a result of having failed to remember the qualifications, prudences, ambiguities.

The culs-de-sac – or if you wish to be generous, the theoretical conundra – are well known. The emphasis on the key role of the urban industrial proletarians meant that Marxists were ceaselessly explaining, or explaining away, the role of (the very existence of) nationalities, peasants, minorities, women, and the whole peripheral zone. How much ink has been spilled – and blood – over Marxism and the national question, Marxism and the peasant question, Marxism and the woman question! Nine-tenths of the world became "questions," anomalies," "survivals" – objectively progressive for a while perhaps, but destined to disappear, sociologically, analytically, politically.

And as if this weren't curious enough, Marxists have had to face the disturbing fact that in many ways what was supposed to be the locus of world revolution – that is, the core of the core – turned out to the most refractory zone of all. No revolutions, no immiserization, and surely no withering away of the state.

The biggest conundrum of all has been the Soviet Union. Born out of a revolution that wasn't supposed to have occurred, Marxists have spent the last 65 years facing up to the particular structures and policies that have prevailed, all unanticipated by and largely unaccounted for by prior theorizing. On the whole, Marxists have reacted to this phenomenon either by apologetics or by denunciation. A few have tried to find an uncomfortable niche in-between these two polar responses. What Marxists have not done is to see whether or not, within the framework of Marxist theory, one could have expected to have happened exactly what did happen, whether the Soviet Union's policies – from Lenin to Stalin to Khrushchev to Brezhnev to Gorbachev – are not completely explicable as a consequence of the workings of the capitalist world-economy? Does not Marx's question in his 1846 letter to Annenkov apply here still? "Is the whole internal organization of nations, and their international relations, anything but the expression of a given division of labor?"

I would like to argue that if we take what I consider to be the six major theses of the Marx corpus, they can account for, do account for, the history of the last 150 years (indeed the history of the last 400 years) quite adequately, and also indicate both the hopeful possibilities and the great dangers of the immediate future.

1 Social reality is a process of ceaseless contradictions, which can only be apprehended dialectically.
2 Capitalism is a process of ceaseless accumulation of capital, which distinguishes it from precapitalist modes of production.
3 Capitalism as a historical system involves the transformation of the productive processes such that they create surplus-value which is appropriated by bourgeois in order to accumulate capital.
4 Capitalism over time polarizes the social organization of life such that more and more persons are grouped as either bourgeois or proletarians, and that the proletariat suffers immiserization.
5 In a capitalist world, the state is an instrument of capitalist oppression; socialism involves the withering away of the state.
6 The transition from capitalism to socialism cannot be evolutionary; it can only be revolutionary. To believe otherwise is utopian in the negative sense of that term.

Where into all of this does the concept of "underdevelopment" come? The answer is very simple. It is only when we move to the center of our consciousness the fact that the whole set of characteristics we call to mind with the locution "underdevelopment" – that is, non-wage-labor forms of market production, marginalization and squatting, a distended tertiary sector, the emergence of the social role of the housewife, ethnicity, clientelism, corrupt and oppressive state-machineries, etc. – are neither anomalies nor survivals, but creations of the capitalist mode of production which are integral parts of its functioning, that we can arrive at a coherent account of capitalism as a historical system in which the six theses of Marx listed above are seen to be valid.

As long as Marx's ideas are taken to be theses about processes that occur primarily within state boundaries and that involve primarily urban wage-earning industrial workers working for private industrial bourgeois, then these ideas will be easily demonstrated to be false, misleading, and irrelevant – and to lead us down wrong political paths. Once they are taken to be ideas about a historical world-system, whose development itself involves "underdevelopment," indeed is based on it, they are not only valid, but they are revolutionary as well.

In this case, we have the following kind of broad account of the actual historical development of the capitalist world-economy over time. In the late Middle Ages, as the result of the so-called crisis of feudalism which threatened the ability of Europe's upper strata to extract significant amounts of surplus from the direct producers by the methods central to the feudal system, emphasis began to be placed on an alternative mode of surplus-extraction, that occurring via market mechanisms. We call this system capitalism.

It required new forms of production processes, new modes of labor control, and new institutional frameworks. It also required new social roles, those we have come to call the roles of bourgeois and proletarian. Within the relatively short period of 200 years (by say 1650), this new "mode of production" was so successful that it had completely reversed the previously declining rates of upper strata extraction and had indeed made possible new levels far beyond the imagination of feudal society. The new system consolidated itself in Europe and went on from there to take over the world, in the process eliminating all alternative modes of social organization and establishing eventually a single division of labor throughout the globe for the first time in human history.

By 1650, we not only had in place a capitalist world-economy located primarily in Europe; we also had a functioning interstate system, composed of so-called sovereign states. The world-economy was structured by an integrated set of production processes which involved a pattern of exchange that ensured not only the transfer of surplus-value from direct producers to upper strata but a concentration of the accumulation in the so-called core areas of this world-economy, essentially by means of unequal exchange mechanisms that gave the advantage to upper strata in core areas at the expense of smaller numbers of upper strata in the peripheral areas. The sovereign states became the primary political units organizing the necessary flow of the factors of production. Placed in a hierarchical order, these states were all constrained (even the strongest among them) by emerging "rules" or the interstate system, these "rules" providing the crucial political superstructure of capitalism as a mode of production.

To make such a system work, more and more productive processes had to be commodified, that is, oriented to production for a world market, which developed long "commodity chains." These commodity chains, when subjected to empirical analysis by tracing backwards the multiple inputs to some major consumables such as finished cloths, revealed two traits from the beginning. First, the chains crossed many frontiers, primarily moving from periphery to core. Secondly, the inputs to these chains were produced by a very variegated set of relations of production, only a small part of which were what we have wrongfully come to think of as "classically capitalist." These two traits have remained largely true up to today.

The shape of the chains and perhaps most importantly the price structures of the multiple transactions were not shaped in an absolutely free market, but fashioned in a market whose rules for price-setting were framed by the vector of all political authorities (the unequally strong sovereign states, acting directly and via the "rules" of the interstate system). Price-setting practices have been stable in the medium run but changeable in the long run, the outcome of the continuing class struggle.

The inherent contradictions of capitalism as a mode of production resulted with relatively predictable frequency in cycles of economic expansion and stagnation of the world-economy as a whole (causing a very complex set of changes in its component parts). One of the many aspects of these cyclical shifts has been an internally generated but discontinuous need of the capitalist world-economy to expand its zone of operation, both extensively and intensively. Extensive expansion involved the incorporation of new, previously external, areas into the division of labor of the capitalist world-economy. Internal expansion (or deepening of capitalist processes) involved socially rewarded technological innovations (with the concurrent practices of increased concentration of capital, increase of the ratio of fixed to variable capital, and continuous deskilling of the work force). The two processes of extensive and intensive expansion went to some extent in opposite directions. Indeed, the major impulse for extensive expansion was to counteract the reduction in the overall ratio of surplus-value extraction as a result of the economic *and political* consequences of an increase in intensive expansion.

The central social consequence of this capitalist process, however, has been the *creation* of the proletariat and the bourgeoisie as social categories. In order to have an adequate work force for the production processes producing for the world market, this work force has had to be compelled to work in ways that were different from those in which its predecessors did. This is the famous and crucial insight of Marx about the alienation of the proletariat and the elimination of his ownership and control of the means of production. Yet this crucial insight has been misread, in part by Marx himself, as a simple sequence of taking land away from an independent small peasant which thereby drove him to be an urban wage-worker.

Historically, the picture is so much more complex than that imagery conveys that we can only call it flagrantly misleading. In fact, what has happened is that the process of commodification of labor has been accompanied by a reshaping of "subsistence" forms of labor such that they have remained an integral element of the reproduction of the labor force in the capitalist mode of production. It is precisely this fact, that the vast majority of the work force depends only *partially* on wage-labor for their lifetime income needs, that has made the work force totally integrated into the logic of the world-economy. And it has done so in ways that have been far more efficacious – and profitable – for the upper strata than if the work force were in fact composed only of full-time wage-earning industrial workers with no sources of income other than that received from the employer as wages.

Instead, workers have been regrouped in complex structures we may call households, collectivities of individuals of both sexes and of different ages, which have been, however, neither necessarily close kin nor necessarily co-residential. These households typically have assembled their income from multiple sources, one of which to this day has remained various forms of "subsistence" activity (consecrated indeed by the devalued work symbolized by the social role of the "housewife"). In addition, household income has been assembled from petty commodity production, rents, transfer payments and gifts, and of course wage-work (this last being statistically less important than we usually assert).

The resulting households have found themselves under two continuing pressures: to commodify even further all aspects of social reproduction; to funnel surplus-value to the upper strata indirectly by permitting significant reductions in the lifetime wage levels of wage-workers, even of that minority who are paid more than the real minimum wage. Not only are there therefore a wide range of social combinations reflected in these household structures, but it is only a minority – even today, even in the core zones – which come close to the "classical" image of the proletariat. Yet, paradoxically – a paradox to which we shall return – it is true that the degree of proletarianization has in fact been nonetheless increasing over time, both in terms of the percentages of the work force involved in production for the world market, and in terms of the degree of dependence upon wage-labor as a percentage of household income.

Parallel to this process of proletarianization has been a process of bourgeoisification. Just as more and more of the work force has been oriented to production for the world market, so more and more upper strata have been oriented to deriving their surpluses from the current operations of the world market. Bourgeois households too have become structures that pool diverse forms of income in complex ways, profits from managerial ownership being only one of them, and (as with wage-labor for the work force) a minority form. The parallel to the work force's "subsistence" income has been the upper strata's "feudal rent" (*lato sensu*) income. Just as "subsistence" in a capitalist system provides greater profit to the bourgeosie than if all labor sales were through the market, so "feudal rent" in a capitalist system provides greater profit to the bourgeoisie than if all labor purchases were through the market.

Not only therefore is there a wide range of bourgeois households but it is only a minority – even today, even in the core zone – which come close to the "classical" image of the bourgeoisie. Yet, paradoxically, it is true that the degree of bourgeoisification has been increasing, in the same double sense we invoked for proletarianization. The percentage of upper strata involved in market surplus-extraction operations has been growing, and an ever greater percentage of their income has in fact been coming from current market operations.

I have used the word "paradox" twice, once about proletarianization and once about bourgeoisification. What is the paradox? The paradox is that these central processes of capitalist development as described by Marx, and which in turn account for the material and social polarization of the world, have come about not because of but *despite* the will and interests of the bourgeoisie as a class. It is the low level of proletarianization, not the high level, that has created and preserved the profit-making potential of capitalism as a system. It is the low level of bourgeoisification, and not the high level, that has created and preserved the political structures that ensured its survival. Neither proletarianization nor bourgeoisification are of intrinsic interest to capitalist. "Accumulate, accumulate! That is Moses and the prophets!" (Marx 1967: vol. 1, 595).

Proletarianization and bourgeoisification have come about not because of the demiurge of the capitalists but as mechanisms to resolve repeated short-run crises which have had the contradictory effect of undermining the system in the long run. It is as though capitalist economic policies which pushed at the level of the world-economy as a whole to ever greater material polarization (the increasing real work load of the majority of the world's population and the real historical reductions in their quality of life) have been countermanded by the ever greater social polarization (the increasing elimination of the "neo-feudal" structures that were created by capitalists to make possible the material polarization). For it is the social polarization far more than the material polarization which has created the main base for the rise of the capitalist world's antisystemic movements in the last 150 years.

And here we come to the last paradox. The political configuration of the capitalist world-economy – sovereign states ensconced in an interstate system – has forced upon the movements a Hobson's choice. They have been forced to choose between seeking power within the framework of separate sovereign states, or not to have a plausible possibility of achieving some power. But obtaining power within a sovereign state that is constrained by an interstate system based on a functioning division of labor has not meant, probably could not have meant, the ability to opt out of the capitalist world-economy. It has meant instead the ability to achieve some limited reallocation of world surplus, in short, the power to bring about reforms, without necessarily undermining the system as such.

Quite the contrary. The coming to power in state after state of antisystemic movements has undoubtedly undermined the system by providing models and support for other antisystemic movements. But it has simultaneously reinforced the system by providing means of taming the rebelliousness of the world's work force. The Soviet Union – both in its "Stalinist" tendencies and in its "revisionism" – is neither a distortion nor logically a surprise. It is the model of what we should have expected as a consequence of the development of capitalism as a world-system, precisely if we had taken Marx's theses seriously, especially in the light of the concept of "underdevelopment." It is the model of a weak state trying to become a strong state, thereby changing the economic role of this region in the world-economy. Marxism has served both as an instrument to struggle against the world capitalist system, and as ideological cover and ideological constraint on those who came to hold power. Ergo, the ambiguous balance sheet.

But history is not yet over. The "socialist states" have emerged as an integral part of the developmental history of capitalism. So have the continuing and expanding ethno-nationalisms of the twentieth century. So have racism and sexism. Capitalism is more of a hydra-headed monster than anyone could imagine in the nineteenth century, to say nothing of the sixteenth. Like all monsters, it is lumbering along to its doom, but in the meantime it is destroying many lives and much of our ecological heritage.

This then brings me to the seventh thesis, the one about which Marx was unequivocally wrong. Thesis number 7 is that capitalism represented progress over what existed before, and it will ineluctably be followed by the dawning of the classless society. This is socialism utopian, not socialism scientific. Capitalism has represented historically moral regression and for the vast majority of the world's population material regression, even while it has ensured for the upper strata of the world (now enlarged from 1 percent to maybe 20 percent of the world's population) a material standard of living and style of life that far surpasses the possibilities of even the "Oriental potentates" of yore.

In fact, as the dilemmas of the antisystemic movements show us, the world today is faced not with inevitable progress but with a real historical choice. The bourgeoisie of the world, reluctantly bourgeoisified, is struggling to survive. Just as the aristocracy of feudal Europe survived their great structural crisis by transforming themselves into bourgeois reigning over a new mode of production, so the bourgeoisie of today are already in the process of trying to survive their structural crisis by transforming themselves into "x" reigning over a new mode of production.

This is neither impossible nor inevitable. The alternative possibility is the creation in the next 100 years of a socialist world order, one based on a system of production for use, one that will involve the withering away of the states because of the withering away of the interstate system, one which will result in a reasonably egalitarian distribution of resources, time, space, and social roles. Such a system will not be utopia, nor beyond history. And it is quite impossible today to predict its institutional forms. But this alternative would indeed be progress.

The question before us, the only one of any moral or political interest, is how in this twilight-zone of capitalism as a historical social system, we can make more likely the relatively egalitarian outcome as opposed to the relatively inegalitarian one. I have no easy answer to that question. I have observed that, in the last 100 years or so, the most progressive upsurges of collective sentiment and action, those that have left the most positive residue, have come in the late stages of political mobilization by the movements – the stages where these movements "get out of hand" Once these movements achieve "power," these upsurges become more practical and less effervescent, and eventually die down through inanition, disillusionment, active suppression.

I do not conclude that movements should never take state power, nor that it is hopeless if they do. I do conclude that unless a broader, more complex strategy of the struggle is evolved, we shall not arrive at an egalitarian socialist world order. I have some specific suggestions, none of which is completely thought through, and all of which together may not suffice. But they do seem to me hopeful lines of action.

First, three different kinds of antisystemic movements have emerged in the three political "worlds" existing since the Second World War. There are the national liberation movements in the "pre-revolutionary" states of the periphery. There are the multiple forms of "new" movements in the principal core states, organizing all sorts of groups who have been left out previously. There are the emerging efforts to create movements within and without the parties of the "post-revolutionary" states. Insofar as each segment reflects a different form of antisystemic impulse (that is, opposition to the capitalist world-economy and all of its outgrowths), these movements need to figure out how they can become one family of movements, not three.

Secondly, these movements need to rethink how they relate to existing "workers" movements. Indeed the question is one of fundamental definition. If indeed Marx was right and the world is socially polarizing into bourgeois and proletarians, then at least 80 percent worldwide are indeed proletarians (though this percentage would be different as calculated within particular state boundaries), and all three of the new kinds of antisystemic movements are primarily composed of proletarians.

Thirdly, state power is only one form of power within the modern world-system. There are many other forms – economic, social, cultural. We must cease thinking of these other forms of power as mere byways en route to state power. We must think of them as coordinate parts of a whole, in which the battle is fought. We must defetishize state power without neglecting it.

Fourthly, we must systematically and thoroughly reopen the nineteenth-century consensus of social thought, of which liberalism and classical Marxism are the two principal variants and, in the light of the real evolution of the world we must rewrite our theory and above all our historiography. We must do as Marx counseled: *Hic Rhodus, hic salta*!

Finally, it would be well to rethink our metaphor of transition. Since the late nineteenth century, we have been embroiled in a pseudo-debate about evolutionary versus revolutionary paths to power. *Both* sides were and always have been essentially reformist, because both sides believed that transition is a controllable phenomenon. A transition that is controlled, that is organized, is bound to involve some continuity of exploitation. We must lose our fear of a transition that takes the form of crumbling, of disintegration. Disintegration is messy, it may be somewhat anarchic, but it is not necessarily disastrous. "Revolutions" may in fact be "revolutionary" only to the degree they promote such crumbling. Organizations may be essential to break the crust initially. It is doubtful they can actually build the new society.

If this sounds too adventurous for you, and too vague, I ask you to reflect upon the alternative scenarios – both the one represented by the historical transition of Europe from feudalism to capitalism, and the one that seems indicated by the very ambiguous and uneven story of our antisystemic movements up to now. I am not recommending any form of passivity. I am recommending the use of active intelligence and active organizing energy that is simultaneously reflexive and moral, in the class struggle of the majority against the minority, of those who are exploited against the exploiters, of those who are deprived of the surplus-value they create against those who seize this surplus-value and live off it.

12

Marxisms as Utopias: Evolving Ideologies

I

We are all to some extent prisoners of our education. For me the concept of utopia brings immediately to mind three writings: Sir Thomas More's *Utopia*, Friedrich Engels's *Socialism: Scientific and Utopian*, and Karl Mannheim's *Ideology and Utopia*. In fact, these involve three rather different meanings and usages of the concept of utopia, which reflect in fact three different moments of the history of the modern world-system as reflected in its intellectual currents.

More left us in no doubt about what was utopian in his *Utopia*, that place that is nowhere:

> As long as you have private property, and as long as cash money is the measure of all things, it is really not possible for a nation to be governed justly or happily. For justice cannot exist where all the best things in life are held by the worst citizens: nor can anyone be happy where property is limited to a few, since those few are always uneasy and the many are utterly wretched.
>
> So I reflect on the wonderfully wise and sacred institutions of the Utopians who are so well governed with so few laws. Among them virtue has its reward, yet everything is shared equally, and all men live in plenty. (More 1975: 30–31)

Utopia then, for More, was quite simply the criticism of capitalist reality in the name of egalitarian ideals. More made it clear, furthermore, that he believed these criticisms could lead to social action that would rectify the situation. Like the good civil servant that he was, More believed that legislated reform could bring utopia into being.

There are two elements one should not miss in More's *Utopia*. One is its homogeneity. This comes out clearly in the very opening description of the geography of utopia: "There are fifty-four cities on the island, all spacious and magnificent, identical in language, customs, institutions, and laws. So far as the location permits, all of them are built on the same plan, and have the same appearance. The nearest are at least twenty-four miles apart, and the farthest are not so remote that a man cannot go on foot from one to the other in a day" (More 1975: 35). This homogeneous egalitarian world is composed of highly moral persons – "a second conviction of adultery is punished by death" (More 1975: 67) – who work hard at rural and artisanal tasks during the day, prize intellectual and cultural activities in their leisure time, and remember to devote a certain part of the collective surplus to sustaining an intellectual and cultural elite.

The second thing to note, however, is that alongside the homogeneity, utopia contains one small inequality, slipped into the description without too much fanfare. There is a certain amount of "dirty and heavy work" (More 1975: 47), it seems, even in utopia. For this, one has slaves. And for the perilous work, one hires mercenaries "at extravagant rates of pay" (More 1975: 50). This is because, apparently, utopia is only a single country. It is not the entire world. Happily, it is well protected against any danger of invasion by its natural surroundings – a detail so important that it opens More's description of the place. Utopia is a large, crescent-shaped island, whose inhabitants live along the shores of the immense inner coast of the bay formed by the horns of this crescent, 11 miles apart:

> What with shallows on one side, and rocks on the other, the entrance into the bay is very dangerous. Near the middle of the channel, there is one rock that rises above the water, and so presents no danger in itself; on top of it a tower has been built, and there a garrison is kept. Since the other rocks lie under water, they are very dangerous to navigation. The channels are known only to the Utopians, so hardly any strangers enter the bay without one of their pilots; and even they themselves could not enter safely if they did not direct themselves by some landmarks on the coast. If they should shift

these landmarks about, they could lure to destruction an enemy fleet coming against them, however big it was. (More 1975: 34)

Thus well fortified against enemy fleets, one might think utopia is isolationist. But it seems utopia is subject to demographic vagaries and hence to a pressure for expansion. The problems are initially resolved by interhousehold and then by intercity (but intraisland) transfers. Still, sometimes this is not enough.

And if the population throughout the entire island exceeds the quota, then they enroll citizens out of every city and plant a colony under their own laws on the mainland near them, wherever the natives have plenty of unoccupied and uncultivated land. Those natives who want to live with the Utopian settlers are taken in. When such a merger occurs, the two peoples gradually and easily blend together, sharing the same way of life and customs, much to the advantage of both. For by their policies the Utopians make the land yield an abundance for all, which had previously seemed too barren and paltry even to support the natives. But if the natives will not join in living under their laws, the Utopians drive them out of the land they claim for themselves, and if they resist make war on them. The Utopians say it's perfectly justifiable to make war on people who leave their land idle and waste, yet forbid the use of it to others who, by law of nature, ought to be supported from it. (More 1975: 44–45)

How much of the outer world egalitarian utopians submit to their rule via their "extravagantly paid" mercenaries is never made clear by More. Paying the mercenaries seems as good a use as any of their ample money in any case, since "they hold gold and silver up to scorn in every conceivable way" (More 1975: 51).

This rereading of More's *Utopia* makes Engels's attitude to the later utopians quite understandable. Utopia was simply the culminating idea of the bourgeoisie's "kingdom of reason" (Engels 1959: 69). It is a version of socialism, that is, of egalitarian communal life, that "is the expression of absolute truth, reason and justice, and has only to be discovered to conquer all the world by virtue of its own power. And as absolute truth is independent of time, space, and of the historical development of man, it is a mere accident when and where it is discovered" (Engels 1959: 81). But this "eternal reason was in reality nothing but the idealized understanding of the eighteenth-century citizen, just then evolving into the bourgeois" (Engels 1959: 71). It therefore reflected the interests of this bourgeoisie as a social class that had become dominant. More represented an early expression of this viewpoint, which had become more widespread among Enlightenment thinkers.

Utopia was, in short, for Engels, an ideology, class-bound as are all ideologies. The opposite of ideology for Engels was science, the opposite of utopian socialism was therefore scientific socialism. Scientific socialism was the product of the developments in the real capitalist world: "The class struggle between proletariat and bourgeoisie came to the front in the history of the most advanced countries in Europe, in proportion to the development, on the one hand, of modern industry, on the other, of the newly acquired political supremacy of the bourgeoisie.... From this time forward socialism was no longer an accidental discovery of this or that ingenious brain, but the necessary outcome of the struggle between two historically developed classes – the proletariat and the bourgeoisie" (Engels 1959: 88–89). Hence for Engels, subjective lucubrations about the moral society were both intellectually irrelevant and politically noxious. Utopia as a concept had no virtue. It was at best a subjective fantasy, but social transformation was an objective process out of the hands of reform-minded technocrats: "While the capitalist mode of production more and more completely transforms the great majority of the population into proletarians, it creates the power which, under penalty of its own destruction, is forced to accomplish this revolution.... The proletariat seizes political power and turns the means of production into state property" (Engels 1959: 105–06). And then what? Then followed Engels's one clear (and famous) image of the future: "The first act by virtue of which the state really constitutes itself the representative of the whole of society – the taking possession of the means of production in the name of society – that is, at the same time, its last independent act as a state. State interference in social relations becomes, in one domain after another, superfluous, and then dies out of itself; the government of persons is replaced by the administration of things, and by the conduct of processes of production. The state is not 'abolished.' It withers away [The translation reads 'It dies out.' I have substituted the more famous 'It withers away.']" (Engels 1959: 106). Unlike More, Engels does not even broach the topic of the relationship of this socialist zone in which the state has withered away with the rest of the world. No crescent-shaped natural fortress; no mercenaries; but also no imperialism – a more utopian utopia, no doubt, than More's *Utopia*.

Karl Mannheim presented himself neither as the self-confident
civil servant nor as the self-confident revolutionary but as the self-
confident intellectual. Faced with the political realities of a world in
which Nazism and fascism were riding strong, disabused of the
approaches of both More and Engels, he sought and thought he
found another way out to a better world. Mannheim's basic instrument was the distinction between two kinds of intellectual con-
structs – ideologies and utopias. His starting point, as he said, was
Marxist theory, "which first gave due emphasis to the role of class
position and class interests in thought" (Mannheim 1936: 74). But,
as he continued, the resulting relativism placed us before an epistemological dilemma: "Once we recognize that all knowledge is
relational knowledge, and can only be formulated with reference to
the position of the observer, we are faced, once more, with the task
of discriminating between what is true and what is false in such
knowledge. The question then arises: which social standpoint vis-à-
vis history offers the best chance for reaching an optimum of truth?
In any case, at this stage the vain hope of discovering truth in a
form which is independent of a historically and socially determined
set of meanings will have to be given up" (Mannheim 1936: 79–80).
Nonetheless, Mannheim did not really solve the problem he posed.
On the one hand, he offered as the optimal standpoint for truth
Alfred Weber's "socially unattached intelligentsia," whom he put
forward as an "unanchored, *relatively* classless stratum" (Mannheim 1936: 155). But even Mannheim italicized the word "relatively," and the thesis is hardly defensible. For one thing, it is too
self-serving, which is after all what the concept of ideology is
supposed to expose. Furthermore, quite aside from the question of
who would be the bearers of synthetic truth, Mannheim also is
weak on the criteria of truth. He argued that a theory "is wrong if
in a given practical situation it uses concepts and categories which,
if taken seriously, would prevent man from adjusting himself at that
historical stage" (Mannhein 1936: 95). But that of course merely
shifts the original issue to another locus. For how, and via whom,
will we know what an "adjustment" is, and even more, what it
ought to be?

Having seen the problems inherent in Engels's view that utopianism is an ideology but having failed to resolve this problem other
than by legerdemain, Mannheim did somewhat better in his discussion of what he called the utopian mentality. He started by saying
that if we define a utopian state of mind as one that is "incongruous
with the state of reality within which it occurs" and hence is

inefficacious, we are tilting against windmills. For there exist some states of mind that not only "transcend reality" but also simultaneously "break the bonds of the existing order" (Mannheim 1936: 192). And it is to such states of mind that he would confine the usage of the term "utopia," eliminating the inefficatious ones. For Mannheim it is the inefficacious ones that are precisely the ideologies, which are to be defined as those "situationally transcendent ideas which never succeed *de facto* in the realization of their projected contents" (Mannheim 1936: 194). In this usage, Engels may well have been right to denounce the utopias of Saint-Simon, Fourier, and Owen as mere ideologies. The question nonetheless remains, Was Marx a utopian in Mannheim's sense?[1]

Mannheim himself ended his discussion on a curious note, albeit a provocative one. He recounted the history of utopian ideas in the modern world-system, outlining what he saw as four "forms" of the utopian mentality: the orgiastic chiliasm of the Anabaptists, the liberal-humanitarian idea, the conservative idea, and the socialist-communist utopia. It may seem that this is an unusual order in which to discuss the four forms, until one realizes that Mannheim is ranging them in an order of increasing historicity and determinateness. Chiliasm was a totally ahistorical world view, in which neither past nor future exists. All was present, and all was possible: "We always occupy some here and now on the spatial and temporal stage but, from the point of view of Chiliastic experience, the position that we occupy is only incidental. For the real Chiliast, the present becomes the breach through which what was previously inward bursts out suddenly, takes hold of the outer world and transforms it" (Mannheim 1936: 215).

Liberalism brought us closer to the spatio-temporal here and now but still in a form that "appealed to the free will and kept alive the feeling of being indeterminate and unconditioned" (Mannheim 1936: 229). In conservatism, the process of approximation to the here and now was completed: "The utopia in this case is, from the very beginning, embedded in existing reality.... It is either in us, as a 'silently working force' (Savigny), subjectively perceived, or as an entelechy which has unfolded itself in the collective creations of the community, of the folk, the nation, or the state as an inner form which, for the most part, is perceivable morphologically" (Mannheim 1936: 233).

---

[1] This has been argued by E. K. Hunt (1984), without, however, any reference to Mannheim.

For Mannheim, it was the socialist-communist utopia that was in some sense the true *Aufhebung* of this process:

> The economic and social structure of society becomes absolute reality for the socialist. It becomes the bearer of that cultural totality which the conservatives had already perceived as a unity.... The utopia which achieves the closest relationship to the historical-social situation of this world manifests its approximation not only by locating its goal more and more within the framework of history, but by elevating and spiritualizing the social and economic structure which is immediately accessible. Essentially what happens here is a peculiar assimilation of the conservative sense of determinism into the progressive utopia which strives to remake the world. (Mannheim 1936: 242)

The curious but very contemporary and relevant note on which Mannheim ended his historical panorama was to suggest a historical sequence for social movements. As their class base grows "broader" and as they are more successful, their viewpoint shifts to one of great historical concreteness and hence to conservatism (but why not to socialism-communism, just demonstrated to be the most historically concrete of all four world-views?). Mannheim thus ended on a pessimistic note, the very thing his whole book was designed to counter:

> Socialist thought, which hitherto has unmasked all its adversaries' utopias as ideologies, never raised the problem of determinateness about its own position. It never applied this method to itself and never checked its own desire to be absolute. It is nevertheless inevitable that here too the utopian element disappears with an increase in the feeling of determinateness. Thus we approach a situation in which the utopian element, through its many divergent forms, has completely (in politics, at least) annihilated itself. If one attempts to follow through tendencies which are already in existence, and to project them into the future, Gottfried Keller's prophecy – "The ultimate triumph of freedom will be barren" – begins to assume, for us at least, an ominous meaning. (Mannheim 1936: 250)

Thus ideology is dead, or dying, Mannheim said. Marxism exposed it and buried it. All hail! But, alas, utopia is dying too. And if it dies, rationalism will have been its own undoing: "Thus, after a long tortuous, but heroic development, just at the highest stage of awareness, when history is ceasing to be a blind fate, and is becoming more and more man's own creation, with the relinquishment of utopias, man would lose will to shape history and therewith his ability to understand it" (Mannheim 1936: 263).

II

I have outlined at some length the various usages of the concept of utopia in order to place them in some relation to the various Marxisms. Marxism has, of course, been under steady attack throughout its existence as a world-view linked to a social movement. But it has been attacked on two seemingly quite contradictory grounds. It has been attacked on the one hand because it is (too) utopian, and on the other hand for not being utopian enough (or at all). As we have seen, it depends on the content one gives to the concept of utopia. It also depends on what one calls Marxism.

In my view, there have been three Marxian eras. The first is the era of Marx himself, from the 1840s to his death in 1883. It is not that his death was itself a turning point but that it made possible the development of a trend that had already existed but was impossible to formalize as long as he lived. With his death began the era of "orthodox Marxism."

Orthodox Marxism is a curious, very specific phenomenon. It was the product of the historical experience of the German Social-Democratic Party (circa 1880–1920) plus the historical experience of the Bolsheviks (circa 1900–50). It was, in short, Kautsky plus Lenin plus Stalin, so to speak. It came to be a relatively codified set of ideas, which in its worst moments was reduced to a catechism. And like all catechisms, it had the somewhat disconcerting characteristic of being a set of external, unchanging verities that were revised with some frequency and in response to the most immediate and fleeting of political concerns. It was, to use a French metaphor, *histoire structurelle* seen through the prism of *histoire événementielle*.

Orthodox Marxism was the Marxism of the parties.[2] It may be said to have come into existence at the Congress of Gotha, whose platform was the object of Marx's fury. It died a slow but painless

---

[2] It is for this reason that Norbert Elias has suggested to me that it might be better to substitute for the appellation "orthodox Marxism" the appellation "Marxism of the parties," thus underlining the "material basis" of these ideas.

death in Second International, to be given a formal burial at Bad
Godesburg in 1959. It died a convulsive and painful death in the
Third International, as did the Third International itself. It received
a death blow in Khrushchev's Secret Report at the Twentieth Party
Congress in 1956, despite the fact that its ghosts still haunt the odd
corners of the globe (as, for example, in the Portuguese Communist
Party). When I say that orthodox Marxism is dead, I mean, of
course, it died as a utopia. As an ideology it has shown considerable resistance, despite Mannheim's somewhat naive presumption
that Marx's unmasking of ideologies sufficed to make all modern
ideologies noncredible and hence nonviable.

The third Marxian era commenced somewhere in the 1950s, and
we are still living in it. It is the era of a thousand Marxisms, the era
of Marxism "exploded" (Lefebvre 1980). In this era not only is
there no orthodoxy but it is also hard to say that any version is even
dominant. Marxism is being used to paper over so many different
world-views that its content seems very diluted indeed. We are
approaching a linguistic transformation parallel to that which occurred when Constantine made Christianity the official religion of the
the Roman Empire. Was there any paganism to which a veneer of
Christianity could not be added? And yet, of course, among the
thousand Marxisms, there are even Marxist Marxisms, still critical
of existing capitalist reality, still in search (in renewed search) of a
utopia without which, as Mannheim put it so aptly, we cannot
understand the world.

The Marxist utopia that prevailed in the era of Marx was in fact
More's *Utopia*. This utopia was, first and foremost, a criticism of
capitalist reality in the name of a possible human alternative – a
possible alternative that had merely to be proclaimed in order to
be realized in a relatively short period of historical time. Engels
could thunder all he would at Saint-Simon. Everything he said
applied almost verbatim to the writings of Marx and Engels themselves. Indeed, Marx and Engels were extraordinarily Saint-Simonian
in their visions of a moral, productivist, intellectual utopia (see
Meldolesi 1982) which, as we have seen, More had already spelled
out in his pioneer treatise.

The politics of this first Marxian era were, when all is said and
done, essentially chiliastic. One day the working class would rise
up, make the revolution, and then the state would wither away.
When this did not happen in 1848, Marx wrote very detailed,
sophisticated, and subtle analyses of why the moment had not yet
been ripe. This kind of revolution came closer to realization in

the Paris Commune, which thereupon became the very symbol of utopian possibilities of this first Marxian era. The Paris Commune, however, we now know, represented not a harbinger of future political happenings but the last gasp of chiliastic socialism.

The Marxism of the era of orthodox Marxism essentially rejected the utopia of the era of Marx. The trick was to do it without saying so. Bernstein at least admitted he was doing this. Kautsky, Lenin, and Stalin denied doing it quite loudly, but they did it all the same. In this way Marxism moved from being the expression of a chiliastic brotherhood to being the expression of organized parties operating in the real world. To be sure, sometimes the organization was perforce clandestine. The parties nonetheless sought a very concrete and very worldly objective – state power, that is, control of the apparatus of rule of a particular sovereign state.

The language that orthodox Marxism used about utopia was in general the language of Engels. Utopia represented the impractical propositions of naive, impatient, or treacherous others. Utopia was an ideological deception. The party incarnated not wish-fulfillment but science, which was rational, orderly, and efficacious. Of course, the internal debates about which particular set of policies was the most rational, orderly, and efficacious were, to say the least, vigorous. This was after all what the split between the Second and Third International was about.

Was there nonetheless a utopian mentality visible in these parties of orthodox Marxism that disavowed the very concept? Yes, there was, just as we find one in Engels's pamphlet. Utopia, unavowed, was expressed in the little-described, but clearly presumed perfect, classless society that was located at the end of history, just over the horizon. One got there by walking there (even running there) in the here and now along the rational, orderly, efficacious path that the party laid out. One concentrated on the politics of the present, made them the be-all and end-all of political attention, and utopia would take care of itself. One day, and suddenly, several mini-moments of time after the revolution, we would become aware that the government of persons had been replaced by the administration of things. We would rub our eyes and sing praises. But for the moment, comrades, back to the hard work of the present, securing and advancing the revolution via strengthening the political position of the party.

The Marxist utopia of the era of a thousand Marxisms is a utopia in search of itself. The view of utopia reflects the same kind of perspective developed by Mannheim. About the Marxist utopia of the first era, proponents of the present view agree that it was inefficacious and therefore not a true utopia. About the Marxist utopia of the second era, they agree on the importance of the here and now and on the denunciation of utopian ideology, but they insist on applying this analysis to orthodox Marxism too. Is this not what all the endless critiques of "real, existing socialism" are about?

The Marxist utopia of the era of a thousand Marxisms seeks to present itself, as Mannheim sought to present his concepts, as the solution to these dilemmas, as a utopia that is efficacious and not a mere ideology. But if one poses the question how does one know that this new utopia truly represents an efficacious, nonideological "adjustment" to reality, the answer has to be that the case has not yet been proven. But then the era of a thousand Marxisms is not yet over. It has barely begun.

III

The three eras of Marxism are not a mere accident. As Marx taught us, sets of ideas linked to social movements are products of larger historical processes. It will therefore come as no surprise that the three eras of Marxism occur alongside three eras of social science whose periodization is roughly parallel and which are not unlinked with the three meanings or usages of utopia.

Social science took a long time to be born. Christian theology had absorbed and subordinated Greek philosophy. The difficult rebirth of philosophy in Christian Europe as a category of knowledge separate from theology resulted from a protracted effort to create an arena in which the modern world could be analyzed as a changing, developing reality as opposed to theological verities that by definition had to be eternal. The measure of the success of this effort and the limitations of this success can be seen in the fact that by the end of the eighteenth century the intellectual autonomy of all that went under the flowing robes of philosophy (whose breadth is to this day celebrated by the name of the highest academic diploma of our universities, the Ph.D.) was clearly established, requiring no more than a formal, ritual obeisance to the existence of God. But the limits were there in that this knowledge remained philosophy, that is, it reposed on a constant pressure to formulate the analysis of this world in terms of the human potential, the good that is the true. Thus history was instructive history, and social enquiry centered on what ought to be done. More's *Utopia* was in this sense quintessential social science of the first era. But so were the writings of Rousseau and Hegel. It is probably wisest to perceive even the classical economists up to and including Marx as the culmination of this philosophical era of social science, every bit as much as the beginning of the next era.

The next era was the scientific era. Its moment of birth (albeit not of conception) was no doubt the French Revolution, and the birth trauma was profound. It is less that the French Revolution changed the world than that the French Revolution forced us to change our ways of looking at the world. The events from 1789 to 1815 impressed on everyone's consciousness that institutions were transmutable. They also impressed on everyone the irremediable tension of the modern world-system between its global structures (the networks of the world-economy, the interstate system, the culture of universal science) and its political loci (the nation-states then in creation with their boundaries and the particularities that were in their interest to develop).

To create utopia, it was necessary to do more than describe utopia. Such description in fact was now seen as a waste of time. Work had to be done on the here and now in a rational, orderly, efficacious way. This meant writing history "as it really happened." This meant social analysis that was scientific – logical, empirical, quantified. This meant a corps of researchers who were specialized and professionally trained in the multiple so-called disciplines that now came to be given names and to be institutionalized within each university and in the wider academy of national and international disciplinary societies.

Social science involved, of course, the rejection of utopia as ideology. What is the difference between Engels denouncing Saint-Simon as subjective and Weber calling for value-free sociology? What is the difference between the party of orthodox Marxism as the only interpreter of scientific socialism (along with relentless, continuing party activity as the only meaningful path to revolution) and the corps of professional social scientists as the only interpreter of the scientific method (along with relentless, continuing research activity as the only meaningful path to scientific truth)? In the end, the same implicit utopia was just over the horizon.

The intellectual history of the nineteenth and twentieth centuries has tended to be written as if it were one gigantic battle between liberalism and Marxism. Liberalism dominated the state structures and the universities (most notably, social science), and Marxism represented the opposition, outside the state structures (at least until 1917) and largely outside the universities (at least until very recently). But it is less interesting to look at the differences between these two giant *Weltanschauungen* than to perceive the many elements that they shared in common, thereby constituting what should be thought of as the gigantic liberal-Marxist consensus that in fact underlay both university soical science and orthodox Marxism. Both social science and Marxism took the modern state as the basic entity within which social reality occurred, and they both did this implicitly rather than explicitly. They both took science, in the Baconian-Newtonian version, as the only rational world-view conceivable, and they both dedicated themselves to its fulfillment. They both tied the successful manipulation of the world to the work of an elite defined in terms of intellectual criteria. And above all they both believed in the supreme validity of progress – progress as desirable, progress as possible, progress as evolutionary (revolution being for the Marxists a necessary moment in evolutionary transition), and progress as inevitable. It was in the idea of progress as inevitable that lurked their common utopian mentality.

We are today in a third era of social science. It has no obvious name. After philosophical social science and scientific social science we are in the era, or coming into the era, of what might be thought of as social science as interpretation of process. It is hard too to say when this era began. It began somewhere after the Second World War, perhaps only in the 1960s. We are still in a great sea-change of transition. This new social science rejects "philosophy" as ideological utopia on the same grounds as did scientific social science. But it says to scientific social science, you too are ideology. It searches (again the same theme) for a resolution of the dilemmas by looking for a truly efficacious utopia – a social science that is neither moral instruction nor value free, a social science that is truly efficacious in its ability to enable us to "adjust" the world. It is a social science engaged in a "search for a method."

Its starting point is the rejection of the utopia implicit in the liberal-Marxist consensus of the second era. The unit of analysis becomes itself an object of reflection. This third era is skeptical of Baconian-Newtonian science as the only defensible version of science.[3] It sees as the object of scientific activity a kind of controlled interpretation rather than the statement of universal laws. It

---

[3] It joins in this respect a movement in the physical sciences. See Prigogine and Stengers (1984).

doubts that the corps of scientists must be or ought to be thoroughly insulated from the masses whose interests they claim to represent. It does so, however, without denying the distinction between scientific reflection and political action. And above all it looks with some doubt on our received view of progress. It does so not in the name of a neoconservatism that denies that progress is really possible or even desirable but in opposition to the idea that progress is evolutionary and inevitable. Progress as possible but not inevitable, regression as possible but avoidable – this reopens all the issues of utopia, restores the possibility, indeed imposes the necessity, of historical choice. The only problem is that this choice is by no means easy.

IV

What then do we conclude about the multiple utopias, the multiple Marxisms, the multiple social sciences? First of all, that in this third era of utopias, of Marxisms, of social sciences, we cannot rely on the acquired wisdom of the second era. No doubt there is wisdom there, but we have to tear it into very small bits in order to reassemble it in forms that are usable. Not to do so is simply to fall further into the monumental culs-de-sac in which, as of the 1960s, both orthodox Marxism and scientific social science found themselves.

Second, we need to think directly about our utopias. Mannheim was absolutely right in his conclusion that if we dispense with utopias, we have dispensed with rational will. Furthermore, he was also right that an inefficacious utopia does not deserve to be called a utopia. But he probably misled us by counterpoising ideology and utopia, as though they were in some sense alternatives.

Utopias are always ideological.[4] Here Engels (and Marx) was right, provided one remembers that they were wrong in the implicit utopia involved in believing that there could ever be an end to

---

[4] Here we might bear in mind Norbert Elias's assessment of why Mannheim wished to discuss utopia as something different from ideology: "I have often wondered if the fact that Mannheim attributes to the concept of utopia, surely also ideological in character, a sort of special position outside of ideologies, despite his concept that all theories are ideological, did not derive from his instinctive search for a way out for socialism of the implications of his relativizing of it as an ideology" (Elias 1984: 36).

history, a world in which ideologies no longer existed. If we are to make progress, it seems to me we have not only to accept contradiction as the key to explain social reality but also to accept its enduring inescapability, a presumption alien to orthodox Marxism. Contradiction is the human condition. Our utopia has to be sought not in eliminating all contradiction but in eradicating the vulgar, brutal, unnecessary consequences of material inequality. This latter seems to me intrinsically a quite achievable objective.

It is in this sense that utopia is a process, always defining the better in a way that is critical of existing reality. Such a definition can, by its very nature, never be brought to fruition by some (a few) on behalf of others (the many). That can only be done by the many on behalf of themselves. If some believe this view to be utopian, it is, but in Mannheim's sense of an agent of efficacious, rational transformation. However, neither a socially unattached intelligentsia nor a party, any party, can bring about this transformation – which is not to say, on the other hand, that they cannot play any role at all.

The task before us is precisely to place the activities of the intelligentsia that is, social science) and the activities of political organizations in a framework in which, in tension and tandem with each other, they illuminate the historical choices rather than presume to make them. In this situation, how different are the intellectual and the social tasks facing social science of the third era and the Marxism of the era of a thousand Marxisms? They seem to me similar and overlapping, albeit not identical. The political task is to reconstruct a strategy of change that in fact will work, in the sense of being utopian. Our present strategies have not really worked and threaten to lead us into a new historical system as inegalitarian and as little libertarian as the one out of which we are moving. The intellectual task is to create a methodology that will seize the unseizable – process – in which A is never A, in which contradiction is intrinsic, in which the totality is smaller than the part, and in which interpretation is the objective. This too is utopian, but only such an intellectual utopia will make possible the political utopia. The two tasks are obverse and therefore inseparable.

Part V
Revisiting Braudel

13

Fernand Braudel, Historian, *"homme de la conjoncture"*

In the tradition of *Annales*, all historical writing should be organized as *histoire-problème*.[1] An appreciation of Fernand Braudel and his historiography must start with its *problème*: how can we account for his success – the success of the *Annales* school – against the dominant ideology of the Establishment in France (and in the world), and how can we account for the fact that success led to the creation of a new Establishment over which Fernand Braudel reigned and against which he protested?[2]

Since *Annales* teaches us that the way to respond to a *problème* is with *histoire pensée* and not *histoire historisante* (that is, with analytical rather than a chronological history), I shall organize my answer in terms of the trinity of social times Braudel set forth: structure, *conjoncture*, and event (Braudel 1972a). I shall try to

[1] I have not been able to track down the original use of this code-phrase. It is probably the invention of Lucien Febvre. A typical statement of Febvre is: "To pose a problem is precisely the beginning and the end of all history. No problems, no history" (Febvre 1953d: 22). In the editorial inaugurating *Annales ESC*. Febvre promised to "offer history that is not automatic, but problematic" (Febvre 1953c: 42). François Furet, in discussing the merits of serial history, asserts, "It is a *histoire-problème(s)* rather than a *histoire-récit*" (Furet 1971: 71).

[2] Other accounts of Braudel, which pose different "problems" are to be found in Hexter (1972), Kinser (1981), and Stoianovich (1976).

remember that, even in biography, events are "dust"[3] and that what ultimately serves as explanation is the combination of structure and *conjoncture*. I shall also try to remember that *very* long time (that is eternal, ahistorical time) is very unlikely to be real and I shall be careful not to invoke it. *The Mediterranean*, Braudel's major work, treats the three temporalities in the order: structure, *conjoncture*, event. I believe this is the one serious error in the book, and that its explanatory persuasiveness would have been increased had Braudel begun with events, then dealt with structure, and culminated with *conjoncture*. Believing this, I shall follow that order here, and begin with the events of the life of Fernand Braudel.

Fernand Braudel was born in 1902 in a small village in eastern France. He tells us he is of "peasant stock" (Braudel 1972b: 449), but his father was a *professeur* of mathematics, (which may explain why, unlike most historians of his generation, he has never been dismayed by exact figures and arithmetic calculations). In any case, his "peasant stock" seems reflected in his lifelong concern with agricultural production patterns. He reminds us that he (and others of the *Annales* school) came from that part of France that was "next door to Germany" (Braudel 1972b: 467). That proximity has led to a lifelong sympathetic interest in German scholarship which even five years in a prison camp did not seem to erase. For whatever reason, German historical thought has had a great deal of influence on Braudel and the *Annales* – the Germany of Gustav von Schmoller, however, and not that of Leopold von Ranke: Germany protesting rather than Germany decreeing. And finally he "loved the Mediterranean with passion, perhaps because I am northerner" (Braudel 1973: vol. 1, 17). Mere poetry? Perhaps, but perhaps also, at the psychological level, it is an expression of that flight beyond his province that constitutes Braudel's historical imagination.

After his *agrégation*, it was Braudel's luck that his first teaching post was in Algeria where he stayed for a decade. It was from a base in Algiers that his study of the diplomatic history of Philip II of Spain would blossom into his larger and very different study of the Mediterranean as a physical-temporal locus within which to place the *conjonctures* of the sixteenth century. It was in Algeria

---

[3]   Braudel says in the opening of part III of *the Mediterranean*: "Les événements sont poussière" (Braudel 1966: vol. 2, 223). In the English edition, this has been translated: "Events are the ephemera of history" (Braudel 1973: vol. 1, 901).

that Braudel developed a different perspective on Spain and, perhaps, on Europe as well. After more than a decade in Algeria, he spent several years in Brazil, which could only have deepened his ability to stand outside his Europe to see his Europe as a whole. When, on his return from Brazil, he fell into the fortuitous circumstance of traveling on the same relatively small ship as Lucien Febvre, the co-founder of *Annales*, his life was profoundly affected. For his shipboard companionship with Febvre rapidly became friendship and led to his return to Paris and to the direct organizational link with the *Annales* school. It also led to Febvre's "imprudent advice" that he shift the basic emphasis of his thesis from Philip II to the Mediterranean.[4]

France's defeat in 1940 left Fernand Braudel a captured army officer. He was to stay in German military prison, eventually in Lübeck, throughout the war. And he was to be, even there, a leader of men. Prison turned out to have its advantages. For it gave Braudel the enforced time to write his thesis. True, he had no notes and no archival records. But Febvre sent him books and he sent out segments of a manuscript for Febvre to see. Years later, when an Italian historian learned that he had written *The Mediterranean* while in prison, he exclaimed that that explained why he had always thought of it as a "book of contemplation" (Braudel 1972b: 453). In any case, Braudel himself tells us how the events of life in a prison camp affected his writing: "I had to outdistance, reject, deny [events]. Down with occurrences, especially vexing ones! I had to believe that history, destiny, was written at a more profound level" (Braudel 1972b: 454).

After the war, following the path of his master, Lucien Febvre, Braudel was both rejected by the Sorbonne and nominated to the *Collège de France*. Honor without academic power. That too was a sort of luck, since it meant – for Febvre and for Braudel – that they had to look outside the university to create a secure organizational base for their work. This base was to be found in the Vle *Section* of the École Pratique des Hautes Études, a structure authorized since the 1870s but only activated by Febvre and Braudel in 1948. The Vle *Section* flourished, and in 1963 Braudel created a complementary institution, the Maison des Sciences de l'Homme.

---

[4] Lucien Febvre, (1950: 217). Febvre cites a letter he wrote Braudel: *"Philip II and the Mediterranean,* a lovely subject. But why not *The Mediterranean and Philip II?* Another great subject too. For, between the two protagonists, Philip and the Inland Sea, the match is not an even one."

When the May revolt occurred in 1968, Braudel and the *Annales* found themselves, a bit to their surprise, perceived very much as the Establishment. Braudel navigated the crisis months with relative success. Shortly thereafter, however, he withdrew from two of the three structures which had made up his "Establishment." He gave up editorial control of *Annales ESC* in 1969 to the "new" (that is, post-Braudelian) *Annales*. He resigned as President of the VIe *Section* in 1970, which soon thereafter became transmuted into a new university, the École des Hautes Études en Sciences Sociales (EHESS). Retaining only his role as Administrator of the Maison des Sciences de l'Homme, Braudel escaped identification with the *émiettement* so many saw in the "new" *Annales* and in the EHESS.[5]

Were all these turning points mere luck? Surely not. Surely, Fernand Braudel has been a man to seize *fortuna*, not once but each time it was offered him. One does not become a towering figure in world social science by luck. But to seize *fortuna* requires not only the will to seize, but the *fortuna* to be seized. The *fortuna* to be seized is located in the *conjoncture*, and to assess the *conjoncture* we must place it within the structure. Let us therefore turn to structure and then proceed to *conjoncture*.

The long "stagnation" of the European world-economy that ran from 1600 to 1750 led to a major geographical shift of economic roles. The end of Dutch hegemony was followed by a second hundred-years' war, beginning in 1689, between Britain and France for control of a now well-articulated network of world trade linking ever more closely integrated production processes. While Britain may be said to have won this competitive struggle with France by

---

[5] "Emiettement," or "scattering," like "histoire-problème," is a term everyone uses and whose source few seem to know for certain. Jacques Revel, however, has written me his views, in a letter dated 28 September 1979: "You ask me about the origin of the term 'émiettement.' The original version may be found in the little text Nora edited as the prospectus for the *Bibliothèque des histoires*, published by Gallimard, which states: 'Nous vivons l'éclatement de l'histoire.' You will find the text on the back of the books in the collection. This formula, which was intended to characterize as of 1970 an evolution of research, was reacted to negatively, both by advocates of total history (Braudel in particular) and by the university left (Chesneaux). It was they, I believe, who substituted the term of 'émiettement' (or 'histoire en miettes') to that of 'éclatement.'" See also the discussion, *passim*, in "The Impact of the *Annales* School on the Social Sciences," *Review*, 1, 3/4 (Winter-Spring, 1978), especially the contributions of Jacques Revel and Traian Stoianovich.

1763, it was not until 1815 that France might be said to have acknowledged defeat. Once British hegemony was assured, as of 1815, not only economically and militarily but politically as well, there followed a thrust to consolidate and justify this hegemony in the domains of culture and ideology. The middle of the nineteenth century saw the triumph of what may be called "universalizing-sectorializing" thought. Of course, there were many variants of this perspective, but the core of each variant was a pair of premises that the path of knowledge begins with the particular and ends with the abstract – "universalizing thought"; that there are separate, parallel paths for the different "sectors" of knowledge, reflecting separate, parallel processes in the real world – "sectorializing thought."

"Universalizing thought" took two main forms, seemingly opposite, actually structurally parallel. One form argued that by starting with the description of empirical reality one could by induction arrive at the formulation of abstract laws, truths that held over all of time and space. This became the ideology of modern social science. (It became the ideology of the modern physical and biological sciences as well, but I leave them out of this discussion.) In the nineteenth century, this ideology found its heartland in British thought, which was appropriate, since Britain was centralizing at the time all the major world organizational networks.

The second form of "universalizing thought" also started with the description of empirical reality, but there it stopped – denying with more or less vigor the possibility of ever going beyond these descriptions. It was "universalizing" in the sense that all particulars were equal; there were no exogenous *structured* differences. This approach became the ideology of most modern historians (and of a segment of the anthropologists). In the nineteenth century, its heartland was Germany, its high priest was Ranke, and its call was for history *"wie es eigentlich gewesen ist."* This locus was appropriate. Dependent thought is outside the metropole but needs the organizational bases of a strong semiperipheral state to support its flourishing. In the late nineteenth century and even in the twentieth, advocates of these two varieties of "universalizing thought" made a great show of engaging in a debate, claimed to be fundamental, between the nomothetic and idiographic disciplines, but the argument was essentially a diversion.

The second premise, that knowledge was sectorialized and parallel, gave rise to the various so-called "disciplines" in the social scences. Whereas, in the eighteenth century, philosophy, moral economy, political economy were all descriptive terms that were inclusive and overlapping (that is, all part of one body of knowledge), by the twentieth century, not only had "history" become quite distinct from the "social sciences," but the latter had been split into at least five separate "disciplines": anthropology, economics, geography, political science, and sociology. The separation was not merely intellectual, but administrative. It was justified in terms of "universalizing thought." Since we were in search of general laws, we must find those that are appropriate for each sector of the real world, which if formally parallel are, however, substantively distinctive and distinguishable. Those who argued the idiographic variation merely amended this proposition to say that, since general laws are impossible, we must narrowly restrict our descriptions to zones of immediate knowledge, which led not merely to "sectorializing" knowledge, but to hyper-specialization within each "discipline," especially in history and ethnography.

It is clear what advantage the beneficiaries of British hegemony drew from such doctrines. "Universalizing thought" led to the vulgar translation (vulgar, but nonetheless very influential) that the British path was the model of a universal path. This thesis had two implications: that the advantages the British enjoyed they had earned; and if others were to earn parallel advantages, they must perforce imitate the British. This "Whig interpretation of history" became extraordinarily pervasive, even among those it implicitly denigrated. It was such a consoling and efficacious ideology that when the United States succeeded to Britain's hegemonic role in the twentieth century, American scholars simply adopted the ideology lock, stock, and barrel.

As for "sectorializing thought," its purpose was negative. It prevented analysis from ever seeing the whole and from ever appreciating the dialectical flow of the real historical world. In this way, it made it far more difficult for anyone to perceive the underlying structures that sustained the world-system and therefore more difficult to organize to change them.

Difficult, but not impossible. There did in fact grow up three major currents of resistance to "universalizing-sectorializing" thought. The first was *Staatswissenschaften*, whose homeland was Germany from List to Schmoller. Its message was in essence very simple: liberal, free-trade Britain was not a model that any other country could or should follow. The social patterns of different areas of the world were the consequence of their differing histories, which had necessarily led to different institutional structures which, in turn, determined different contemporary social processes.

It was called *Staatswissenschaften* to emphasize the central role of the state structures in the modern world. The state, it was implicitly believed, was in fact the key defense mechanism of the non-hegemonic area of the world economy against the economic, political, and cultural domination of the center (in this case, primarily Great Britain). This argument led its proponents to seek to identify particularities that were both national and structural (ergo, attacking "universalizing thought" in both is variants). Its key terms – *Nationalökonomie* (national economy) and *Volkswirtschaft* (traditional economy) – reflected these concerns.

It is no accident that the key intellectual debate that surrounded this school – and one much more profound than the largely specious nomothetic-idiographic battle – was the so-called *Methodenstreit* in which Carl Joseph Menger, a civil servant in the office of the prime minister of Austria-Hungary, took on in 1870 the German historical school of Schmoller. In this debate, where the Austrians symbolically cast in their lot with the British against the Prussians, as they had done in the War of the Austrian Succession, and for essentially the same reasons, Menger defended the "universalizing" premises against what was obviously a very serious assault on them in the world of Germanic scholarship.

The second current of resistance, born somewhat later, was what we have come to call the *Annales* school. French historiography had become a "discipline" in the contemporary sense with the foundation of the *Revue historique* in 1876, a journal consciously based on the Rankeian model and focused on empirical data, primary sources, and political and diplomatic history. Later, Febvre was to describe it as "history as written by those defeated in 1870, whose penchant for diplomatic history reflected the feeling: 'Ah, if we had studied it more carefully, we should not be where we are today'" (Febvre 1953a: vii). As Gabriel Monod and Emile Bourgeois derived their historiographic model from Leopold von Ranke, so Lucien Febvre and Marc Bloch in 1929 chose the name of their new journal, *Annales d'histoire économique et social*, by almost direct translation from the title of Germany's leading journal in the Schmoller tradition: the *Vierteljahrschrift für Sozial- und Wirtschaftsgeschichte*. Of course, the "*Annales* tradition" predated the founding of the journal in 1929, and is conventionally traced to Henri Berr and the *Revue de synthèse historique*.

The *Annales* school asserted holism against "segmentalized thought" – the economic and social roots against the political facade, the *longue durée* against the *événementielle*, "global man" against "fractional man."[6] And against "universalizing thought," it concentrated its fire on the idiographic variant so widespread in France. It advocated the study of quantified trends against chrono-logical narrative, the blending of history and the "social sciences" against a belief in historical uniqueness, *histoire structurelle* against *histoire historisante*. If *Annales* spent less time attacking the nomothetic variant of "universalizing thought," it nonetheless felt this variant to be as illegitimate as the other which may be seen in Braudel's various strictures on Lévi-Strauss.[7]

When all is said and done, there was a large dose of nationalism in the rebellious thought of the *Annales* school, which substained it and eventually made it flourish. This sentiment explains the pecu-liarly French cultural channels of its internationalist thrust, which was nonetheless genuinely felt and generously expressed, and this also explains why its great practitioners have remained to this day Frenchmen (Huppert 1978). (Comparable statements could be made about *Staatswissenschaften*.) Nationalism is not usually consi-dered respectable as an intellectual motive, but this negative appre-ciation of cultural nationalism is itself part of the cultural domination of hegemonic forces with the world-system. The nationalism of the *Annales* school provided the underlying passion that sustained its ability to serve as a locus of antisystemic resistance.

The third great school of resistance was Marxism, which was born and thrived (at least until the 1970s) outside acedeme within the antisystemic (anticapitalist) movements of the working classes. Marx from the outset attacked a fundamental philosophical premise of "universalizing thought," the concept of human nature (Ollman 1971: part II) He asserted that human behavior was social and not individual, historically rooted and not transhistorical, but yet struc-turally analyzable – "all history is the history of the class struggle." As for "sectorializing thought," the Marxists conceived of these assertions as the quintessence of bourgeois thought, to be overcome by truly holistic proletarian thought.

These three schools of resistance – *Staatswissenschaften*, *Annales*, and Marxism – shared some common premises, deriving from their

---

[6] The last antithesis is not in Febvre's writings, but in Ernest Labrousse, (Labrousse: 1970: 740).

[7] See Braudel, (1972a: 32–35; 1978: 247). In the latter text, Braudel says: "Lévi-Strauss has [always] been impervious to history. He doesn't know what it is, and doesn't want to know. . . . There is no society, even a primitive one, which does not develop, does not have a history."

common attack on universalizing-sectorializing thought, but they were, of course, almost totally separate in organizational terms. There was some sense among the early figures of *Annales* that they were drawing from the tradition of *Staatswissenschaften*, but it was never emphasized in their writings. It is doubtful if later generations of *Annales* scholars even read Schmoller. As for Marxism, since it was outside the academy, it could have no organizational links with the other two very academic schools of thought. Nor did it really wish to have these links. By the turn of the twentieth century, the heirs of *Staatswissenschaften* were engaged in major polemical debates with Marxism; while in France, at least up to the Second World War, *Annales* and the Marxists simply largely ignored each other.

After the Second World War, *Staatswissenschaften* had essentially disappeared as an identifiable school of thought – in Germany or elsewhere. It had run its course. But *Annales* was just reaching its apogee, and Marxism was entering into a new phase as an intellectual perspective. It is in this particular *conjoncture* that went from 1945 to 1967/73 that we must place the work and the influence of Fernand Braudel.

Before 1945, the *Annales* school had great ideas, had even produced great works, but it was still essentially an obscure intellectual force. The subscribers to the journal were counted in the hundreds and were largely to be found in France. From 1945 to 1968, *Annales* climbed to worldwide fame (although true renown in the inner sanctum of the English-speaking world was delayed until the 1970s). This quarter-century was precisely the period of the "curious confluence, via economic history" (Hobsbawn 1978: 158) of Marxism and the *Annales* school – if not everywhere, then in many countries. After 1968, the *Annales* had become an Establishment; there was *émiettement* (at least according to some); self-doubt set in – is there an *Annales* school? (Huppert 1978: 215).

What was there about the period 1945 to 1967/68 that explains both the meteoric rise of *Annales* and the "curious confluence" with Marxism, and what was Braudel's role in all of this? As we know, although the Allies won the Second World War, France had suffered a humiliating defeat by Germany and seen the creation of a collaborationist regime at Vichy. The exploits of the Resistance and of the Free French forces of General de Gaulle were not sufficient compensation, since neither the United States nor Great Britain was particularly impressed with the real importance of the of these forces in the victory. France was seen by the US and

Britain, and saw itself, as a "great power by sufferance," and this has meant that it has had to fight for its place in the sun ever since.

At the same time, the years immediately following the Second World War constituted the period of the cold war and of the culmination of Stalinism in its most ossified form. The forces who incarnated French nationalism vis-à-vis the United States were also strongly committed to a position of the foreign policy of the USSR. This quandary led to a search in France for ways in which to express a position of "Third Force" – that is, a position of opposition to the USSR which, however, did not involve direct subordination to the United States. The question of where to place the emphasis in this balancing-act was the source of much internal French political debate. One of the easiest realms in which to be non-Anglo-Saxon and non-Soviet simultaneously proved to be the realm of culture and ideas.

In this context, the existence of the *Annales* school provided a very convenient focus for such sentiment. It was a school of resistance to Anglo-Saxon hegemony, but one clearly separate from the French Communist Party (whatever the affinities of its viewpoint analytically to some of the premises of classical Marxism). Thus, it is no surprise that "all the youth of the university turned toward the *Annales* kind of history" (Braudel 1972b: 462). It was of course not the only ideology toward which the youth of the university had turned. Existentialism was very popular too, and for essentially the same reasons. If, however, the *Annales* school has thrived, and existentialism has faded, it is because Febvre and Braudel had the wisdom to create lasting institutional structures to sustain it – the Vle *Section* and the Maison des Sciences de l'Homme. And if they were able to create such structures, it is because their intellectual stance found resonance among the senior civil servants and cabinet ministers who ultimately granted the funds and the political support. Who knows? The existentialists might have been able to do the same, had they tried.

World Marxism at this time was its most sclerotic. The era of Stalin, from 1923 to 1956, whatever else it was, was one in which Marxist theory was increasingly and unremittingly transformed into a set of simplified dogmas at the service of a particular party-state. This had the consequence of eliminating almost all creative Marxist scholarship – in the USSR and elsewhere. Either one was a Stalinist (or a Trotskyist, which became the counter-dogma), or one ceased to proclaim aloud one's Marxism. No doubt there were small pockets of good work, but the situation was bleak. The parlous state of world Marxist scholarship was a matter of especial concern in those Western countries which had a strong, if limited, tradition of such scholarship – to wit, France, Italy, and, to a lesser extent, Great Britain. There were thus at least some Marxist scholars in these countries searching for ways to end the sclerosis without making an overt political break with the existing Marxist political movements.

The "curious confluence" is thus not difficult to explain. Fernand Braudel wrote in 1957:

> Marxism is a whole collection of models. Sartre protests against the rigidity, the schematic, inadequate nature of models, and he does so in the name of the particular and the individual. I shall protest, as he does, more or less, not against the model, but rather against the use to which people have thought themselves entitled to put it. The genius of Marx, the secret of his enduring power, lies in his having been the first to construct true social models, starting out from the long-term. These models have been fixed permanently in their simplicity; they have been given the force of law and they have been treated as ready-made, automatic explanations, applicable in all places to all societies. Instead, by submitting them again to the changes wrought by time, we should reveal their true structure, which is strong and well-knit and would always recur, with subtle variations, blurred or brightened by the proximity of other structures, themselves definable in terms of other rules and models. In this way has the creative power of the most powerful social analysis of the last century been shackled. It will be able to regain its strength and vitality only in the long-term.... Shall I add that present-day Marxism seems to me to be the very image of the danger facing any social science devoted to the model in its pure state and for its own sake? (Braudel 1972: 38–39).

The hand was thus extended, intellectually, if not politically – *Annales* "did not hold [Marxism] at a distance" (Braudel 1978: 249). It was extended to all those Marxists who were concerned with the real, empirical world, who were concerned with both structures and *conjoncture,* and who were willing in turn to collaborate with *Annales.*

Marxists who were not caught up in Stalinist or Trotskyist dogmas – whether they were ex-party members, still party members, or totally outside the various parties – responded to the extended hand, sometimes tacitly, sometimes overtly. Hobsbawm, speaking of British Marxists, says that "in general [they] thought of themselves as fighting on the same side as *Annales*" (Hobsbawm 1978:

158). The response was particularly great in places like Poland and Hungary, where it was especially difficult at the time to be a non-Stalinist Marxist (Pomian 1978). But it was also great in a place like Quebec, where it was equally difficult at the time to call oneself any kind of a Marxist (Dubuc 1978).

And in the key Western countries – France, Britain, Italy – the response of the Marxists was divided. Some found the confluence congenial; others found it uncomfortable and rejected it. The British Marxists, who were the most isolated, were the most willing to respond. The Italian Marxists, with their Crocean non-empirical traditions (which made *Annales* less congenial) and with their ability to use Gramsci as a mode of being legitimately non-dogmatic (which made the link to *Annales* less necessary), responded the least.[8] The French response was the most varied. Pierre Vilar could be considered an *Annaliste*, but not Albert Soboul. The French Communist Party itself moved from a stance of hostility to *Annales* to one of lower-key skepticism. The "curious confluence," furthermore, did not exist at all, at least in the pre-1967 period, in the two epicenters of the cold war, the United States and the USSR, nor in their two most ideologically dependent allies, West and East Germany. Once détente set in, this would change, but even then, it took a long time before the *Annales* school was given *droit de cité*.

The *conjoncture* of 1945–67, then, was favorable to *Annales*, at least in certain parts of the world-system, and it was favorable to *Annales* with the particular Braudelian emphases: more economic than social history, history that emphasized the so-called "early modern period," history informed by an analysis of the multiple social temporalities, historiography that "did not hold Marxism at a distance."

The *conjoncture* changed somewhere around 1967. For one thing, the A-phase (of economic expansion) had come to an end, and a B-phase (of economic stagnation) was beginning – with all the economic and political changes in the world-economy such a shift always entails. One expression of the shift was the worldwide political crises of 1968, which took their most acute form in France with the May events. In the B-phase, a "new" *Annales* began to

---

[8] See Pomian, "Discussion," (1978: 121). And see Maurice Aymard (1978). See also the discussion in which the editors of *Storia d'Italia* are asserted by others to be of the *Annuales* school, an assertion they in turn deny, claiming that they should be perceived *rather* as Marxists (Caracciolo et al. 1974).

crystallize, and a "new" Marxism, and the "curious confluence" became somewhat unstuck.

The "new" *Annales* was in some senses not new at all. It took traditional *Annales* concerns and pushed them further. *Annales* had always emphasized the importance of systematic data. This concern led to an increasing sense of affinity with a new stream of scholarship in the United States of quantitative "sociological" history, which was neopositivist in that it tended to take techniques of structural-functionalist sociology and apply them to historical data.[9]

Annales had always emphasized the importance of analyzing the totality of the social fabric. This concern led to an increasing sense of affinity with structuralist anthropology and its detailed analyses of the formal structures of everyday social interactions, which tended in the long run, however, to be ahistorical, if not antihistorical.[10] *Annales* had always emphasized the importance of comprehending *mentalités,* by which it meant the set of ideas and presuppositions into which particular groups were socialized at particular points of time. This concern led to an increasing sense of affinity with the emerging field of psychohistory (Le Goff 1974; Elmore 1978), whose approach tended to reduce attention to longterm economic and social structures in favor of a new sophisticated form of biography and the individual as the unit of analysis.

In all these ways, the "new" *Annales* found itself edging towards a different intellectual stance in the cultural debates of the worldsystem. From being an antisystemic school of thought, which some Marxists used as a cover in order to be antisystemic (whether for the motives that applied in Poland or those that applied in Quebec), it was in danger of becoming a system of thought which was more congential to and felt more affinity for the dominant world-view, and one which some anti-Marxists would use as a cover in order to be prosystemic.

What was happening in the "new" Marxism was of quite another order. The Stalinist era came to an end not in 1953, when Stalin died, but in 1956 when Khrushchev made his secret speech at the Twentieth Party Congress. The official revelations broke the crust

---

[9] US "sociological" history has its own new journals, such as the *Journal of Interdisciplinary History,* and *Social Science History.* For the "new" *Annales* version, see the discussion in Furet (1971).
[10] Tilly (1978). See also Copans (1978) on why there emerged a new "curious confluence" between "structural Marxism" and "structural anthropology" in the "post-Stalinist" era.

of ideology in such a way that it could never re-created. This was followed by split between the USSR and China, The Chinese Cultural Revolution, and, after the death of Mao Zedong, by the return to power of Deng Xiaoping.

The rise of the New Left in the Western countries, whose high point was in fact the student uprisings of 1968 and afterwards, may have been transitory in term of the ideological positions and organizational forms the New Left espoused. But this movement, more than anything else, ended the unquestioned and unquestioning dominance of liberal ideology in key countries like the United States, West Germany, and Great Britain. It relegitimated the left, after the anathema of cold war days, and it thus, more or less for the first time, made possible the entry of Marxism into the universities of these countries and into the realm of legitimate discourse.

On the one hand, Marxist heresies now abounded. There was no longer one Marxism (or even two – Stalinist and Trotskyist). A thousand Marxisms now bloomed. On the other hand, non-sclerotic Marxists no longer needed the cover, or the aid, of *Annales* or anyone else, to pursue their enterprise. With multiple *Annales* schools and multiple Marxisms, was it meaningful in this new *conjoncture* to talk of "confluence" or even of divergence? The generalizations of an earlier *conjoncture* were no longer easy to apply.

As this present *conjoncture* goes on, what may we expect to see happen to *Annales* and Marxism? Will *Annales* survive? I'm not sure it will, and if it does, I'm not sure there will be more than a formal continuity with the *Annales* of Febvre and Bloch, and above all that of Braudel. If we can now write that *Staatswissenschaften* has had its day, will someone not write not write that about *Annales* 20 years from now? Probably, but it is not clear we should mourn this. Intellectual movements like *Staatswissenschaften* and *Annales* have tended to be partial and partisan, responding to problems which were real but often *conjoncturel*, rather than structural. As such, when the *conjoncture* passes, it serves not too much purpose to preserve a name. It often hurts the memory to hold on to the name.

Marxism is quite a different story. It was conceived as an ideology not of the *conjoncture* but of the structure. It has laid claim to being *the* ideology of all antisystemic forces in the capitalist world-economy, the ideology of the world transition from capitalism to socialism. It seems to be making good its claim. To the extent that antisystemic political forces have grown, Marxism as an ideology has spread. Someday soon, it may be that we will discover that Marxism has suddenly become the universal *Weltanschauung* of the late capitalist era and its successor system as Christianity became the *Weltanschauung* of the late Roman Empire and beyond with the proclamation of Constantine.

When that happens, and it may happen very soon, then we shall have the true *émiettement*. For if everyone (or almost everyone) is a Marxist, will anyone be? We shall have Marxists on the left, center, and right. We already do. We shall have determinist and voluntarist Marxists. We already do. We shall have empirical and rationalist Marxists. We already do. We shall have "universalizing-sectorial-izing" Marxists and Marxists of resistance. We already do. In the next century, the political turmoil of transformation will be reflected in great intellectual confusion, to which the early triumph of Marxism as a way of thought will no doubt contribute greatly. It may be that in that period, the memory of the *Annales* school as a school of re-sistance will help us to preserve a Marxism of resistance amid the Marxists.

Fernand Braudel, historian, thus emerges as the *homme de la con-joncture*, a *conjoncture* that coincided precisely with his period of intellectual and organizational preeminence. He was responsible to an important degree for the continuity of the traditions of resist-ance in a *conjoncture* that was otherwise unfavorable to it, both by the intellectual themes he stressed and by the organizational frameworks he created. He may thereby have contributed in a major way to the transition to a reassessment in the period to come of the premises of historical social sciences, a reassessment that may possibly be as fundamental as the one that occurred in the period 1815–73. Above all, Braudel provided a standard of intellec-tual passion and human concern to which we can safely repair, and which can serve as a reminder of the possibility of integrity in difficult times.

14

Capitalism:
The Enemy of the Market?

Forty years ago the role of the market in capitalism seemed quite straightforward. The market was thought to be a defining feature of capitalism, not only because it was a key element in its operation but because it distinguished capitalism from the two antitheses to which it was usually compared: on the one hand, from feudalism which preceded it; and on the other hand, from socialism which was supposed to come after it. Normally one presented feudalism as a pre-market system and socialism as a post-market one.

Today it is no longer possible to use such a schema as the basis of analysis. This is not because this schema is simplistic; rather, the schema is unquestionably false, for at least three reasons

First of all, research on feudal society, considerably advanced since 1945, makes it quite clear that it is not possible to think of it as a closed system living on subsistence farming within a so-called natural economy. In reality, markets existed everywhere and were deeply enmeshed in the logic of the operation of this historical system. To be sure, there were many differences between it and a capitalist system. Commodification was limited, and the markets were usually either quite local or long-distance, but seldom "region-al." The long-distance trade was primarily a trade in luxury goods. Nonetheless, the contrast with what developed later under capital-ism has become increasingly blurred as we have come to study the realities of feudal society more closely.

In the same way, really existing socialism has seemed to show a tendency to develop the market, in two ways. First of all, analysts

are more and more in agreement that it is simply not true that the
so-called socialist/Communist countries have truly and definitively
withdrawn from the world market. Secondly, at the national level,
practically every country in the socialist camp has been the scene
of a long internal debate about the virtues of some liberalization
of the internal market. There is even a new concept these days,
"market socialism."

Thus the reality of feudalism and the reality of socialism have
contradicted the old theoretical schema. But it is also true that
capitalist reality contradicts it as well. And here Braudel's work has
been of central importance in understanding this. The central point
of his recent trilogy (Braudel 1981–84) is to discern three parts to
capitalist reality, and to argue that the word "market" should be
used to designate only one of these parts, the stratum between
"everyday life" at the bottom and "capitalism" at the top. In
particular Braudel wishes to reformulate the relation between the
market and monopolies. Normally one thinks of competition and
monopoly as two poles of the capitalist market, which in some way
alternates between them. Braudel sees them rather as two structures in perpetual struggle with each other, and of the two, he
wants to use "capitalist" as the label only of the monopolies.

By doing this, he turns the intellectual debate upside down.
Rather than thinking of the free market as the key element in
historical capitalism, he sees monopolies as being the key element.
Monopolies dominating the market are the defining element of our
system and it is this that distinguishes capitalism quite clearly from
feudal society – and perhaps as well from an eventual world socialist system, one that has been insufficiently noticed up to now.

Adam Smith and Karl Marx agreed on certain things. One of the
most fundamental of their common views was to consider that
competition is what is normal in capitalism – normal ideologically
and normal statistically. Consequently, monopoly was exceptional.
Monopoly had to be explained, and to be fought against. This
ideology is still deeply rooted in the views of people today, not only
in the general public but among social scientists.

However, it is not true that monopoly is statistically rare. Quite
the contrary. The evidence mounts up on all sides, and one has but
to read the work of Braudel to see how far back this goes. Not only
have there always been monopolies in capitalism but they have
always been of the utmost importance. Furthermore, it has always
been the powerful and largest accumulators of capital who have
controlled these monopolies. In fact, one could argue that the

ability to accumulate a very large amount of capital has depended
on the ability to create monopolies.

It seems to me one can draw three main lessons from reading
Braudel. All three go against the grain of accepted truths, or at
least against dominant views. Let us begin with the famous categorization of the bourgeoisie or capitalists into merchants, industrialists, and financiers. How much ink has been spilled, is still being
spilled, trying to figure out which variety of capital was dominant at
specific times and places? How many different theories have been
developed, purporting to show a sort of natural progression from
the dominance of merchant capital to that of industrial capital and
then to that of finance capital? How much confusion has there been
about the role, the very existence, of agrarian capitalists?

And yet it's a non-problem. Braudel shows us very clearly that
the big capitalists have always sought to do everything – trade,
production, finance. It is only by having their fingers in all the
sectors that they have been able to have a hope of achieving
monopolistic advantage. It is only the second-rate who specialize,
who are merely merchants or merely industrialists.

Thus the key distinction among capitalists is not between merchants, industrialists, and financiers. It is between nonspecialists
and specialists. And this distinction correlates very strongly with
large vs. small, transnational vs. local/national, monopoly sector vs.
competitive sector, that is, between what Braudel designates as
"capitalism" and what he designates as "the market."

Once we have this straight, several other non-problems drop out
as a consequence: when capital was internationalized (monopolies
have always been "international"); or how to explain the multiple
"treasons" of the bourgeoisie (transferring capital between sectors
is part and parcel of the logic of monopolies faced with conjunctural shifts). The explanation of the so-called industrial revolution in
England at the end of the eighteenth century now becomes quite a
different question: how was it that at that particular moment there
were enough monopolistic profits in textile production to attract big
capital?

The second lesson is less specifically Braudelian. Nonetheless, his
writings allow us to combat the resistance to admitting this particular verity: all monopolies are politically based. No one can ever
succeed in dominating an economy, stifling it, constraining market
forces, without political support. It requires force, the force of
some political authority, to create noneconomic barriers to entry
into the market, to impose outrageous prices, to ensure that people

buy things they do not urgently need. The idea that one can be a capitalist (in Braudel's sense of the term) without the state, not to speak of in opposition to the state, is quite absurd. I say without the state, but of course this is not necessarily the capitalists' own state. Sometimes it is some quite other state.

But if that is true, it changes the meaning of the left–right political struggles in the modern world. It is not and has never been a struggle over the legitimacy of state interference in the economy. The state is a constitutive element of the functioning of the capitalist system. The debate is rather about who will be the immediate beneficiaries of state interference. Seeing this helps in demystifying many a political debate.

Finally, Braudel allows us to be a bit reserved in our enthusiasm for new technology, normally defined as "progress" by most acolytes of Smith and Marx. Every great technological advance has given new life to the monopoly sector. Every time the competitive market seems to regain ground against the monopoly sector, by enlarging the number of economic actors, by reducing the costs of production, and therefore prices and profits, someone (but who is this "someone"?) seeks to make some great new technological leap forward, to put the capitalist world-economy back into an expansionary phase – and to line the pockets of the big capitalists, by creating for them once again some closed and highly profitable sector which will last perhaps another 30 years.

I have outlined Braudel's merits. I should point out a great dangerous turning one can make by using these arguments. It is very easy to take a jump into a renewed romanticism about the freedom-loving small guy against the villainous and freedom-constraining big guy. That is only one step away from a neo-Poujadist view of the world.

To save us from such an unfortunate inference, to save Braudel, allow me to speak about the great slogan of the French Revolution: liberty, equality, fraternity. These concepts have always been treated as three different ones. For nearly 200 years we have been arguing about how compatible they are with each other. Is freedom possible if there is equality? Is freedom an obstacle to the achievements of equality? Do not freedom and equality lead to the opposite of fraternity? And so on.

Perhaps we should reconsider this trinity in the light of Braudel's analysis. If the "market," domain of the small person, domain of liberty, is in perpetual struggle with "monopolies," domain of the big, domain of constraint, and if monopolies only exist thanks to some kind of state action, does it follow that the struggle against the various inequalities – economic, political, cultural – is in fact one and the same struggle? Monopolies dominate by denying liberty and equality in the economic arena and therefore necessarily in the political arena and quite as much (though we haven't discussed it) in the cultural arena. To be in favor of a Braudelian "market" seems to me in the end to be for the egalitarianization of the world. That is to say, it is to struggle for human liberties. And therefore for fraternity (since the logic of such a struggle does not permit the existence of subhumans). And that brings us to the final reversal of perspective. It may be that the triumph of the market (in Braudel's sense), no longer being the sign of the capitalist system, turns out to be the sign of world socialism. What a stunning reversal!

Obviously we are now discussing not the historical past but a future that is difficult to construct. And that is the last lesson we can learn from Braudel. It will not be in the least easy to bring about the triumph of Braudel's market. In a way one could say that the story of the last 500 years has been that of the constant defeat of this market. The only hope that Braudel offers us is that this market, or rather the people who constitute it, have never accepted this defeat. Every day they take up the hard struggle anew to constrain the constrainers, by sabotaging them economically and undermining their essential political structures.

15

Braudel on Capitalism,
or Everything Upside Down

Fernand Braudel asked us to take seriously the concept of capitalism as a way of organizing and analyzing the history of the modern world, at least since the fifteenth century. He was not alone in this view, of course. But his approach must be said to have been an unusual one, for he developed a theoretical framework which went against the two theses that both of the two great antagonistic world-views of the nineteenth century, classical liberalism and classical Marxism, considered central to their approach. First, most liberals and most Marxists have argued that capitalism involved above all the establishment of a free, competitive market. Braudel saw capitalism instead as the system of the anti-market (*contre-marché*). And secondly, liberals and most Marxists have argued that capitalists were the great practitioners of economic specialization. Braudel believed instead that the essential feature of successful capitalists was their refusal to specialize.

Thus, Braudel viewed capitalism in a way that, in the eyes of most of his colleagues, could only be termed seeing it "upside down." I shall try to expound clearly what I take to be Braudel's central arguments, and then to analyze the implications of this reconceptualization for present and future work, and to assess its importance.

I

Braudel starts with an analogy of a house with three stories – a ground floor of material life "in the sense of an extremely elementary economy" (Braudel 1981–84: vol. 2, 21), a second story that he usually calls "economic life," and a third or top story he designates as "capitalism," or sometimes "true capitalism." So here we have the first surprise. A distinction is being made among the two upper stories between, on the one hand, "economic life" (or "the market") and, on the other hand, "capitalism." What can this possibly mean in reality? Braudel suggests that there are six elements in the distinction.

(1) He begins by distinguishing economic life from the ground story. Economic life moved "outside the routine, the unconscious daily round" of material life. It was nonetheless involved in "regularities," but these were derived from market processes that helped organize and reproduce an "active and conscious" division of labor (Braudel 1981–84: vol. 1, 562). The world of these markets was therefore one "in which everyone would be sure in advance, with the benefit of common experience, how the processes of exchange would operate" (Braudel 1981–84: vol. 2, 455). Thus self-conscious open activity distinguished economic life from material life, the domain of consumption and production for immediate consumption. Capitalism was, of course, also different from material life but it differed from the regularities of economic life as well. "The capitalist game only concerned the unusual, the very special, or the very long distance connection. . . . It was a world of 'speculation'" (Braudel 1981–84: vol. 2, 456). One might think this latter description, even if valid for the fifteenth to eighteenth centuries, were no longer true today. We shall return to this question.

(2) The market economy was a world of " 'transparent' visible realities" and it was on the basis of "the easily observed processes that took place within them that the language of economic science was originally founded." By contrast, below and above the market, the zones were "shadowy" or opaque.[1] The zone below, the zone of material life, is "often hard to see for lack of adequate historical documents." Its opaqueness is in the difficulty of observation for the analyst. The zone above, on the other hand, the zone of

---

[1] The English translation, "shadowy zones," is less strong, I think, than the French original "zones d'opacité" (Braudel 1979: vol. 1, 8). Opaqueness suggests a greater density, more difficulty in seeing clearly, than shadows.

capitalism, was also opaque, but in this case because capitalists wanted it so. It was the zone in which "certain groups of privileged actors were engaged in circuits and calculations that ordinary people knew nothing of." They practiced "a sophisticated art open only to a few initiates at most." Without this zone that existed "above the sunlit world of the market economy," capitalism, that is "*real* capitalism" was "unthinkable" (Braudel 1981–84: vol. 1, 23–24).

(3) The zone of the market, which he occasionally calls the zone of "micro-capitalism," was a zone of "small profits." Its "face was not unacceptable." The activities there were "barely distinguishable from ordinary work." How different this was from real capitalism, "with its mighty networks, its operations which already seemed diabolical to common mortals" (Braudel 1981–84: vol. 1, 562). The zone of capitalism was "the realm of investment and of a high rate of capital formation" (Braudel 1981–84: vol. 2, 231), the zone of "exceptional profits" (Braudel 1981–84: vol. 2, 428). "Where profit reaches very high voltages, there and there alone is capitalism, yesterday like today" (Braudel 1979: 378).[2] But although profits of capitalists were high, they were not regular, like an annual harvest. "Profit rates varied all the time" (Braudel 1981–84: vol. 2, 430).

Still, it was not merely a question of choice, of some who were willing to settle for small steady profits versus others who, being more adventurous, were ready to take the risk of exceptional, but variable, profits. Not everyone had this choice. "What is clear … is that the really big profits were only attainable by capitalists who handled large sums of money – their own or other people's…. Money, ever more money was needed: to tide one over the long wait, the reverses, the shocks and delays" (Braudel 1981–84: vol. 2, 432).[3]

(4) "The market spells liberation, openness, access to another world. It means coming up for air" (Braudel 1981–84: vol. 2, 26). This description presumably fits the late Middle Ages. It might also be said to reflect the sentiments of post-Cultural Revolution China.

---

[2] For some reason, probably an editor's *lapsus*, this sentence is not translated in the English version. See the parallel English paragraph in Braudel (1981–84: vol. 2, 428).

[3] Braudel is speaking here of long-distance merchants, but the description fits quite well for a contemporary firm like Boeing Aircraft.

By contrast, the zone of the anti-market is that "where the great predators roam and the law of the jungle operates" (Braudel 1981–84: vol. 2, 230).[4]

Originally, the anti-market particularly flourished in long-distance trade. It was not distance per se, however, which accounted for the high profits. "The indisputable superiority of *Fernhandel*, long-distance trading, lay in the *concentrations* it made possible, which meant it was an unrivalled machine for the rapid reproduction and increase of capital" (Braudel 1981–84: vol. 2, 408). In short, economic life is being defined by Braudel as those activities which are truly competitive. Capitalism is being defined as the zone of concentration, the zone of a relatively high degree of monopolization, that is, an anti-market.

(5) The zone of the market economy was a zone of "horizontal communications between the different markets [note the plural – I.W.]: here a degree of automatic coordination usually links supply, demand and prices" (Braudel 1981–84: vol. 2, 230). The zone of capitalism was fundamentally different. "Monopolies were the product of power, cunning and intelligence" (Braudel 1981–84: vol. 2, 418). But power above all. Describing "exploitation, that is unequal or forced exchange," Braudel asserts: "When there was a relationship of force of this kind, what exactly did the terms supply and demand mean?" (Braudel 1981–84: vol. 2, 176).[5]

(6) The issue of power then brings us to the role of the state. Here Braudel makes two points, one concerning the state as regulator, the other concerning the state as guarantor. And his argument is paradoxical. As regulator, the state preserves freedom; as guarantor, it destroys it. His logic runs as follows. The state as regulator means price control. The ideology of free enterprise, which has always been an ideology that served the monopolists, has always attacked price control by governments in its many forms. But for Braudel, price control ensured competition:

[4]   The original French is perhaps less vivid: "la zone du contre-marché est la règne de la débrouille et du droit du plus fort" (Braudel 1979: vol. 2, 197).
[5]   I have changed one phrase in the English translation. I believe that, in the context, Braudel's phrase "rapport de force" should not be translated as "balance of power;" but as "relationship of force." The original French reads: "Quand il y a ainsi rapport de force, que signifient exactement les termes 'demande' et 'offre'?" (Braudel 1979: vol. 2, 149).

Price control, which is used as a key argument to deny the appearance of the "true" self-regulating market before the nineteenth century, has always existed and still exists today. But when we are talking of the pre-industrial world, it would be a mistake to think that the price-lists of the markets suppressed the role of supply and demand. In theory, severe control over the market was meant to protect the consumer, that is competition. One might go so far as to say that it was the "free" market, such as the "private marketing" phenomenon in England, that tended to do away with both control and competition. (Braudel 1981–84: vol. 2, 227)

Here the role of the state was to contain the forces of the anti-market. For private markets did not arise merely to promote efficiency, but also to "eliminate competition" (Braudel 1981–84: vol. 2, 413).

But the state was a guarantor as well, a guarantor of monopoly, indeed its creator. This was not true of every state, however; only some states were able to do this. It was not only that the biggest monopolies, the great merchant companies, "were set up with the regular cooperation of the state" (Braudel 1981–84: vol. 2, 421). There were many monopolies that "were taken so much for granted that they were all but invisible to those who enjoyed them" (Braudel 1981–84: vol. 2, 423). He cites the example of currency as a monopoly that is taken for granted – in the Middle Ages, monopolists possessing gold and silver and most people only copper; today, monopolies utilizing so-called strong currencies and most people only "weak" currencies. But the biggest monopoly of all was that possessed by the hegemonic power, the guarantor of the whole system. "The position of Amsterdam as a whole constituted a monopoly in itself, and that monopoly was the pursuit not of security but of domination" (Braudel 1981–84: vol. 2, 423).

Here then is our picture. Economic life is regular, capitalism unusual. Economic life is a sphere where one knows in advance, capitalism is speculative. Economic life is transparent, capitalism shadowy or opaque. Economic life involves small profits, capitalism exceptional profits. Economic life is liberation, capitalism the jungle. Economic life is the automatic pricing of true supply and demand, capitalism the prices imposed by power and cunning. Economic life involves controlled competition, capitalism involves eliminating both control and competition. Economic life is the domain of ordinary people; capitalism is guaranteed by, incarnated in the hegemonic power.

II

The distinction among merchants, industrialists, and bankers is an ancient and an obvious one. They are the practitioners of the three main economic activities from which entrepreneurs can make profits: trade, manufacturing (or, more generally, productive activities), and handling money (lending it, safeguarding it, investing it). It is normally thought that these are differentiated occupational or institutional roles, and often they are reified into three distinct social groups, as for example in the trinity: merchant capital, industrial capital, finance capital.

Many analysts indeed use such categories to construct a categorical chronology of capitalism: first the era of merchant capital, then the era of industrial capital, and finally the era of finance capital. Furthermore, both in the liberal and in the Marxist traditions, there has been a sense that trading activities are both more dubious ethically and less "capitalist" than industrial production. This is the legacy above all of Saint-Simon and his concept (itself derived from the Physiocrats) of distinguishing between productive and nonproductive labor. In any case, the centrality of the presumed moment of historical transformation labeled the industrial revolution depends on these distinctions and their ontological reality.

Braudel purely and simply attacks the distinctions at their root:

> One's impression then (since in view of the paucity of the evidence, impressions are all we have) is that there were always sectors in economic life where high profits could be made, but that these sectors varied. Every time one of these shifts occurred, under the pressure of economic development, capital was quick to scent them out, to move into the new sector and prosper. Note that as a rule it had not precipitated such shifts. This differential geography of profit is a key to the short-term fluctuations of capitalism, as it veered between the Levant, America, the East Indies, China, the slave trade, etc., or between trade, banking, industry or land. . . .
>
> It is difficult then to establish a classification, valid once and for all, as between the profits from agriculture, industry and trade. Broadly speaking, the standard classification in descending order: trade, industry, agriculture, corresponds to a certain reality, but there were a number of exceptions which justified shifts from one sector to another.
>
> Let me emphasize the quality that seems to me to be an essential feature of the general history of capitalism: its unlimited flexibility, its capacity for change and adaptation. If there is, as I believe, a

certain unity in capitalism, from thirteenth-century Italy to the present-day West, it is here above all that such unity must be located and observed. (Braudel 1981–84: vol. 2, 432–33)

Once it is established that profit opportunities determine the shifting location of the capitalist in the circuit of capital, it remains to be seen how the capitalist achieves this "unlimited flexibility." The answer for Braudel is simple. The real capitalist always resisted specialization, and thus being trapped in one arena by past investment, past networks, past skills. Specialization exists, of course, but for Braudel, it is the work of the lower stories:

Specialization and division of labour usually operated from the bottom up. If modernization or rationalization consists of the process whereby different tasks are distinguished and functions subdivided, such modernization began in the bottom layer of the economy. Every boom in trade led to increased specialization of shops and the appearance of new professions among the many hangers-on of trade.

Curiously enough, the wholesaler [*le négociant*] did not in fact observe this rule, and only specialized very occasionally. Even a shopkeeper who made his fortune, and became a merchant, immediately moved out of specialization into non-specialization. (Braudel 1981–84: vol. 2, 378–79)

The attitude of the capitalist is quite different from the attitude of the shopkeeper:

The characteristic advantage of standing at the commanding heights of the economy, today just as much as in the days of Jacques Coeur (the fourteenth-century tycoon) consisted precisely of not having to confine oneself to a single choice, of being eminently adaptable, hence non-specialized. (Braudel 1981–84: vol. 2, 381)[6]

III

What implications does it have to see capitalism "upside down" in this manner? For one thing, it changes the historiographical

---

[6] I have altered the translation of the last four words, because the English translation "able ... to keep one's options open," while perfectly correct, loses the explicitness of the French original: "D'être éminemment adaptable, donc non spécialisé" (Braudel 1979: vol. 2, 335).

agenda. For a second, it contains an implicit critique of Enlightenment theories of progress. For a third, it gives a very different
policy message for the contemporary world. These are not implications that Braudel made explicit. It was not his habit to explicate
the implications of his scholarly work in his scholarly work. If he
occasionally did so in interviews, his comments often had an off-
the-cuff quality which reflected less his views about the world than
his views about interviews. Perhaps Braudel believed that the sub-
text has more influence if the reader discovers it himself. Perhaps
he did not want to be drawn into too politicized a controversy,
though he was scarcely shy of intellectual combat. Whatever the
explanations of Braudel's own hesitancies or silences, they should
not prevent us from using his work as a basis for our own inflections.

The agenda of History (with a capital H), since at least the
middle of the nineteenth century, has been dominated by an
explanatory myth[7] which runs as follows. Out of some earlier,
simpler, smaller system, characterized by landlords exploiting
peasants in one way or another, emerged the "middle classes" or
the "bourgeoisie" who eventually became the dominant force of
the modern nation-states. The growing strength of this "new
group" and of the economic system they practiced, capitalism,
accounts for the two great revolutions, the industrial revolution in
Great Britain and the bourgeois French Revolution, which together
constitute a great temporal divide of world history at the turn of the
nineteenth century.

All our periodization is based on this myth: the break between
medieval and modern times; the break between early and late
modern history (or in European terminology, between modern and
contemporary history). But, even more, this mythology is located
in our adjectives, which in fact means that it is lodged in our
unexamined premises. We talk, for example of "pre-industrial"
societies and recently of "post-industrial" ones, both of which
adjectives assume measurable periods of something called an "industrial society." Finally the mythology is located in our problema-
tics: why was the bourgeois revolution so late in Italy? When did
France, or Russia, or India have its industrial revolution? Were
slave owners in the US South feudal patriarchs or capitalist entrepreneurs? Braudel, I hasten to add, was not himself liberated from

---

[7] On the role of historical myths, see McNeill (1986), as well as ch. 4.

all these premises, particularly in the use of adjectives. But he did largely ignore them.

However, his "upside down" view of capitalism is, I would contend, a devastating attack on these mythologies. If the capitalists are the monopolists as opposed to those operating in competitive markets, then the lines of division in reality have been quite different from those to which we are accustomed of thinking. One can trace out multiple forms of monopolistic controls of production or trade or finance. Large plantations are one such form, large trading companies another, transnational corporations a third, state enterprises a fourth. Arrayed in contraposition to them would be the working populations of the world, rural and urban, who inhabit the zone of the material life but who sally forth into the zone of the market to struggle against the power of the monopolists.

These workers have sought to reclaim more of the surplus-value they created by augmenting their wage income, creating forms of petty commodity production and marketing, and defying to the degree possible the price structure imposed by the monopolists and substituting one that truly reflects supply and demand, that is, real value. In this effort at "liberation," they have sought the support of the state as regulator, as protector of "competition," but they have repeatedly encountered the role of the state as "guarantor" of the very monopolies against which they are struggling. Thus they must be ambivalent in their attitudes toward the state.

Since the strength of the capitalists is their adaptability, their flexibility, their rapidity in moving towards the arenas of high profit, the shift towards cotton textile production in 1780 was no more and no less significant than the shift towards investment in agriculture in the Venetian Terraferma in the seventeenth century or the shift towards financial speculation by transnational corporations in the 1980s. In addition, the concept of "controlled competition," with the state as regulator, opens up new ways of thinking about the remarkable rise of "market socialism" as a policy option of the socialist countries in the last decade or so. Braudel offers us the imagery of an ongoing struggle within the capitalist world-economy between monopolists who have power and cunning on their side and the majority of the population who are hampered by the openness and clarity of their operations in economic life. Might not the political history of the past two centuries be conceived as one in which this majority has sought to build up counterpower and systematize its own countercunning?

It should be clear, then, that Braudel's imagery accords ill with the more stultified views of our dominant ideologies. No doubt both Adam Smith and Karl Marx were subtle thinkers and anticipated much of what we can derive from a reading of Braudel. But liberalism as an ideology is different from the views of Adam Smith, and Marxism has been different from the views of Karl Marx. And it is liberalism and Marxism that have dominated our horizons, not the views of either Adam Smith or Karl Marx.

By reconceptualizing capitalism, Braudel has undercut the basic argument that both liberals and Marxists have used to justify their adherence to the theory of inevitable progress. Both liberals and Marxists have seen historical sequence in which capitalists and/or bourgeois and/or the middle class rose and developed their structures in particular ways. For liberals, when completed, this process would culminate in a sort of utopian apotheosis. For Marxists, when completed, this process would culminate in an explosion, which in turn would lead to new structures that would arrive at a sort of utopian apotheosis.

Braudel instead sees not a linear progression, but a continuing tension between the forces of monopoly (so-called real capitalism) and the forces of liberation who seek this liberation through self-controlled economic activities within the framework of a complex of competitive markets, one in which their activities are "barely distinguishable from ordinary work."

Braudel himself goes no further. We can assume this conflict is eternal, or we can look for secular trends that would transform this historical system by making its unstable equilibria increasingly untenable. It is for us to fill this lacuna. I for one believe that such secular trends do exist within the capitalist world-economy, and that the increasing contradictions will result in a systemic "bifurcation" that will force a transformation of the system into something else. I also believe that what the something else will be is open, in the sense that it depends on our collective historical choice, and is not preordained. This is not the moment to develop these views, which I have done elsewhere.

What I think is important to understand is that Braudel's views do not reflect a hidden Poujadism honoring a putative "small businessman." Quite the contrary. Braudel's "liberatory" market is not what we have come to recognize as a market in the real world. It is truly competitive, in that supply and demand really do determine price, that is, potential (or fully realized) supply and demand. The "profits," it would follow, would be miniscule, in effect, a wage for the work. Whether such a system is historically viable remains a question. But his invocation of the "market" cannot be confused with the so-called neo-liberal ideology of the 1980s. It is in fact the very opposite.

Finally, its policy implications for the contemporary world are massive. If capitalism, real capitalism, is monopoly and not the market, real markets, then what is to be done is a question that gets answered perhaps very differently from the ways in which anti-systemic movements have been answering it for the past 100 years.

I have tried here to expound the ways in which Braudel has gone against accepted conceptualizations of capitalism. I have called this seeing capitalism "upside down." I have then tried to do what Braudel restrained himself from doing, make explicit the intellectual and social implications of his reconceptualization. Braudel should not be blamed for the latter effort. Perhaps others will take Braudel's reconceptualization and draw from it other implications. It will in any case be useful for all of us to allow Braudel to blow fresh air into the realm of our unexamined pre-mises about the central institutional forms of the historical system in which we live.

16

Beyond *Annales*?

The *Annales* movement was born as a reaction against the dominant premises underlying the institutionalization of the social sciences in the nineteenth century. Today we are accustomed to dividing knowledge about social processes and structures into a series of named categories, the most prominent of which are (in alphabetical order): anthropology, economics, history, political science, and sociology. At least three of these words did not even exist before the nineteenth century. In the last half of the nineteenth century (let us say, the period 1850–1914), there were three principal ways in which these names were institutionalized: the universities created departments (or at least chairs) bearing these names; national (and later international) scholarly societies were created bearing these names; major libraries began to classify books in systems organized around these names.

It is not the place of this paper to analyze exactly why this institutionalization of categories occurred at this point of time,[1] nor to detail the process by which this occurred.[2] Suffice it to note that the process engendered much debate at the time, but the present schema triumphed fairly widely throughout Europe and North America, and spread subsequently (often only in the post-1945 period) to all the regions of the globe.

---

[1] See, for a first approximation, ch. 1.
[2] The Fernand Braudel Center currently is engaged in research on this topic.

The premises on which nineteenth-century institutionalization was based were, I believe, primarily the following seven:[3]

1 The social sciences are constituted of a number of "disciplines" which are intellectually coherent groupings of subject matter distinct from each other.
2 History is the study of, the explanation of, the particular as it really happened in the past. Social science is the statement of the universal set of rules by which human/social behavior is explained.
3 Human beings are organized in entities we may call societies, which constitute the fundamental social frameworks within which human life is lived.
4 Capitalism is a system based on competition between free producers using free labor with free commodities, "free" meaning its availability for sale and purchase on a market.
5 The end of the eighteenth and the beginning of the nineteenth century represent a crucial turning point in the history of the world, in that capitalists finally achieved state-societal power in the key states.
6 Human history is progressive, and inevitably so.
7 Science is the search for the rules which most succinctly summarize why everything is the way it is and how things happen.

Of course, not everyone agreed with these premises, but they became predominant.

The *Annales* movement is frequently traced to the journal, *Revue de synthèse historique*, which Henri Berr founded in 1900. This journal concentrated its fire against the first of the seven premises, the ghettoization of separate disciplines. It was not very successful intellectually in changing the climate of university opinion, even in France. When Lucien Febvre and Marc Bloch founded the *Annales d'histoire économique et social* in 1929, they were marginal scholars in a marginal university. They concentrated their fire against the second premise, the division of all knowledge into two mutually exclusive (and mutually denunciatory) epistemologies, the idiographic and the nomothetic. While the idiographic particularists (mostly historians and ethnographers) argued that the world could

---

[3] This list is drawn from an article in which I sought to indicate the limitations of each of the seven premises. See ch. 18.

only be usefully perceived in its complex concreteness, the nomothetic universalizers (mostly economists and sociologists) argued that the world could only be usefully perceived by learning its underlying general laws. The *Annales* movement disagreed with both views, and sought to conduct a "war on two fronts" (see Wallerstein 1980a). Febvre, in his Inaugural Lecture at the Collège de France in 1933 proposed the slogan "Histoire science de l'Homme, science du passé humain." He added four caveats: "History as human science, and therefore constituted of *facts*, yes: but these are *human* facts. . . . Written sources, yes: but these are *human* written sources. . . . The written sources, of course: but *all the written sources*. . . . The written sources, to be sure: but not *merely the written sources*" (Febvre 1953b).

While the *Annales* movement continued to remain marginal to French (and world) intellectual life up to the Second World War, it rapidly achieved its apogee and apotheosis in the period 1945–67. This occurred first of all in France, but not only in France. The *Annales* movement became influential in southern Europe, Eastern Europe, Great Britain, and eventually North America.[4] I believe that this sudden intellectual *and institutional* success was due to a particular *conjoncture* which created an increased receptivity to *Annales* views.[5] The *conjoncture* was that of the cold war. What the *Annales* movement had to offer in this context was an intellectual worldview that seemed to express resistance both to Anglo-Saxon intellectual hegemony and to sclerotic official Marxism simultaneously. As I said in my previous analysis of this *conjoncture* of 1945–67, it was "favorable to *Annales* with the particular Braudelian emphases: more economic than social history, history that emphasized the so-called 'early modern period,' history informed by an analysis of the multiple social temporalities, historiography that 'did not hold Marxism at a distance.' "[6]

But *conjonctures* change, as is their way. And the present post-1967 *conjoncture* has placed the *Annales* movement in a most ambiguous position. The larger social scene of this *conjoncture* is

---

[4] See the special issue of *Review* on "The Impact of the *Annales* School on the Social Sciences," I, 3/4 (Winter/Spring 1978), which provides considerable evidence on this subject.

[5] *Conjoncture* is used here in the French sense of a period of medium length, usually one phase in some cyclical movement.

[6] See ch. 13, p. 198.

composed of two principal elements. Element one is the relative decline of US power, such that its hegemony in the world-system is no longer unquestioned. This relative decline of the United States has multiple different manifestations. One is the relative economic upsurge since the 1960s of Japan and Western Europe (with the institutional consequence for the latter of the new structures that will be established in 1992). A second is the considerably reduced ability of the United States to intervene directly in Third World situations. The third is the remarkable political, economic, and social reorganizations under way today, at varying paces, in the formerly so-called socialist countries. It may seem surprising to cite this last set of developments as an indicator of relative US decline. However, I believe that the Stalinism/Yalta complex of arrangements (both internally for the USSR and internationally for the socialist bloc) were part and parcel of the US hegemonic institutional arrangements of the postwar era (despite the rhetoric to the contrary). These arrangements could not survive the internal confrontations they provoked, once the US outside de facto support system began to crumble. Under these new circumstances of the post-1967 *conjoncture*, the version of the *Annales* movement that had been dominant in the 1945–67 period no longer seemed very pertinent, neither, in quite another domain, did the movement of non-aligned countries continue to be relevant to the new political reality of the world-system.

There was, however, a second and even more fundamental transformation of the post-1967 period, more important, that is, than the decline of US hegemony. It was the world revolution of 1968. The world revolution of 1968 had two objects of its political action. The first, of course, was to struggle against US hegemony (as well as Soviet collusion with that hegemony). But the second, and ultimately more significant, political target was the "Old Left" antisystemic movements in their three main variants: Second International (or similar) movements in the Western world; Third International movements in the socialist countries (and elsewhere where they were strong – e.g. France, Italy, Japan); and national liberation movements in the Third World (see Wallerstein 1989c; Arrighi et al. 1989). The major charge of the movements which thrived in the post-1968 era (women's movements, movements of "minorities," ecology movements, anti-bureaucratic movements, etc.) against the so-called Old Left is that Old Left movements had not been truly antisystemic, and (to the extent that they had come to power, or partial power, in various states) had not transformed the world as they had promised.

Once again, this is not the place to discuss the validity of these assertions, nor to assess the comparative strength of "Old Left" and "new" movements since 1968, nor to discuss the probable trajectory of all these movements in the immediate future. Rather, I wish merely to discuss the impact of 1968 on the world intellectual community. It has, in my view, launched a transformation of the world university system.

I do not refer primarily to the restructuring of the governance system of universities, which has of course occurred. I consider this restructuring important but not fundamental. Were it the only consequence, 1968 would have been a minor event, since it is relatively easy to co-opt and neutralize new participants in governance structures, and indeed for the most part this has already occurred in the last 20 years.

Nor do I believe the impact of 1968 on the world university system has been that it made the universities more socially conscious, or politically relevant. This was indeed a theme of many of the student uprisings in and around 1968, but the actual legacy is small. The university has always been, since its creation in the Middle Ages, a locus of activity *in tension with* political authorities. It has always found it impossible to cut itself completely off from political authorities but it has always tried to create some distance. This has resulted in a see-saw, and will probable always do so. In this sense 1968 simply represented a cyclical swing of the pendulum. The universities had come to be *too* closely identified with their states in the 1945–67 period. The movements of 1968 pushed in the other direction. We are in fact already swinging back in the first direction.

The real impact of 1968 was rather on the *intellectual* life of the universities. It represented a challenge not only to the immediate consensus of the 1945–67 period, but to the deeper consensus that had governed world intellectual life since at least the mid-nineteenth century. What 1968 did was to weaken gravely the legitimacy of the nineteenth-century consensus, without, however, destroying its institutional base. Prior to 1968, the range of what was intellectually permissible for dicussion in universities was in fact largely circumscribed by the consensus. Other views were essentially *ultra vires*. The attack of 1968 shattered the arrogance of the defenders of consensus views, emboldened its challengers (coming from multiple intellectual horizons), and made of the universities for the first time somewhat open (or pluralist) intellectual arenas. Whereas a "centrist liberalism" was virtually the only acceptable position for historians and social scientists in most Western universities before 1968, after 1968 both neo-conservative and Marxist views received *droit de cité*. Whole new fields of study were legitimated, such as "ethnic" studies (of various names) and not least women's studies. This was of course a positive legacy. But it has also been an unsettling one. Intellectuals do not appreciate it, any more than anyone else, when "things fall apart; the centre cannot hold."[7]

But what was this consensus that was no longer unquestioned? The key epistemological premise was the second one on my list, the famous distinction between nomothetic and idiographic ways of knowing. It is this premise which the *Annales* movement – under Febvre and Bloch, and under Braudel – sought to refute. The strongest theoretical statement of this position is to be found in Braudel's essay, "Histoire et les sciences sociales," which appeared in *Annales ESC* in 1958. In this essay, Braudel first details the limitations of *histoire événementielle*, which is the social time of idiographic historians. Then he turns his fire on the proponents of "la très longue durée," about which Braudel comments "if it exists, [it] can only be the time period of the sages" (Braudel 1972a: 35). In the text it is Lévi-Strauss who incarnates this latest vision of nomothetic science, which pushes empirical research "the intersection of the infinitely small and the very long term" (Braudel 1972a: 34).

What solution did the *Annales* movement offer to the epistemological squeeze between concentration on the infinitely small in space and time by idiographic historians and the concentration on the infinitely small in scope and eternal in time of nomothetic social scientists? The answer of the *Annales* movement was to analyze large space and long time, using the double temporality of persisting structures slow to change and cyclical *conjonctures* within these structures.

But in practice, what did this mean in terms of the university system? In fact, the *Annales* movement addressed itself primarily to persons trained as historians and used to working in archives, and said to them: read and embrace the knowledge that is being created by the various kinds of social scientists, and utilize their hypotheses or generalizations to organize your research and interpret your

---

[7] William Butler Yeats, "The Second Coming," stanza 1.

findings. In short, it preached: Historians – be "open" to the social sciences! The second practical message of the *Annales* movement was that history was more than the story of princes and diplomats. It was the story of humans collectively (as seen in economic and social patterns over time) and humans at the level of life as they lived it (as seen in the patterns of everyday life). In short, it preached: be open to demography, to family history, to *mentalités*, etc.

Up to a point, as we well know, this worked. Indeed it worked magnificently well. The libraries are full of excellent books that are testimony to this program of total history "open" to the social sciences. There was nonetheless a fatal flaw in this program, which sharply limited the ability of the *Annales* movement to transcend or sublate the idiographic-nomothetic antinomy, that is, to arrive at an epistemological *Aufhebung*. The *Annales* movement proposed in effect "multidisciplinarity." Of course, it was not the only movement to recommend this practice in that epoch. The same period of 1945–67 saw the flourishing in the United States of the concept of "area studies," another form of multidisciplinarity, and one of which Braudel (as we know from his writings) was well aware. Multidisciplinarity has the appearance of trying to transcend the disciplines. In practice, however, it often merely reinforces them. It does so because the very term presumes the legitimacy and meaningfulness of the separate disciplinary categories and argues for the integration of distinctive wisdoms. The underlying message therefore is that there do exist distinctive wisdoms.

Concentrating on multidisciplinarity leads to a second flaw: forgetting the reason why the *Annales* movement had originally sought to transcend the disciplines. In the so-called third generation, some *Annalistes* became so bemused with the quantitative data they could collect and the theory testing in which they could engage that it became hard to distinguish their work from that of the nomothetic social scientists against whom the *Annales* movement presumably stood. And some other *Annalistes* became so bemused by the incredible complexity of everyday life and the *mentalités* that could be seen to be reflected therein that it became hard to distinguish their work from that of the idiographers concentrating on the small of scale and time, against whom the *Annales* movement presumably stood. The *Annales* movement was losing its singularity, which is the real meaning behind the frequent observation about its *émiettement*. If everything becomes *Annales*, nothing remains *Annales*.

The key limitation of the *Annales* movement was institutional. Now you may find this strange, since it is often said that the genius of the *Annales* movement was in their collective talent for organization – creation of a central journal; monumental book series; establishment of the VIe *Section* of the EPHE, which then became the Ecole des Hautes Etudes en Sciences Sociales; and last, but surely not least, the invention of the Maison des Sciences de l'Homme. And this is to leave out structures inspired by *Annales* outside France. Surely few intellectual movements have created as many important institutions to advance and defend their intellectual approach.

The limits of the accomplishment are nonetheless easy to gauge. The basic university system that grew out of the nineteenth-century premises which the *Annales* movement sought to attack has essentially remained in place; indeed it may be stronger than ever. Yet the moment for grand-scale organizational transformation is approaching. The structures have been evolving in the wider social scene as I have tried to show, and the *conjoncture* is or soon will be ripe.

Ripe for what? Precisely to go "beyond *Annales*," beyond multi-disciplinarity, beyond (above all) the idiographic-nomothetic antinomy. The historical social sciences are a single discipline and there is no intellectual justification for the existing set of categorizations we call the "disciplines" of the social sciences. Even if it would be heuristically useful to divide the historical social sciences into sub-disciplines, there is little reason to believe these subdisciplines should utilize the current "names"; probably, quite the contrary.

The historical social sciences can only proceed on the premise that humans live inside historical systems that are large in scale, long in time, but nonetheless have natural lives. These historical systems come into existence and eventually they go out of existence. All systems are systemic, that is, they have structures. But all systems are simultaneously historical, that is, they have not only cyclical rhythms (or *conjonctures*) but secular trends, which is why their natural lives come to an eventual end. No scholarly work is useful unless it simultaneously analyzes the unchanging or repetitive and the constantly and eternally changing.

Furthermore, we must abolish the nineteenth century's holy trinity of politics, economics, and culture as the three presumedly autonomous spheres of human action, with separate logics and separated processes. We must invent new language that will permit us to talk about the eternal, instantaneous, continuous movement of all social processes in and among these three supposedly distinctive arenas.

And finally then we must be ready to draw the organizational implications of this kind of reconceptualization by reorganizing the departmental structures of our universities and the associational structures of our scholarly meetings. Then and only then will the promise of the *Annales* movement as critique have a chance of lasting fulfilment. If this does not occur, the *Annales* movement will in another decade or two have become only a vague memory of historians of ideas and have as much resonance as the *Staatswissenschaft* movement has today, that is to say, not very much. The heirs of the *Annales* movement – in France, in the USSR, in the US, and everywhere else – are the natural ones to offer the lead in the search for a new consensus based upon a new epistemology as well as a new organizational structure so that the twenty-first century will not need to chew the cud of the outmoded consensus of nineteenth-century social science, in which few today have faith and from which only a few can still profit.

Part VI

World-Systems Analysis as Unthinking

17

Historical Systems as Complex Systems

The term "historical system" is not commonly used in the social sciences. Indeed, in general most social scientists would consider it an anomalous phrase. Those who emphasize the historical by and large downplay or deny the systemic. And those who emphasize the systemic normally ignore the historical. It is not that, as an abstract issue, the importance of reconciling this standard dichotomy or distinction between the static and the dynamic, the synchronic and the diachronic, is not acknowledged. The curtsey is made, but in practice, there has been strong institutional pressure to proceed in the one direction or the other of what was in the late nineteenth century designated as the *Methodenstreit* between idiographic and nomothetic modes of scholarship in the domain of social life.

And yet it seems obvious, at least to me, that everything that is historic is systemic, and everything that is systemic is historic. All complex phenomena have their rules, their constraints, their trends or vectors, that is, their structures. Any real structure (as opposed to imagined structures) has its particularities, due to its genesis, its life history, and its environment, hence has a history which is central to its mode of functioning. The more complex the structure, the more crucial its history. The problem is not to state this as some metaphysical truth, but to manipulate this truth in our study of any real complex phenomenon. My mode of handling this is to conceive the social world as a succession and coexistence of multiple large-scale, long-term entities I call historical systems which have three defining characteristics. They are relatively autonomous, that is, they function primarily in terms of the consequences of processes internal to them. They have time-boundaries, that is, they begin and they end. They have space-boundaries, which, however, can change in the course of their life-history.

This seems simple, perhaps obvious. It poses considerable problems when one wishes to operationalize these criteria, and indeed the historiography of the last 150 years is filled with debates about systemic boundaries of particular historical systems, even though this language is often avoided. I have tried to approach the issue of boundaries by starting with the social division of labor, the conditions of ensuring social survival. I assume that a historical system must represent an integrated network of economic, political, and cultural processes the sum of which hold the system together. This presumes that, if the parameters of any particular process change, the other processes must somehow adjust. This banality enables us, however, to locate that which is outside the historical system. If something can or does occur in zone X, a zone thought or suspected to be part of a given historical system at time Y, and the rest of the system in effect ignores this happening, then zone X is outside this historical system, even though there may seem to be some visible social interaction between zone X and this system. Perhaps if I translate that statement into discussion of a concrete issue, it will become clearer. In my book on the European world-economy in the long sixteenth century, I argued that Poland could be said to have been part of its social division of labor, but that Russia was not. To be sure, both Poland and Russia had sea trade links with various countries of western Europe (and Poland overland links as well with the Germanies). The difference, however, between the two cases was that, in my view (for which I offer some empirical evidence), any more than momentary interruption of the links between Poland and say the Low Countries (a serious but unfulfilled possibility in 1626–29) would have resulted in significant alteration of the production processes in both locales, whereas the actual efforts of Tsar Ivan IV in the 1550s and 1560s to cut such links as existed at the time did not in fact result in such an alteration. Hence Poland and the Low Countries could be said to have been located in a single social division of labor, but Russia was located outside this historical system.[1]

[1] For the details of my argument, see Wallerstein (1974: Ch. 6, *passim* and esp. pp. 304–5, 315). For a view which takes issue with me empirically on whether or not Russia in the long sixteenth century was part of the European world-economy, see Nolte (1982: 32–48).

If then one uses a measuring rod, I believe it is true that such autonomous social divisions of labor can only be found historically in rather small entities, small both spatially and temporally – I call these mini-systems – and in relatively large scale, long-term ones – I call these world-systems. Furthermore, I divide the world-systems into two major structural variants: those with a single overarching political structure, the world-empires; and those without one, the world-economies (Wallerstein 1979: ch. 9; Wallerstein 1984: ch. 14).

I believe we know almost nothing today about how mini-systems work. For one thing. I believe they no longer exist. Furthermore, I think most of what has been described as mini-systems have in fact been merely local components of world-systems, since one of the prerequisites for their study seems to have been up to now their inclusion in such a world-system. Finally, I think such mini-systems had short lives and, almost by definition, had no method of recording their life-history. Hence, we are up against a problem analogous to that faced by physicists seeking to study those extremely small particles with a fleeting existence. Perhaps one day we shall devise modes of perceiving these particles (the mini-systems) which cover such a large portion of the social history of mankind, but for the moment we do not seem to be able to do this. Therefore, what I shall have to say concerns world-systems primarily.

I start by noting a historical shift in the relationship of the world-empires and the world-economies. From circa 10,000 BC to circa AD 1500, there have existed (and coexisted) a large but countable number of such world-systems (as well as an unknown, probably very large, number of mini-systems). During this period, the world-empire form seemed "stronger" than the world-economy form, in that, with some regularity, expanding world-empires absorbed nearby world-economies (as well as nearby mini-systems). World-empires seem to have had built-in space and time limits, since the expansion outwards always seemed to reach a point where the central authority's power was overtaken by disintegrative forces and these world-empires then contracted. In the spatial "voids" thus created, new world-economies and mini-systems subsequently reemerged. As far as we can tell, two generalizations can be made about the coexistence of world-empires and world-economies in this long period. Those world-empires that succeeded (that is, there were no doubt in addition a large number of abortive attempts to establish world-empires) lasted for significant lengths of time (say, on the order of a half-millennium from beginning to end). On the

other hand, world-economies seemed more fragile and not one
lasted this long in this period.

Circa 1500, something strange occurred, for which in my view
there is as yet no truly satisfatory explanation. The relative strength
of the world-economy and world-empire form became inverted.
That is to say, one particular world-economy, the one established in
a large area of Europe at this time, proved to be less fragile. It
survived and therefore was able to serve as the framework for the
full development of a capitalist mode of production, which requires
and can only exist within a world-economy form. Once this capitalist world-economy consolidated itself, it expanded spatially by virtue of the logic of processes internal to it, absorbing the surrounding world-empires (for example, the Russian Empire, the Ottoman
Empire, the Mughal Empire, the Chinese Empire), as well as, of
course, the surrounding mini-systems. Furthermore, unlike what
had previously occured with world-empires the expansion process
seemed to have had no in-built spatial limits. By the end of the
nineteenth century, the capitalist world-economy had expanded to
cover the entire planet, absorbing, it seems, all other existing
historical systems. Ergo, for the first time in the history of the
planet there existed only one historical system on the planet. This
created an entirely new structural situation, since now there were
no coexisting historical systems external to the one surviving system
called the capitalist world-economy.

This poses three intellectual problems. (a) What explains the
transition circa 1500? I have already said that explanations previously given, including I may add my own, are weak; I shall not
pursue this question for the moment. (b) What is it about the
current system which explains its ceaseless expansion? (c) What are
the consequences of the fact that this historical system operates
today without other systems external to it?

The ceaseless spatial expansion of the capitalist world-economy
has been a function of its central dynamic, the ceaseless accumulation of capital. This dynamic operates in three ways. In the first
place, lateral spatial expansion has specific effects in recreating the
margin of surplus-extraction each time that this margin is reduced
globally in order to contribute to extricating the world-economy
from a conjunctural downturn by means of expanding global effective demand via some partial redistribution of this surplus to relatively low-income sectors. The process of geographical expansion
serves to incorporate new sectors of direct producers receiving low
remuneration which reexpands the percentage of surplus central-

ized in the hands of a small number of relatively large accumulators of capital.[2]

Secondly, the capitalist world-economy involves structures which specifically reward technological advance more often than not. In world-empires, there were also rewards for technological advance, but there were significant penalties as well (which tended to slow the process down considerably), since centralized authorities were constantly faced with the difficult political problem of controlling their geographically dispersed senior cadres, and technological advance made this more difficult, through what might be called its tendency to democratize the use of force. The rapid technological progress thus ensconced in the normal workings of the capitalist world-economy made it technically possible, because militarily possible, to overcome the resistance of world-empires to incorporation within the world-economy.

Thirdly, a capitalist mode of production involves mechanisms that specifically penalize behavior that is non-responsive to the shifting optimal modalities of maximizing the accumulation of capital. Those who control economic operations and who do not act to maximize capital accumulation eventually go bankrupt and are removed as actors. Conversely, there are no mechanisms (such as might exist in a world-empire) to penalize irrational modes of consuming the world product. Indeed, there is no way of intruding systematically and persistently anti-market values into decision making. Consequently, there is no basis on which opposition to geographical expansion could have been effectively mounted, once it was shown to serve the interests of capital accumulation.

The deepening of the capitalist processes and the geographical expansion of the boundaries of the social division of labor were then the outcome of very strong forces involved in the very creation and consolidation of a world-economy. They have been thus far unstoppable. One might even talk of a juggernaut effect. Of course, this has been a historical process in which every parameter is constantly changing. Historical systems are preeminent examples of the nonreversible arrow of time. Yet we purport to analyze this system structurally, which implies the existence of some kinds of repetitive phenomena, and at some level (however limited) some kinds of thrusts towards equilibrium, even of moving ones. We thus come back to the original contradiction of the phrase "historical

[2] The process of course involves other elements as well. See Wallerstein (1982: 15–22).

system" – something which is always changing directionally but something which is also always the same essentially, at least provisionally.

Intellectually, the issue is one of distinguishing cyclical rhythms, secular trends, and crises that are transitions and therefore ruptures. It is part of the governing social ideology of our present world-system to give moral priority to the new. Since the world is changing at each moment, it is consequently always intellectual child's play to discover and to illuminate what is novel. It is in fact much more difficult to discover what has not changed "essentially." I therefore pose as methodological admonition number one – exhaust first the description of the unchanged, that is of the repetitive, the cyclical. Obviously, to do this, we have to begin by deciding on the unit of analysis, and it is in this fashion that my discussion of the boundaries of historical systems becomes crucial. What is repetitive or cyclical is that measured within the time and space boundaries of a given historical system.

Given in fact that everything always changes, the cycle, the repetition is at best approximate, never exact. But the changes are not random. They are in principle predictable within the rules of functioning of the system – else it would not be a system. For example, I argued previously a particular sequence: economic stagnation; some redistribution of surplus and hence both new effective demand and reduced global surplus-appropriation; lateral systemic expansion and hence incorporation of new low remuneration productive zones and consequent increased global surplus-appropriation. This is a small part of a more complex picture and I will not for the moment elaborate the merits of this analysis. I merely wish to point out that if the sequence is true, there are hidden in its operation secular trends. One is obvious, that of lateral spatial expansion. Another is not obvious from the material I have given you here, but let me say that I could demonstrate that located within this sequence there is a trend to the proletarianization of the labor force. Now if we draw each of these trends as a simple linear curve in which the abscissa represents the percentage of the whole (percentage of the planet included in the boundaries of the capitalist world-economy, percentage of the work force of this world-economy which is proletarian), then it follows that the secular trends move towards asymptotes.

This simple reality accounts for crisis, transition, rupture. If, in order to solve a middle-run problem, that of repetitive economic stagnations, it is essential (among other things) internally to proletarianize and laterally to expand boundaries, then as one approaches over the long run these asymptotes one can no longer solve the repetitive middle-run problems. Of course, I would have to demonstrate that there are not effective alternative modes of solving the problem. But once again this is an empirical argument about the structural rules governing a particular hisorical system. If I am wrong on these rules, then there will be found other rules. But whatever the rules, the contradiction between middle-run solutions for conjunctural, cyclical problems (disequilibria if you wish) and long-run possibilities of using these solutions (the approach to the asymptote) will remain.

Hence every historical system must therefore remain historical. If it has a beginning, it will have an end. The end can take many forms. I think, however, it is most useful to think of this end not as some sharp line but as a band of time, a "transition" during which the oscillations around whatever line one measures become greater and more erratic. What I think this means, not in the language of the physical sciences but in that of traditional philosophy, is that the range of choice of social actors, the degree to which free will prevails over necessity, expands. Basically what I am arguing is that within a functioning historical system, there is no genuine free will. The structures constrain choice and even create choice. Both the oppression by the strong of the weak and the resistance of the weak to the strong, for example, are structured, predictable, measurable phenomena. However, when the system enters that band of time marking its period of demise or rupture (which by definition only happens once and only at its end), everything (or almost everything) is up for grabs. The outcome is indeterminate. I suppose that at some higher level of abstraction we might be able to explain these outcomes, but at the level at which life is really lived we cannot. That is the meaning of the old adage that "history reserves its surprises."[3]

[3] In the language of the physical sciences, the approach to the asymptote corresponds to the evolution of a system towards a stationary state "characterized by the minimum entropy production compatible with the constraints imposed upon the system." Prigogine and Stengers (1984: 138) continue: "The stationary state toward which the system evolves is then necessarily a nonequilibrium state at which dissipative processes with non-vanishing rates occur." The existence of dissipative processes with non-vanishing rates seems to me the condition within which what philosophers have called "free will" tends to prevail, or at least to have wider scope. The outcome is then "indeterminate."

I believe we have entered into such a band of transition now. I believe the oscillations – both political and intellectual – are becoming greater and more erratic. I believe the outcome is de facto indeterminate. I belive equally that our real range of choice has thereby increased enormously, and that our political choices and our intellectual choices thereby become profoundly choices of morality in ways that were not true a century ago. In such moments, therefore, the working distinction between political, intellectual, and moral choices becomes narrower (albeit I don't think it ever disappears) and each choice thereby becomes more difficult, not easier. I have no doubt this is true for the physical and the biological sciences. It is truest of all when we come to the study of the most complex systems of all, historical social systems.

18

Call for a Debate about the Paradigm

"World-systems analysis" is not a theory about the social world, or about part of it. It is a protest against the ways in which social scientific inquiry was structured for all of us at its inception in the middle of the nineteenth century. This mode of inquiry has come to be a set of often-unquestioned a priori assumptions. World-systems analysis maintains that this mode of social scientific inquiry, practiced worldwide, has had the effect of closing off rather than opening up many of the most important or the most interesting questions. In wearing the blinkers which the nineteenth century constructed, we are unable to perform the social task we wish to perform and that the rest of the world wishes us to perform, which is to present rationally the real historical alternatives that lie before us. World-systems analysis was born as moral, and in its broadest sense, political, protest. However, it is on the basis of scientific claims, that is, on the basis of claims related to the possibilities of systematic knowledge about social reality, that world-systems analyses challenges the prevailing mode of inquiry.

This is a debate, then, about fundamentals, and such debates are always difficult. First of all, most participants have deep commitments about fundamentals. Second, it is seldom the case that any clear, or at least any simple, empirical test can resolve or even clarify the issues. The empirical debate has to be addressed at a very complex and holistic level. Does the sum of derived theorizing starting from one or another set of premises encompass known descriptions of reality in a more "satisfactory" manner? This involves us in all sorts of secondary dilemmas. Our known "descriptions" of reality are to some extent a function of our premises; future "descriptions" may of course transform our sense of reality. Does the "theorizing" said today to encompass reality really encompass it? And last but not least, what does it mean to encompass reality "in a satisfactory manner"? Is this latter criterion anything more than an aesthetic adjunct?

Not only are debates about fundamentals frustrating for all these reasons, but each side has a built-in handicap. The defenders of existing views must "explain away" the anomalies, hence our present challenge. But the challengers must offer convincing "data" in a situation where, compared to the 150 years or so of traditional social scientific inquiry, they have had far less time to accumulate appropriately relevant "data." In a subject matter inherently recalcitrant to experimental manipulation, "data" cannot be accumulated rapidly. So a dispute about fundamentals may be thought of as analogous to a heavyweight championship bout, but without a referee and between two somewhat dyspeptic boxers, each with his left hand tied behind his back. It may be fun to watch, but is it boxing? Is it science?

And who will decide? In some sense, the spectators will decide – and probably not by watching the boxers, but by fighting it out themselves. So why bother? Because the boxers are part of the spectators, who are of course all boxers.

Lest we get lost in analogies, let me return to the discussion of fundamentals. I propose to take seven common assumptions of social scientific inquiry and indicate what it is that makes me feel uncomfortable about them. I shall then explore whether alternative (or even opposing) assumptions are not as plausible or more plausible and indicate the direction in which these alternative assumptions would lead us.

I

The social sciences are constituted of a number of "disciplines" which are intellectually coherent groupings of subject matter distinct from each other.

These disciplines are most frequently listed as anthropology, economics, political science and sociology. There are, to be sure, potential additions to this list, such as geography. Whether history is or is not social science is a matter of some controversy, and we shall return to this later (see section II). There is a similar debate about psychology, or at least about social psychology.

It has been a growing fashion, since at least 1945, to deplore the unnecessary barriers between the "disciplines" and to endorse the merits of "interdisciplinary" research and/or teaching. This has been argued on two counts. One is the assertion that the analysis of some "problem areas" can benefit from an approach combining the perspectives of many disciplines. It is said, for example, that if we wish to study "labor," pooling the knowledge offered by the disciplines of economics, political science, and sociology might be of great advantage. The logic of such an approach leads to multi-disciplinary teams, or to a single scholar "learning several disciplines," at least insofar as they relate to "labor."

The second presumed basis for "interdisciplinary" research is slightly different. As we pursue our collective inquiry it becomes clear, it is argued, that some of our subject matter is "at the borderline" of two or more disciplines. "Linguistics," for example, may be located at such a "border." The logic of such an approach may lead eventually to the development of a new "autonomous discipline," which in many ways is what has been happening to the study of linguistics during the last 30 years.

We know that there are multiple disciplines, since there are multiple academic departments in universities around the world, graduate degrees in these disciplines and national and international associations of scholars of these disciplines. That is, we know *politically* that different disciplines exist. They have organizations with boundaries, structures and personnel to defend their collective interests and ensure their collective reproduction. But this tells us nothing about the validity of the *intellectual* claims to separateness, claims which presumably justify the organizational networks.

The lauding of the merits of interdisciplinary work in the social sciences has so far not significantly undermined the strengths of the organizational apparatuses that shield the separate disciplines. Indeed, the contrary may be true: what has enhanced the claim of each discipline to represent a separately coherent level of analysis linked to appropriate methodologies is the constant assertion by practitioners of the various disciplines that each has something to learn from the other which it could not know by pursuing its own level of analysis with its specific methodologies, and that this "other" knowledge is pertinent and significant to the resolution of the intellectual problems on which each is working. Interdisciplinary work is in no sense an intellectual critique per se of the existing compartmentalization of social science, and lacks in any case the political clout to affect the existing institutional structures.

But are the various social scientific disciplines really "disciplines?" For a word so widely used, what constitutes a "discipline" is seldom discussed. There is no entry for this term in the *International Encyclopaedia of the Social Sciences* nor in the *Encyclopaedia of Philosophy* nor in the *Encyclopaedia Britannica*. We do better by going to the *Oxford English Dictionary*, which tells us that:

> Etymologically, *discipline*, as pertaining to the disciple or scholar, is antithetical to *doctrine*, the property of the doctor or teacher; hence, in the history of the words, *doctrine* is more concerned with abstract theory, and *discipline* with practice or exercise.

But having reminded us of the term's origins, the *OED* does no better for us in the actual definition than describing it as "a branch of instruction or education; a department of learning or knowledge; a science or art in its educational aspect." The emphasis here seems to be on the reproduction of knowledge (or at least its dissemination) and not on its production. But surely the concept, "discipline," cannot be unrelated to the process of producing knowledge?

The history of the social sciences is quite clear, at least in broad brush strokes. Once, there were no social sciences, or only "predecessors." Then slowly but steadily there emerged over the course of the nineteenth century a set of names, and then of departments, degrees, and associations, that by 1945 (although sometimes earlier) had crystallized into the categories we use today. There were other "names" which were discarded and which presumably involved different "groupings" of "subject matter." What is, or was, encompassed by such terms as "moral economy" or *Staatswissenschaft* is not entirely clear. This is not because their advocates were insufficiently clear thinking but because a "discipline" in some real sense defines itself over a long run in its practice. An interrupted practice means an unfulfilled discipline. For example, the famous quadripartite subdivision of anthropology (physical anthropology, social or cultural anthropology, archaeology, and linguistics) was (and to some extent still is) a "practice" rather than a "doctrine." It then became a doctrine, taught and justified by doctors or teachers. But did the whole add up to a coherent, defensible level of analysis or mode of analysis, or just to segregated subject matter?

We know where all these divisions of subject matter came from. They derive intellectually from the dominant liberal ideology of the nineteenth century which argued that state and market, politics and economics, were analytically separate (and largely self-contained) domains, each with their particular rules ("logics"). Society was adjured to keep them separate, and scholars studied them separately. Since there seemed to be many realities that apparently were neither in the domain of the market nor in that of the state, these realities were placed in a residual grab-bag which took on as compensation the grand name of sociology. There was a sense in which sociology was thought to explain the seemingly "irrational" phenomena that economics and political science were unable to account for. Finally, since there were people beyond the realm of the civilized world – remote, and with whom it was difficult to communicate – the study of such peoples encompassed special rules and special training, which took on the somewhat polemical name of anthropology.

We know the historical origins of the fields. We know their intellectual itineraries, which have been complex and variegated, especially since 1945. And we know why they have run into "boundary" difficulties. As the real world evolved, the contact line between "primitive" and "civilized," "political" and "economic," blurred. Scholarly poaching became commonplace. The poachers kept moving the fences, without, however, breaking them down.

The question before us today is whether there are any criteria which can be used to assert in a relatively clear and defensible way boundaries between the four presumed disciplines of anthropology, economics, political science, and sociology. World-systems analysis responds with an unequivocal "no" to this question. All the presumed criteria – level of analysis, subject matter, methods, theoretical assumptions – either are no longer true in practice or, if sustained, are barriers to further knowledge rather than stimuli to its creation.

Or, put another way, the differences between permissible topics, methods, theories or theorizing *within* any of the so-called "disciplines" are far greater than the differences *among* them. This means in practice that the overlap is substantial and, in terms of the historical evolution of all these fields, is increasing all the time. The time has come to cut through this intellectual morass by saying that these four disciplines are but a single one. This is not to say that all social scientists should be doing identical work. There is every need for, and likelihood of, specialization in "fields of inquiry." But let us remember the one significant organizational example we have.

Somewhere in the period 1945–55, two hitherto organizationally separate "disciplines," botany and zoology, merged into a single discipline called biology. Since that time, biology has been a flourishing discipline and has generated many sub-fields, but none of them, as far as I know, bears the name or has the contours of botany or zoology.

The argument of world-systems analysis is straightforward. The three presumed arenas of collective human action – the economic, the political, and the social or socio-cultural – are not autonomous arenas of social action. They do not have separate "logics." More importantly, the intermeshing of constraints, options, decisions, norms, and "rationalities" is such that no useful research model can isolate "factors" according to the categories of economic, political, and social, and treat only one kind of variable, implicitly holding the others constant. We are arguing that there is a single "set of rules" or a single "set of constraints" within which these various structures operate.

The case of the virtually total overlap of the presumed domains of sociology and anthropology is even stronger. By what stretch of the imagination can one assert that Elliot Liebow's *Tally's Corner* and William F. Whyte's *Street-Corner Society* – both "classic" works, one written by an "anthropologist" and the other by a "sociologist" – are works in two different "disciplines?" It would not be hard, as every reader knows, to assemble a long list of such examples.

II

History is the study of, the explanation of, the particular as it really happened in the past. Social science is the statement of the universal set of rules by which human/social behavior is explained.

This is the famous distinction between idiographic and nomothetic modes of analysis, which are considered to be antithetical. The "hard" version of this antithesis is to argue that only one of the modes (which one varies according to one's views) is legitimate or interesting or even "possible." This "hard" version is what the *Methodenstreit* was about. The "soft" version sees these two modes as two ways of cutting into social reality. Though undertaken separately, differently, and for dissimilar (even opposing) purposes, it would be fruitful for the world of scholarship to combine the two modes. This "soft" view is comparable to arguing the merits of "interdisciplinary" work in the social sciences. By asserting the merits of combining two approaches, the intellectual legitimacy of viewing them as two separate modes is reinforced.

The strongest arguments of the idiographic and nomothetic schools both seem plausible. The argument of the idiographic school is the ancient doctrine that "all is flux." If everything is always changing, then any generalization purporting to apply to two or more presumably comparable phenomena is never true. All that one can do is to understand empathetically a sequence of events. Conversely, the argument of the nomothetic school is that it is manifest that the real world (including the social world) is not a set of random happenings. If so, there must be rules that describe "regularities," in which case there is a domain for scientific activity.

The strongest critiques of each side about the other are also plausible. The nomothetic critique of the idiographic view is that any recounting of "past happenings" is by definition a selection from reality (as it really happened) and therefore implies criteria of selection and categories of description. These criteria and categories are based on unavowed but nonetheless real generalizations that are akin to scientific laws. The critique of the nomothetic view is that it neglects those transformational phenomena (due in part to the reflexiveness of social reality) which makes it impossible to "repeat" structural arrangements.

There are various ways of dealing with these mutual criticisms. One way is the path of "combining" history and the social sciences. The historian is said to serve the social scientist by providing the latter with wider, deeper sets of data from which to induce his law-like generalizations. The social scientist is said to serve the historian by offering him the results of research, reasonably demonstrated generalizations that offer insight into the explication of a particular sequence of events.

The problem with this neat division of intellectual labor is that it presumes the possibility of isolating "sequences" subject to "historical" analysis and small "universes" subject to "social scientific" analysis. In practice, however, one person's sequence is another's universe, and the neutral observer is in some quandary as to how to distinguish between the two on purely logical as opposed to, say, stylistic or presentational grounds.

The problem, however, is deeper than that. Is there a meaningful difference between sequence and universe, between history and social science? Are they two activities or one? Synchrony is akin to a geometric dimension. One can describe it logically, but it can be drawn only falsely on paper. In geometry, a point, a line, or a plane can be drawn only in three (or four) dimensions. So is it in "social science." Synchrony is a conceptual limit, not a socially usable category. All description has time, and the only question is how wide a band is immediately relevant. Similarly, unique sequence is only describable in non-unique categories. All conceptual language presumes comparisons among universes. Just as we cannot literally "draw" a point, so we cannot literally "describe" a unique "event." The drawing, the description, has thickness or complex generalization.

Since this is an inextricable logical dilemma, the solution must be sought on heuristic grounds. World-systems analysis offers the heuristic value of the *via media* between transhistorical generalizations and particularistic narrations. It argues that, as our format tends toward either extreme, it tends toward an exposition of minimal interest and minimal utility. It argues that the optimal method is to pursue analysis within systemic frameworks, long enough in time and large enough in space to contain governing "logics" which "determine" the largest part of sequential reality, while simultaneously recognizing and taking into account that these systemic frameworks have beginnings and ends and are therefore not to be conceived of as "eternal" phenomena. This implies, then, that at every instant we look both for the framework (the "cyclical rhythms" of the system), which we describe conceptually, and for the patterns of internal transformation (the "secular trends" of the system) that will eventually bring about the demise of the system, which we describe sequentially. This implies that the task is singular. There is neither historian nor social scientist, but only a historical social scientist who analyzes the general laws of particular systems and the particular sequences through which these systems have gone (the grammatical tense here deliberately not being the so-called ethnographic present). We are then faced with the issue of determining the "unit of analysis" within which we must work, which brings us to our third premise.

III

Human beings are organized in entities we may call societies, which constitute the fundamental social frameworks within which human life is lived.

No concept is more pervasive in modern social science than society, and no concept is used more automatically and unreflectively than society, despite the countless pages devoted to its definition. The textbook definitions revolve around the question: "what is a society?" whereas the arguments we have just made about the unity of historical social science lead us to ask a different question: "when and where is a society?"

"Societies" are concrete. Furthermore, society is a term which we might do well to discard because of its conceptual history and hence its virtually ineradicable and profoundly misleading connotations. Society is a term whose current usage in history and the social sciences is coeval with the institutional emergence of modern social science in the nineteenth century. Society is one half of an antithetic tandem in which the other is the state. The French Revolution was a cultural watershed in the ideological history of the modern world-system in that it led to the widespread acceptance of the idea that social change rather than social stasis is normal, both in the normative and in the statistical sense of the word. It thereby posed the intellectual problem of how to regulate, speed up, slow down, or otherwise affect this normal process of change and evolution.

The emergence of social science as an institutionalized social activity was one of the major systemic responses to this intellectual problem. Social science has come to represent the rationalist ideology that if one understands the process (whether idiographically or, more commonly, nomothetically) one can affect it in some morally positive manner. (Even "conservatives," dedicated to containing change, could broadly assent to this approach.)

The political implications of such an enterprise escaped (and escapes) no one. This is of course why social science has remained to this day "controversial." But it is also why in the nineteenth century the concept "society" was opposed to that of "state." The multiple sovereign states that had been and were being constituted were the obvious focuses of political activity. They seemed the locus of effective social control, and therefore the arena in which social change could be affected and effected. The standard nineteenth-century approach to the intellectual-political issue was concerned with the question of how to "reconcile" society and state. In this formulation, the state could be observed and analyzed directly. It operated through formal institutions by way of known (constitutional) rules. The "society" was taken to mean that tissue of manners and customs that held a group of people together without, despite, or against formal rules. In some sense "society" represented something more enduring and "deeper" than the state, less manipulable and certainly more elusive.

There has ever since been enormous debate about how society and state relate to each other, which one was or should be subordinate to the other, and which incarnated the higher moral values. In the process we have become accustomed to thinking that the boundaries of a society and of a state are synonymous, or if not should (and eventually would) be made so. Thus, without explicitly asserting this theoretically, historians and social scientists have come to see current sovereign states (projected hypothetically backward in time) as the basic social entities within which social life is conducted. There was some sporadic resistance to this view on the part of anthropologists, but they resisted in the name of a putative earlier political-cultural entity whose importance remained primary, many of them asserted, for large segments of the world's population.

Thus, by the back door, and unanalyzed, a whole historiography and a whole theory of the modern world crept in as the substratum of both history and social science. We live in states. There is a society underlying each state. States have histories and therefore traditions. Above all, since change is normal, it is states that normally change or develop. They change their mode of production; they urbanize; they have social problems; they prosper or decline. They have the boundaries, inside of which factors are "internal" and outside of which they are "external." They are "logically" independent entities such that, for statistical purposes, they can be "compared."

This image of social reality was not a fantasy, and so it was possible for both idiographic and nomothetic theorists to proceed with reasonable aplomb using these assumptions about society and state, and to come up with some plausible findings. The only problem was that, as time went on, more and more "anomalies" seemed to be unexplained within this framework, and more and more lacunae (of uninvestigated zones of human activity) seemed to emerge.

World-systems analysis makes the unit of analysis a subject of debate. Where and when do the entities within which social life occurs exist? It substitutes for the term "society" the term "historical system." Of course, this is a mere semantic substitution. But it rids us of the central connotation that "society" has acquired, its link to "state," and therefore of the presupposition about the "where" and "when." Furthermore, "historical system" as a term underlines the unity of historical social science. The entity is simultaneously systemic and historical.

Having opened up the question of the unit of analysis, there is no simple answer. I myself have put forth the tentative hypothesis that there have been three known forms or varieties of historical systems, which I have called mini-systems, world-empires, and world-economies. I have also suggested that it is not unthinkable that we could identify other forms or varieties.

I have argued two things about the varieties of historical systems: one concerns the link of "logic" and form; the other concerns the history of the coexistence of forms. In terms of form, I have taken as the defining boundaries of a historical system those within which the system and the people within it are regularly reproduced by means of some kind of ongoing division of labor. I argue that empirically there have been three such modes. The "mini-systems," so-called because they are small in space and probably relatively brief in time (a life span of about six generations), are highly homogeneous in terms of cultural and governing structures. The basic logic is one of "reciprocity" in exchanges. The "world-empires" are vast political structures (at least at the apex of the process of expansion and contraction which seems to be their fate) and encompass a wide variety of "cultural" patterns. The basic logic of the system is the extraction of tribute from otherwise locally self-administered direct producers (mostly rural) that is passed upward to the centre and redistributed to a thin but crucial network of officials. The "world-economies" are vast uneven chains of integrated production structures dissected by multiple political structures. The basic logic is that the accumulated surplus is distributed unequally in favor of those able to achieve various kinds of temporary monopolies in the market networks. This is a "capitalist" logic.

The history of the coexistence of forms can be construed as follows. In the preagricultural era, there were a multiplicity of mini-systems whose constant deaths may have been largely a function of ecological mishaps plus the splitting of groups grown too large. Our knowledge is very limited. There was no writing and we are confined to archaeological reconstructions. In the period between, say, 8,000 BC and AD 1500, there coexisted on the earth at any one time multiple historical systems of all three varieties. The world-empire was the "strong" form of that era, since whenever one expanded it destroyed and/or absorbed both mini-systems and

world-economies and whenever one contracted it opened up space
for the re-creation of mini-systems and world-economies. Most of
what we call the "history" of this period is the history of such
world-empires, which is understandable, since they bred the cultural scribes to record what was going on. World-economies were a
"weak" form, individual ones never surviving long. This is because
they either disintegrated or were absorbed by or transformed into a
world-empire (by the internal expansion of a single political unit).

Around 1500, one such world-economy managed to escape this
fate. For reasons that need to be explained, the "modern world-
system" was born out of the consolidation of a world-economy.
Hence it had time to achieve its full development as a capitalist
system. By *its* inner logic, this capitalist world-economy then
expanded to cover the entire globe, absorbing in the process all
existing mini-systems and world-empires. Hence by the late
nineteenth century, for the first time ever, there existed only one
historical system on the globe. We are still in that situation today.

I have sketched my hypotheses about the forms and the history
of the coexistence of historical systems. They do not constitute
world-systems analysis. They are a set of hypotheses within world-
systems analysis, open to debate, refinement, rejection. The crucial
issue is that defining and explicating the units of analysis – the
historical systems – becomes a central object of the scientific enterprise.

Within the discussion I have just related there lies hidden a
further debate about the modern world and its defining characteristics. This is a debate in which the two main versions of nineteenth-
century thought – classical liberalism and classical Marxism – share
certain crucial premises about the nature of capitalism.

IV

Capitalism is a system based on competition between free producers
using free labor with free commodities, "free" meaning its availability for sale and purchase on a market.

Constraints on such freedoms, wherever they exist, are leftovers
from an incomplete evolutionary process and mean, to the extent
that they exist, that a zone or an enterprise is "less capitalist" than
if there were no such constraints. This is essentially the view of

Adam Smith. Smith thought of the capitalist system as the only system consonant with "human nature" and saw alternative systems as the imposition of unnatural and undesirable constraints on social existence. But this was also essentially the view of Karl Marx. In characterizing the system, Marx placed particular emphasis on the importance of free labor. He did not regard the capitalist system as eternally natural, and he did not consider it desirable. But he did regard it as a normal stage of humanity's historical development.

Most liberals and Marxists of the last 150 years have regarded this picture of "competitive capitalism" as an accurate description of the capitalist norm, and have therefore discussed all historical situations that involved non-free labor/producers/commodities as deviations from this norm and thus as phenomena to be explained. The norm has largely reflected an idealized portrait of what was thought to be the quintessential exemplar of the norm – England after the "industrial revolution," where proletarian workers (essentially landless, toolless urban workers) labored in factories owned by bourgeois entrepreneurs (essentially private owners of the capital stock of these factories). The owner purchased the labor-power of (paid wages to) the workers – primarily adult males – who had no real alternative, in terms of survival, than to seek wage-work. No one has ever pretended that all work situations were of this model. But both liberals and Marxists have tended to regard any situation that varied from this model as less capitalist to the extent that it varied.

If each work situation could be classified on a degree-of-capitalism scale, as it were, then each state, as the locus of such work situations, can be designated as falling somewhere on that scale. The economic structure of a state, then, can be seen as "more" or "less" capitalist, and the state structure itself can be viewed as reasonably congruent with the degree of capitalism in the economy, or as inconsistent with it – in which case we might expect it somehow to change over time in the direction of greater congruence.

What is to be made of work situations that are less than fully capitalist under this definition? They can be seen as reflecting a not-yet-capitalist situation in a state that will eventually see capitalist structures become dominant. Or they can be seen as anomalous continuances from the past in a state where capitalist structures are dominant.

How the "dominance" of a particular way of structuring the work units within a spatial entity (the state) can be determined has never been entirely clear. In a famous US Supreme Court decision, Justice William Brennan wrote of the definition of pornography: "I know it when I see it." In a sense, both liberals and Marxists have defined dominance of capitalism in a similar fashion: they knew it when they saw it. Obviously, there is implicitly a quantitative criterion in this approach. But insofar as there is such a counting of heads, it is crucial to know what heads are being counted. And thereby hangs a tale.

A distinction was made between productive and unproductive labor. Although the exact definitions of the Physiocrats, Saint-Simon and Marx were quite different, they all wished to define certain kinds of "economic activity" as non-work, that is, as non-productive. This has created an enormous and very useful loophole in the definition of capitalism. If among the various kinds of activity eliminated as nonproductive fall a significant number which do not meet the model of a capitalist work situation – the most obvious but certainly not the only example, is housework – then it becomes far easier to argue that the "majority" of work situations in some countries are of the kinds described in the model, and thus we really do have some "capitalist" countries in terms of the definition. All this manipulation is scarcely necessary were the deduced "norm" in fact the statistical norm. But it was not, and is not. The situation of free laborers working for wages in the enterprises of free producers is a minority situation in the modern world. This is certainly true if our unit of analysis is the world-economy. It is probably true, or largely true, even if we undertake the analysis within the framework of single highly industrialized states in the twentieth century.

When a deduced "norm" turns out not to be the statistical norm, that is, when the situation abounds with exceptions (anomalies, residues), then we ought to wonder whether the definition of the norm serves any useful function. World-systems analysis argues that the capitalist world-economy is a particular historical system. Therefore if we want to ascertain the norms, that is, the mode of functioning of this concrete system, the optimal way is to look at the historical evolution of this system. If we find, as we do, that the system seems to contain wide areas of wage and non-wage labor, wide areas of commodified and non-commodified goods and wide areas of alienable and non-alienable forms of property and capital, then we should at the very least wonder whether this "combination" or mixture of the so-called free and the non-free is not itself the defining feature of capitalism as a historical system.

Once the question is opened up, there are no simple answers. We discover that the proportions of the mixes are uneven, spatially and temporally. We may then search for structures that maintain the stability of any particular mix of mixes (the cyclical trends again) as well as for underlying pressures that may be transforming, over time, the mix of mixes (the secular trends). The anomalies now become not exceptions to be explained away but patterns to be analyzed, so inverting the psychology of the scientific effort. We must conclude that the definition of capitalism that dominated the nineteenth-century thought of both liberals and Marxists accounts for the central historiographical insight that has been bequeathed to us.

V

The end of the eighteenth and the beginning of the nineteenth century represent a crucial turning point in the history of the world, in that the capitalists finally achieved state-societal power in the key states.

The two great "events" that occurred in this period, the industrial revolution in England and the French Revolution, were, it is argued, crucial in the development of social scientific theory. A simple bibliographical check will verify that a remarkably large proportion of world history has been devoted to these two "events." Furthermore, an even larger proportion has been devoted to analyzing other "situations" in terms of how they measure up to these two "events."

The link between the historical centrality accorded these two "events" and the prevailing definition of capitalism is not difficult to elucidate. We have already pointed out that the concept of degrees of capitalism leads necessarily to an implicit exercise in quantification so that we can ascertain when capitalism becomes "dominant." This theory assumed that a mismatch between "economic" dominance and state-societal power is possible, and that it can be overcome.

The industrial revolution and the French Revolution are of interest because they presumably represent the overcoming of a mismatch. The French Revolution highlights the political arena. According to the now strongly challenged but long predominant "social interpretation," the French Revolution was the moment when the bourgeoisie ousted the feudal aristocracy from state power and thereby transformed the precapitalist *ancien régime* into a capitalist state. The industrial revolution highlights the fruits of such a transformation. Once the capitalists achieve state power (or in Smithian terms reduce the interference of the state) then it is possible to expand significantly the triumphal possibilities of a capitalist system.

Given these assumptions, it is possible to treat both these phenomena as "events" and to concentrate on the details of what happened and why they happened in that particular way. Books on the industrial revolution typically debate which factor (or factors) was more important to its occurrence, what its precise dating was and which of the various features encompassed by the term was the most consequential for future transformations. Books on the French Revolution typically debate when it started and ended, what factor or factors triggered it, which groups were involved in key processes and how and when there were alterations in the cast of characters, and what legacy the revolution left.

Of course such a close and ultimately idiographic scrutiny of these "events" inevitably breeds skepticism. Increasingly there are voices doubting how revolutionary the revolutions were. Nonetheless, virtually all these analyses (of both believers and skeptics) presume the analytical frame of reference that led to these two "events" being singled out in the first place: the assumption that capitalism (or its surrogate, individual freedom) had in some sense to "triumph" at some point within particular states.

Furthermore, lest one think that history is central only to historians, we should notice how it immediately became central to the analytical exercises of social scientists. The idea of *the* industrial revolution" has been transformed into the process of *an* industrial revolution" or of "industrialization" and bred a whole family of sub-categories and therefore of sub-issues: the idea of a "take-off," the notions of both "pre-industrial" and "post-industrial" societies, and so on. The idea of the "bourgeois revolution" has become the analysis of when and how a "bourgeois revolution" (or the middle classes in power) could or would occur. I do not suggest that these debates are not about the real world. Clearly, twentieth-century Brazil can be discussed in terms of industrialization, or of the role of the national bourgeoisie, or of the relation of the middle classes to the military. But once again, key assumptions are being made which should be examined.

What world-systems analysis calls for is an evaluation of the centrality of these purportedly key "events" in terms of the *longue durée* of the historical system within which they occurred. If the unit of analysis of the modern world-system is the capitalist world-economy (and this remains an "if"), then we will need to ask whether the received categorical distinctions – agriculture and industry, landowner and industrialist – do or do not represent a leit-motif around which the historical development centered. We can only be in a post-industrial phase if there was an industrial phase. There can only be disjunctures of the tenants of state power and economic power if we are dealing with analytically separable groups. All these categories are now so deep in our subconscious that we can scarcely talk about the world without using them. World-systems analysis argues that the categories that inform our history were historically formed (and for the most part only a century or so ago). It is time that they were reopened for examination.

Of course, this prevailing history is itself informed by the dominant metaphysics of the modern world. The triumph of this modern metaphysics required a long struggle. But triumph it did, in the Enlightenment, which brings us to the sixth premise.

VI

Human history is progressive, and inevitably so.

To be sure, the idea of progress has had its detractors, but they have for two centuries been in a distinct minority. I do *not* count in this minority all those who have criticized the *naive* view of progress and have concentrated their efforts on explaining the so-called irrational. These people have been making rational the irrational. Nor do I include the growing number of disabused believers who embrace a sort of hopelessness or despair about progress. They are rather like lapsed Catholics in a Graham Greene novel, always searching for the faith they once had.

The true conservatives, the ones who do not believe that systematic change or improvement in the world is a desirable or fruitful collective activity, are actually quite rare in the modern world. But notice once again how the dominant assumptions have circumscribed the skeptics and the opponents. To the notion that progress is inevitable, the only response seems to have been despair: despair because the thesis is incorrect, or despair because it is correct.

World-systems analysis wants to remove the idea of progress from the status of a trajectory and open it up as an analytical variable. There may be better and there may be worse historical systems (and we can debate the criteria by which to judge). It is not at all certain that there has been a linear trend – upward, downward, or straightforward. Perhaps the trend line is uneven, or perhaps indeterminate. Were this conceded to be possible, a whole new arena of intellectual analysis is immediately opened up. If the world has had multiple instances of, and types of, historical systems, and if all historical systems have beginnings and ends, then we will want to know something about the process by which there occurs a succession (in time-space) of historical systems.

This has typically been discussed as the problem of "transitions," but transitions have been analyzed within the framework of linear transformations. We detail the process of the transformation toward some inevitable endpoint which we presume to be, to have been, the only real historical alternative. But suppose the construction of new historical systems is a stochastic process. Then we have a totally new arena of intellectual activity before us.

The debate of "free will" versus "determinism" is a hoary one. But it has been traditionally pursued as an either/or proposition. what the reopening of the issue of transitions does – transitions as really occurring, transitions as moving toward uncertain outcomes – is to suggest a different formulation of this debate. Perhaps it is the case that what we call "determinism" is largely the process internal to historical systems in which the "logic" of the system is translated into a set of self-moving, self-reinforcing institutional structures that "determine" the long-term trajectory. But perhaps it is also the case that what we call "free will" occurs largely in the process of "transition" when, precisely because of the breakdown of these very structures, the real historical choices are wide and difficult to predict.

This would then turn our collective attention to the study of precisely how these stochastic processes work. Perhaps they will turn out not to be stochastic at all but have an inner hidden key, or perhaps the inner key is some process that keeps these processes stochastic (that is, not really subject to human manipulation). Or perhaps, least acceptable to the present inhabitants of the globe no doubt, God plays dice. We shall not know unless we look. We may of course not know even then. But how do we look? This brings us to the last and deepest of the assumptions, the assumptions concerning the nature of science.

VII

Science is the search for the rules which summarize most succinctly why everything is the way it is and how things happen.

Modern science is not a child of the nineteenth century. It goes back at least to the sixteenth, perhaps to the thirteenth, century. It has come down strongly on the determinist side of the equation, on the side of linearity and concision. Scientists have brought more and more domains of the universe under their aegis, the world of man being no doubt the last such domain. It was in the name of this tradition that nomothetic social science asserted itself.

The methodology that nomothetic social science adopted emulated the basic principles of its socially successful predecessor, the natural sciences: systematic and precise empirical inquiry, then induction leading to theories. The more elegant the theory, the more advanced the science. Practical applications would of course follow. Nomothetic social science has been haunted by its inadequacies – in a comparison with physics – but sustained by its certainty that science was cumulative and unilinear.

In our doubts concerning the previous assumptions there has been implicit – it should now be clear – another view of science. If we reject the utility of the nomothetic–idiographic distinction, then we are casting doubt on the usefulness of the Newtonian view of science. We do not do this, as the idiographers did, on the basis of the peculiarity of social inquiry (humans as reflexive actors). We doubt its utility for the natural sciences as well (and indeed there has emerged in the last two decades a thrust toward a nonlinear natural science, wherein stochastic processes are central).

Specifically, in terms of what we have been calling historical social science, we raise the question of whether the method of going from the concrete to the abstract, from the particular to the universal, should not be inverted. Perhaps historical social science must *start* with the abstract and move in the direction of the concrete, ending with a coherent interpretation of the processes of particular historical systems that accounts plausibly for how they followed a particular concrete historical path. The determinate is not the simple but the complex, indeed the hyper-complex. And of course no concrete situation is more complex than the long moments of transition when the simpler constraints collapse.

History and social science took their current dominant forms at the moment of fullest unchallenged triumph of the logic of our present historical system. They are children of that logic. We are now, however, living in the long moment of transition wherein the contradictions of that system have made it impossible to continue to adjust its machinery. We are living in a period of real historical choice. And this period is incomprehensible on the basis of the assumptions of that system.

World-systems analysis is a call for the construction of a historical social science that feels comfortable with the uncertainties of transition, that contributes to the transformation of the world by illuminating the choices without appealing to the crutch of a belief in the inevitable triumph of good. World-systems analysis is a call to open the shutters that prevent us from exploring many arenas of the real world. World-systems analysis is not a paradigm of historical social science. It is a call for a debate about the paradigm.

19

A Theory of Economic History in Place of Economic Theory?

> Economic history is a morality play on a vast canvas. No less than good and evil wrestled here throughout the ages. Good, though often thrown, came back for more.
>
> E. L. Jones, *Growth Recurring*

Economic historians, it is well known, are sometimes located organizationally within departments of economics, and sometimes within departments of history. It is also well known that some (today, perhaps even many) economics departments do not wish to house economic historians, and that some history departments feel the same way (although less frequently than is the case with economics departments). Occasionally, economic history is the name of an autonomous university department. And finally, there are people who engage in what most people think of as economic history who are found in departments with still other names (anthropology, geography, sociology). This last group is small, but perhaps growing in number.

All of this reflects the somewhat anomalous status of economic history within the university system we have today. It is a bit as through economic history were an unwanted stepchild, a Cinderella in rags. My impression is that many economic historians respond by being somewhat diffident about their subject, seeking to justify its merits in the eyes of somewhat dubious elders. They have been particularly concerned, as a group, to get recognition from economists. Economists seem serious and solid, and certainly think of themselves in this way.

Economists have tended, especially in the post-1945 period, to look down on economic history as empirical, descriptive, atheoretical, and somewhat irrelevant. There have been two main responses by economic historians to such barely disguised scorn. The nomothetic response has been self-flagellation: Economists are right. Too much of the work of economic historians has been atheoretical. We should mend our ways, engage in rigorous modeling and hypothesis testing (preferably using econometrics), showing that we too can contribute to the advancement of orthodox economic science. The idiographic response has been to point to the richness of detail and the complexity of explanation a more narrative approach has to offer, how much is not in the econometric models, how necessary is the analysis of texture, and to insist that a narrative emphasis represents a worthy enterprise.

I do not have the impression that mainstream economists have paid the least bit of attention to either of these responses. Not only the "old" economic historians but even the "new" economic historians have been widely ignored. No significant dent has been made on the protective armor of the members of what is largely an intellectually closed guild. Economists still act as though economic history was at best an eccentric folly and at worst a serious deviation of the intelligent use of scarce scholarly resources. Most of them wish they could divest the world of economic history. In a recent assessment of the "information needs" of social scientists in the United States, the report says of economists: "Most [economists] need data of a relatively recent vintage – no more than ten years old – and some require data that is virtually up to the minute" (Gould and Handler 1989: 7).

Of course, the emperor has no clothes! What of significance can we possibly know with data about only the last ten years of human existence? Precious little! Instead of defending ourselves against academic divestment by the economists, economic historians should lay claim to replacing economists completely. Away with economics! Away with the *ceteris paribus* clause! History *is* theory. Or rather the only economic theory that can possibly be valid is a theory of economic history.

Let us start with two obvious premises that pose the central methodological dilemmas of all science. Insofar as we analyze the real world, we are obliged to abstract this reality by utilizing conceptual language. A concept is by definition an assertion of permanence. If we use the concept "peasant" or "terms of trade" or "inflation" we are making the assertion that there is some set of differentia specifica which can be summarized by the term and therefore remain in a stable internal relationship. If each time we used the concept we meant something different, no communication would occur.

And yet, as we also know, everything always changes. A concept is always relational, which implies that it has no meaning except within its total context, and the total context is of course in eternal swift turmoil. In an era when even physicists have (re)discovered the centrality of the "arrow of time" to the analysis of physical phenomena (even such presumably unchanging phenomena as atoms), it ill behoves social scientists to neglect this reality. If some economists persist in such ostrich-like behavior, they simply mark themselves out by their antiscientific stance, spinning tales about fairyland.

The serious methodological problem is that it is very difficult, perhaps impossible, to assert simultaneously the continuity of structures and the permanence of structural change. And yet we have no choice. We will therefore not be able to advance our collective efforts very far if we do not make this dilemma our central problem, and seek to devise practices that minimize the damage and maximize the heuristic validity of our findings and therefore of our theorizing. I should like therefore to adumbrate six practices which seem to me the methodological basis of elaborating a theory of economic history.

1. SPECIFY AND JUSTIFY THE UNIT OF ANALYSIS

In most writing today, the unit of analysis is usually merely implicit. It is not specified, and virtually never justified. It thereby becomes a highly questionable a priori assumption. All human activity occurs within some contextual whole, which I prefer to call a "historical system." I give it this name to emphasize the dual reality of all such contextual wholes – they are systemic (that is, have continuing structures in analyzable relation one to the other) and they are historical (that is, they have natural lives, beginnings and ends).

At this point, I shall plead no particular criteria by which to define the appropriate unit of analysis, although I have strong views on the subject. But these criteria are a matter of legitimate debate, and it is no doubt intellectually healthy that there be continuing debate about them. The plea I make rather is that these premises by made explicit and openly defended.

Once the unit of analysis is identified, it must by definition have boundaries. Insofar as the endogenous-exogenous debate about causal factors has any relevance, it is only vis-à-vis the boundaries of the historical system in general, and not those of the particular object of enquiry of a specify study. The famous Dobb-Sweezy debate on the transition from feudalism to capitalism is deeply flawed because of lack of attention to, and therefore internally inconsistent positions on, the unit of analysis and its consequent boundaries.

In addition, as becomes immediately obvious, once we think about the boundaries of a historical system, the system's boundaries may and usually do change over time, and necessarily the denominator of any measurements one makes must vary according to the figures relevant to a given set of boundaries at a given historical moment. Easier said than done, to be sure, but essential if we are to have minimally valid conclusions.

2. DISTINGUISH BETWEEN CYCLES AND TRENDS

This seems obvious, but it is seldom explicitly done. One has of course to start with a Braudelian consciousness about the multiplicity of social times. If time is simply chronometry plus chronology, then all phenomena are linear. But if indeed we organize the world according to multiple social times, then it is possible to distinguish more complex patterns.

Once again, we return to our basic dilemma – how to relate unchanging concepts with eternally changing reality. In terms of social time, this is the distinction between cyclical rhythms (or *conjonctures*) and secular trends (phenomena caused by structures, and which ensure that structures cannot be immobile over the long run).

Economic historians tend to be more sensitive than most scholars to the phenomenon of the *conjoncture*. Of course, they constantly quibble about the empirical dating of any and all specific *conjonctures*. And they sometimes analyze the sources of cyclical shift too locally, missing the patterns of the larger whole (which brings us back to the issue of the unit of analysis). But at least they tend to recognize the reality of the *conjoncture* and its power as an analytic tool.

It is the secular trend which is more often missing from the analysis. It is not that secular trends are not discussed in broad brush strokes. Witness such standard themes concerning the modern world as the rise of the middle classes, urbanization, population growth, etc. What is needed, however, is less the broad brush strokes than some coherent explanations of the precise shape of the curves. And of course what we also need is the drawing of these curves within the appropriate boundaries, those of the unit of analysis as well as of the subunit under direct inspection, so as to understand the significance of the latter's curves.

Furthermore, and this is the crucial element, it is necessary to argue the specific relationship between a set of cyclical rhythms and the corresponding secular trends. Cyclical rhythms are in fact the only possible source of the secular trends. This is because a B-phase is never the mirror image of an A-phase and therefore, the *conjonctures* never return us to the point of origin. This is the explanation of how phenomena can be simultaneously repetitive and changing. Nonetheless, this is not a mere piety. We shall want to know exactly what it is in the operation of the cyclical rhythms that makes it inevitable that there be secular trends. We thereupon come to the issue of contradictions.

3. IDENTIFY AND SPECIFY THE CONTRADICTIONS INHERENT IN THE SPECIFIC STRUCTURES OF A SPECIFIC TYPE OF HISTORICAL SYSTEM

Contradictions, of course, are *not* mere conflicts. Conflicts to be sure are endemic in all historical systems and need to be described as part of any valid analysis. But contradictions are a separate phenomenon. Contradictions are the result of constraints imposed by systemic structures which make one set of behavior optimal for actors in the short run and a different, even opposite, set of behavior optimal for the same actors in the middle run. Obviously then, contradictions are unresolvable in principle. Or rather, to the degree that actors solve problems in the short run they create problems in the middle run. It is thus that they transform cyclical rhythms (the result of solutions to short-run problems) into secular trends (the middle-run consequence of these solutions).

It is for this reason that we must always avoid the so-called anthropological present in our writings. Economic historians tend in fact to be quite good about using the past tense in their empirical work, but occasionally slip into the present tense in their theorizing from economic history. But if the existence of contradictions is an epistemological premise, there can be no present tense in theorizing. Theories are abstractions from given empirical realities and must incorporate the "arrow of time" into their formulation.

4.   CAREFULLY DISTINGUISH BETWEEN A SHIFT IN THE *CONJONCTURE* AND A HISTORICAL TRANSITION

The word "crisis" is a nemesis since it is used indiscriminately to describe both phenomena. If there are cyclical rhythms, there must be peak points followed by downturns. This is of course not a structural "crisis" at all, although particular actors may perceive it as such for them. It is a normal shift in the direction of vectors and in the middle-run adjustment to short-run dilemmas.

Transitions are quite another matter. When short-run optimality creates middle-run problems that are solved by middle-run adjustments, the historical system is working normally. But middle-run adjustments add up over time to secular trends that create long-run problems. The key long-run problem created by the contradictions of a system occurs when the secular trend reaches the point that the middle-run adjustments to short-run problems are no longer efficacious even in the middle-run. At that point, we are into what might be called a systemic crisis wherein, in the language of the contemporary physical sciences, there occur severe oscillations and a bifurcation that is transformatory. That is, there must be a *structural* transition from the existing historical system to something else. This is of course a reasonably long process but an irreversible one. It is also one whose outcome is uncertain (or stochastic).

The great methodological error is to analyze such transitions as simply moments in a continuous historical process. They are not. They are moments of major historical choice, which brings us to the question of chronosophy.

5.   SPECIFY AND JUSTIFY THE CHRONOSOPHY THAT UNDERLIES THE THEORIZING

Chronosophy is a word invented by Krzystof Pomian (1977). It refers to the assumptions we make about the relationship between the past, present, and future. The work of all the historical social sciences for the past two centuries has been dominated overwhelmingly by the linear chronosophy incarnated in the theory of progress. The relationship of past, present, and future in this chronosophy is that of an ascending curve. In its strong version, and the strong version has been the most widespread, this upward ascent of humanity has been inevitable and irreversible.

Occasionally, in this period, this chronosophy has been challenged. But the challengers have tended to put forward a cyclical chronosophy, which has not been very persuasive. The protagonists of a chronosophy of an unchanging world, such as there are, have been totally exculded from the institutions of knowledge. Thus, the theory of progress has not met with a serious challenge, until recently. And even now, the challenge tends to take the form of doubting the reality of progress, usually without explicating the alternative possible view of the world. That is, the current challengers have too often merely derided the ideological bases of the theory of the theory of progress without performing the hard work of providing a new framework. It is not enough to proclaim that all is discourse, since even were this true we would want to know the relation between past, present, and future discourse.

May I suggest an alternative chronosophy – the theory of possible progress. If there exist historical systems, each with cyclical rhythms and secular trends, each with contradictions, each ultimately arriving at a bifurcation point that is intrinsically stochastic in nature, it means that there have been successive moments in historical time and space (a relatively large number of them) in which major historical choices have occurred.

To say a transition is stochastic is not to say that anything and everything is possible. The possible vectors are not infinite but are located within a range created by the sum of existing realities. Ergo the choices we have today are quite different from those available in say AD 1450 or 500 BC The arrow of time is irreversible and cumulative – but not inevitably progressive.

Progressive is of course a moral concept and is measured by reference to some set of assumptions about the good society. But of course these very assumptions are part of the *mentalité* of the historical system of which we are a part, and are themselves variable and varying. Still, we can provisionally agree on what we presumably consider progress and can assess historical transformation in the light of these criteria.

If the bifurcation permits radically different outcomes (albeit within certain parameters) it is because the existing structures have become so brittle that a small fluctuation can, at this moment of time, have major consequences as apposed to the probability of small consequences for even large fluctuations in ongoing systems, and hence the seeming tendency to equilibrium). If small fluctuations have large consequences, then it is clear that multiple actors *may* take advantage of this "free will" type of situation to promote particular projects. We have the equivalent of a fast-moving volley between top-rated tennis or ping pong players in which the analyst's ability to keep his eye on the ball simultaneously with calculating all other details is essential to predict or even to understand retroactively the outcome. Here is E. L. Jones's "morality play on a vast canvas." It is antiscientific to ignore it.

We come thereupon to the last of the methodological practices, the most difficult to follow.

6. THERE ARE NO DISTINCTIVELY ECONOMIC
   PHENOMENA, DISTINGUISHABLE FROM POLITICAL
   AND SOCIAL PHENOMENA: THE WHOLE IS A
   SEAMLESS SKEIN

We have been bequeathed a terrible legacy by nineteenth-century social science. It is the assertion that social reality occurs in three different and separate arenas: the political, the economic, and the socio-cultural. We have built our knowledge institutions around this distinction, and in our writings we speak of three sets of factors or variables. We tend to mean by economic phenomena those related to the fictional market, by political phenomena those related ultimately to state decision-making, and by socio-cultural phenomena those presumedly determined by our states of mind (usually thought to be more "subjective" as opposed to the more "objective" constraints of the market and the state). But this is nonsense in terms of how the world really works. No one subjectively has three segregated motivations – economic, political, and socio-cultural. And there are no real institutions that are in fact exclusively in one arena.

Take a typical institution about which economic historians regularly write: production systems in agriculture and industry. Why do we call such writing *economic* history? It is quite clear, if one but reads the writings of economic historians themselves, that these structures are not completely described in terms of how they relate to a "market." Production systems are organized as a set of social relations incarnating particular belief systems. They presume, and are constrained by, particular political processes. In practice, our analysis has to be "holistic" if it is to have even face value validity. So why do we avoid the issue theoretically?

The holy trinity of politics/economics/society-culture has no intellectual heuristic value today. It probably never did, but it certainly does no longer. Economic historians are recognizing this increasingly by becoming "social historians." But of course we must not throw the baby out with the bath water. Yes, let us study the dynamics of family history, but let us not forget price curves in the process. And why not plunge back into the main pool and also analyze specifically the politics of price curves, or of family history? In short, while economic historians are laying claim to replacing economics, they should insist that the adjective "economic" be dropped – not in order to forget economic factors but in order to insist on holistic analysis.

What we need is a fundamental reorganization of knowledge activity in the historical social sciences on a global scale. Economic historians have been the nearest in spirit in the past to the kind of historical social science we must create in the future – one in which we build our theory out of the study of reality, that is, out of history. The only reality is a constantly changing one. It is that historical reality which must be theorized.

20

World-Systems Analysis: The Second Phase

World-systems analysis has existed under that name, more or less, for about 15 years. Some of its arguments, of course, have longer histories, even very long histories. Yet, as a perspective, it emerged only in the 1970s. It presented itself as a critique of existing dominant views in the various social sciences, and primarily of developmentalism and modernization theory which seemed to dominate social science worldwide during the 1960s.

The worldwide revolution of 1968 did not spare the world of social science, and world-systems analysis shared in, was part of, a wider reaction to the ideologized positivism and false apoliticism that had been the counterpart within world social science of the US hegemonic world view. Although world-systems analysis was only one variant of this critique, it stood out in retrospect by the fact that it broke more deeply with nineteenth-century social science than did other critiques, albeit probably not deeply enough.

It is hard to know how to assess "what we have learned." What I shall do is spell out what I think are the major premises or arguments that I believe have been reasonably explicated. I choose carefully the verb "explicited." It does not mean these premises or arguments have been widely adopted or that they have not been contested, in detail at least, even among those who think they share in the world-systems perspective. What it means is that there has been enough elaboration of the arguments such that they are familiar beyond the bounds of the initiates (and thus, for example, they might appear in textbooks as reflecting a "viewpoint"), and such that these premises and arguments might be seen as part of the defining characteristics of a world-systems perspective.

I see three such defining characteristics. The first and most obvious is that the appropriate "unit of analysis" for the study of social or societal behavior is a "world-system." No doubt this assertion has led to enormous discussion around the so-called macro-micro problem, which in this case translates into how much of local and/or national behavior is explained/determined by structural evolution at the level of the world-system. I believe this is a totally false problem, but I shall not argue that here. I merely point our that, formally, the macro-micro issue is no different if one decides that the boundaries of a "society" are those of a "world-system" or that these boundaries correlate more or less with those of "nation-states." There still can be said to be the macro-micro issue. The real novelty, therefore, is that the world-systems perspective denies that the "nation-state" represents in any sense a relatively autonomous "society" that "develops" over time.

The second defining characteristic has been that of the *longue durée*. This of course put us in the *Annales* tradition, as well as in that of the burgeoning field of "historical sociology." But I believe the world-systems perspective was more specific than either, and spelled out some elements that are blurry in the other two traditions. Long duration is the temporal correlate of the spatial quality of "world-system." It reflects the insistence that "world-systems" are "historical systems," that is, that they have beginnings, lives, and ends. This stance makes clear that structures are not "immobile." It insists, in addition, that there are "transitions" from one historical system to its successor or successors. It is this pair, the space of a "world" and the time of a "long duration," that combine to form any particular historical world-system.

The third element of world-systems analysis has been a certain view of one particular world-system, the one in which we live, the capitalist world-economy. Let me list the various elements that have been explicated. Some of these were borrowed, directly or in modified form, from other earlier perspectives. Some others were relatively new. But it has been the combination of these arguments that has come to be associated with world-systems analysis. I merely list now the characteristics presumed to be the description of a capitalist world-economy:

1 the ceaseless accumulation of capital as its driving force;
2 an axial division of labor in which there is a core-periphery

tension, such that there is some form of unequal exchange (not necessarily as defined originally by Arghiri Emmanuel) that is spatial;

3 the structural existence of a semiperipheral zone;

4 the large and continuing role of non-wage labor alongside of wage labor;

5 the correspondence of the boundaries of the capitalist world-economy to that of an interstate system comprised of sovereign states;

6 the location of the origins of this capitalist world-economy earlier than in the nineteenth century, probably in the sixteenth century;

7 the view that this capitalist world-economy began in one part of the globe (largely Europe) and later expanded to the entire globe via a process of successive "incorporations;"

8 the existence in this world-system of hegemonic states, each of whose periods of full or uncontested hegemony has, however, been relatively brief;

9 the non-primordial character of states, ethnic groups, and households, all of which are constantly created and re-created;

10 the fundamental importance of racism and sexism as organizing principles of the system;

11 the emergence of antisystemic movements that simultaneously undermine and reinforce the system;

12 a pattern of both cyclical rhythms and secular trends that incarnates the inherent contradictions of the system and which accounts for the systemic crisis in which we are presently living.

To be sure, this list is merely a set of premises and arguments that have been articulated, and that have become relatively familiar to many. It is not a list of truths, much less a list of creeds to which we all pay allegiance. No doubt much empirical work needs to be done on each of these items, and there may be in the future much theoretical reformulation of them. But, as a relatively coherent and articulated view of historical capitalism, they exist.

I should like now to talk about the "second phase" – the issues that have been raised, but are not yet well articulated, and that should, in my view, preoccupy us in the next decade or two.

The first is the elaboration of world-systems other than that of the capitalist world-economy. This work has been begun by Chris Chase-Dunn and Janet Abu-Lughod, as well as by a number of archaeologists whose writings are largely unread by world-systems analysts doing work on the modern world-system. As we pursue this kind of work, three things will probably happen. (a) We shall reevaluate what is in fact particular to our modern world-system. (b) We shall reevaluate what we mean by a world-system, both in terms of time and space. (c) We shall begin to compare different kinds of world-systems systematically. Whether this will then lead us astray and back into a new nomothetic world-view ("the science of comparative world-systems") or a new idiographic world-view ("the description of the unique world-system that has been evolving for at least 10,000 years") remains to be seen.

The second field is the elaboration of how we define and measure polarization within the capitalist world-economy. In the postwar period, polarization had become a relatively unpopular concept. World-systems analysis revived it, but has never really elaborated it. How do we prove its existence? Indeed, how do we measure its existence? There is first of all the technical difficulty that no measurements are useful or relevant that are not world-system-wide, and that the boundaries of the system have been constantly changing over time. Secondly, polarization is not theoretically between states but between economic zones, and between classes and peoples. Finally, statistics have not been collected by state-machineries in a manner pertinent to such analysis. The problems of measurement are thus daunting.

Quite aside from the necessary invention of new data bases, on which little real progress has been made in the past 15 years, there is the question of how we conceptualize polarization. If we measure it in some kind of monetary income terms, we face relatively well-known and long-considered, but not well-resolved, issues as to how to translate into monetary terms income that is not monetized but is nonetheless real. This is, however, the least of our problems. The bigger issue falls under the label of quality of life. For example, since there are more people in the world today, there is obviously less space per person. Less actual space? Surely. Less usable space? Possibly. How much space do people at polarized ends of the income distribution use, or have at their disposition, and how would we know? And what about trees? Do the world's upper strata have more trees to look at and the world's lower strata fewer than 500 years ago? Then there is the issue of health. If we all live on the average x years longer, but some of us live those x years at a level of health that permits good functioning and others are vegetating, this is a further polarization. The questions here are simultaneously technical (how to measure) and substantive (what to measure). They are knotty. They are also intellectually crucial in the debate with the still very much alive developmentalist perspective. Until we tackle convincingly the question of polarization, we cannot expect to become truly influential.

Thirdly, we must begin to do research on the historical choices that are before us in the future. If we believe that all historical systems come to an end, the one in which we are living will also do so. And if we believe that the secular trends of the existing system have brought it into the zone of systemic crisis or "transition," then it is more than time that we begin to engage in utopistics – not utopianism, but utopistics. Utopistics is the science of utopian utopias, that is, the attempt to clarify the real historical alternatives that are before us when a historical system enters into its crisis phase, and to assess at that moment of extreme fluctuations the pluses and minuses of alternative strategies.

In the rejection of nineteenth-century social science, world-systems analysis necessarily rejects its reigning faith, the belief in inevitable progress. I believe that a viable alternative model of change is that of nonlinear processes which eventually reach bifurcation points, whereupon slight fluctuations have large consequences (as opposed to determinate equilibria in which large fluctuations have small consequences). This is the model Prigogine has suggested for all complex systems ("order through chaos") – and the most complex of all known systems is a historical social system. Even for such simple systems as physical systems, the key variable becomes time, reconceptualizing reality as involving stochastic and irreversible processes, within which deterministic, reversible processes constitute a limited, special case. *A fortiori* for complex historical systems.

The fact that the solution of a bifurcation is indeterminate does not mean that it is something beyond the reach of rational research. We can clarify the network of forces at work, elaborate possible vectors (and therefore loci of possible conscious interference), and thereby illuminate the real historical choices that are before us. This is not a matter of speculation but of serious research. It is work that we should be doing.

I have left for the last what I believe to be the key issue, and the hardest nut to crack. We have said from the outset that our perspective is unidisciplinary. But we have merely paid lip service to this view. There is hard work to do, at three levels: theoretical, methodological, and organizational.

Theoretically, the issue is simple. Everyone in the social sciences uses regularly the distinction of three arenas: the economic, the political, and the socio-cultural. No one believes us when we say there is but a single arena with a single logic. Do we believe it ourselves? Some of us, no doubt, but not even all of us. And all of us fall back on using the language of the three arenas in almost everything we write. It is time we seriously tackled the question.

The theoretical question is whether this trinity of arenas of social action – the economy, or market; the polity, or state; the society, or culture – is at all useful, or whether it is in fact pernicious. Can any of the three be conceived to have, even hypothetically, autonomous activity? All economic activity assumes socio-cultural rules and preferences, and works within political constraints. Furthermore, markets are socio-political creations. Is there, for example, a true economic price that can somehow be stripped of its political and social base? All political activity serves the end of ensuring or pursuing economic advantage or need as well as the reinforcement of socio-cultural objectives. Can there be a pursuit of power that is stripped of these considerations? And socio-cultural activity is itself made possible and explained by economic and political location, and serves ends that are ultimately defined in these terms. How can one imagine social (and/or cultural) activity stripped of these factors?

Nor is it simply a question that the three arenas are closely interlinked. It is that human activity within a given world-system moves indiscriminately and imperceptibly in and among all three arenas. Do they really then constitute separate arenas? It is sometimes suggested that, although they were not separate arenas before the advent of a capitalist world-system, they became so in this system. But the descriptive work of world-systems analysis up to now on how historical capitalism has actually operated leads one to be very skeptical that the separation of spheres has had any functional reality even in that system. If so, then we are pursuing false models and undermining our own argumentation by continuing to use such language. It is urgent that we begin to elaborate alternative theoretical models.

This will then force us to face up to and spell out the methodological implications of world-systems analysis: that neither nomothetic nor idiographic modes of knowing in fact exist and that the only epistemology that is plausible lies in the swampy middle ground of the concept of a historical system. That is to say, our knowledge is about structures that reproduce themselves while they constantly change and consequently never reproduce themselves. We may discover the rules by which the cyclical rhythms seem to operate, except that they never truly describe any given empirical situation. The science of the complex is the science of the optimal description of the inherently imprecise.

We must not merely explicate this methodology. We have in addition the enormous task of creating world-systemic data that reflect this imprecise reality with maximum relevance. This is an intellectually difficult, materially and temporally exhausting, work of imagination and drudgery which will take a good 50 years by tens of thousands of scholars before it begins to pay off significantly. We have been dawdling too long.

Finally, we may be reluctantly forced to face the politically difficult organizational implications of our work: the wholesale reorganization of the social science sector of our universities and our libraries. It has taken 100 years for our present disciplinary divisions to institutionalize themselves, and they are now well entrenched. Social science is a mega-colossus, and even its feet of clay are large and not easy to chip at. Nonetheless, once we confront the theoretical and methodological issues, we may not be able to avoid the organizational implications of our radical views. But this is perhaps the third phase. The second phase is for the moment enormous enough.

References

Amin, S. 1980: Révolution ou décadence? La crise du système impérialiste contemporain et celle de l'Empire romain. *Review*, 4, 1 (Summer), 155–66.

Amin, S. 1982: Crisis, nationalism and socialism. In S. Amin, G. Arrighi, A. G. Frank and I Wallerstein (eds), *Dynamics of Global Crisis*, New York: Monthly Review Press, 167–231.

Arrighi, G. and Drangel, J. 1986: The stratification of the world-economy: an exploration of the semiperipheral zone. *Review*, 10, 1 (Summer), 9–74.

Arrighi, G., Hopkins, T. K. and Wallerstein, I. 1989: *Antisystemic Movements*. London: Verso.

Aymard, Maurice 1978: Impact of the *Annales* school in Mediterranean countries. *Review*, 1, 3/4 (Winter-Spring), 53–64.

Bergeron, Louis 1978: La revolution agricole en Angleterre. In Pierre Leon (ed.), *Histoire économique et sociale du monde*, III, Louis Bergeron (ed.), *Inerties et révolutions, 1730–1840*, Paris: Armand Colin, 226–32.

Bergier, J. F. 1973: The industrial bourgeoisie and the rise of the working class, 1700–1914. In C. M. Cipolla (ed.), *Fontana Economic History of Europe*, III, *The Industrial Revolution*, London: Collins, 397–451.

Bloch, Marc 1930: La lutte pour l'individualisme agraire dans la France du dix-huitième siècle. *Annales d'histoire économique et sociale*, II, 329–83, 511–56.

Braudel, F. 1966: *La Méditerranée et le monde méditerranéen à l'époque de Philippe II*. 2nd ed. enl. Paris: Armand Colin. (First published in 1949.) (English translation 1973: *The Mediterranean and the Mediterranean World in the Age of Philip II*.)

Braudel, F. 1969: Histoire et sciences sociales: la longue durée. In *Ecrits sur l'histoire*, Paris: Flammarion, 41–83. (First published in *Annales ESC* in 1958.) (English translation 1972: *History and the Social Sciences*.)

Braudel, F. 1972a: History and the social sciences: the *longue durée*. In P. Burke (ed.), *Economy and Society in Early Modern Europe*, London: Routledge and Kegan Paul, 11–42.

Braudel, F. 1972b: Personal Testimony. *Journal of Modern History*, 64 (December), 448–67.

Braudel, F. 1973: *The Mediterranean and the Mediterranean World in the Age of Philip II*. 2 vols, New York: Harper and Row.

Braudel, F. 1978: En guise de conclusion. *Review*, 1, 3/4 (Winter-Spring), 243–83.

Braudel, F. 1979: *Civilisation matérielle, Economie et capitalisme, XVe–XVIIIe siècles*. Paris: Armand Colin. (English translation: 1981, 1982, 1984: *Civilization and Capitalism, 15th-18th Century*.)

Braudel, F. 1981–84: *Civilization and Capitalism, 15th-18th Century*. 3 vols, vol. 1 1981, vol. 2 1982, vol. 3 1984, New York: Harper and Row.

Bücher, Carl 1901: *Industrial Evolution*. New York: Henry Holt.

Bücher, Karl 1913: *Die Entstehung der Volkswirtschaft*. 9th ed. Tübingen: H. Laupp'schen Buchhandlung.

Caracciolo, A., Giarrizzo, G., Manselli, R., Ragionieri, E., Romano, R., Villari, R. and Vivanti, C. 1974: "Caratteri originale e prospettive di analisi: ancora sulla 'Storia d'Italia' Einaudi," discussione. *Quaderni storici*, 26 (May–August), 523–58.

Chase-Dunn, C. (ed.) 1982: *Socialist States in the World-System*. Beverley Hills: Sage.

Chaudhuri, K. N. 1981: The world-system east of longitude 20°: the European role in Asia, 1500–1750. *Review*, 5, 2 (Fall), 219–45.

Cole, G. D. H. 1952: *Introduction to Economic History, 1750–1950*. London: Macmillan.

Cole, W. A. and Deane, Phyllis 1966: The growth of national incomes. In H. J. Habakkuk and M. M. Postan (eds), *The Cambridge Economic History of Europe*, VI, *The industrial Revolutions and After: Incomes, Population and Technological Change*, Cambridge: Cambridge University Press, 1–55.

Coleman, D. C. 1966: Industrial growth and industrial revolutions. In E. M. Carus-Wilson (ed.), *Essays in Economic History*, New York: St Martin's Press, III, 334–35.

Copans, Jean 1978: In search of lost theory: Marxism and structuralism within French anthropology. *Review*, 3, 1 (Summer), 45–73.

Crouzet, François (ed.) 1972: *Capital Formation in the Industrial Revolution*. London: Methuen.

Daumas, Maurice 1965: Introduction. In M. Daumas (ed.), *Histoire générale des techniques*, II, *Les premières étapes du machinisme*, Paris: Presses Univ. de France, v–xix.

Davis, Ralph 1973: *The Rise of the Atlantic Economies*. London: Weidenfeld and Nicolson.

Deane, Phyllis 1973: Great Britain. In C. M. Cipolla (ed.), *The Fontana Economic History of Europe*, IV, *The Emergence of Industrial Societies*, London: Collins, part 1, 161–227.

Deane, Phyllis 1979: *The First Industrial Revolution*. Cambridge: Cambridge University Press.

Dubuc, Alfred 1978: The influence of the *Annales* school in Quebec. *Review*, 1, 3/4 (Winter-Spring), 123–45.

Elias, Norbert, 1984: Notizen zum Lebenslauf. In P. Gleichmann et al. *Macht und Zivilization*, Frankfurt am Main: Suhrkamp, 9–82.

Elmore, Richard 1978: View from the Rive Gauche: A comment on *Annales* historiography. *Psychohistory Review*, 7 (Fall), 30–35.

Engels, Friedrich 1880: *Socialism: Utopian and Scientific*.

Eversley, D. E. C. 1967: The home market and economic growth in England, 1750–80. In E. L. Jones and G. E. Mingay (eds), *Land, Labour and Population in the Industrial Revolution*, London: Edward Arnold, 206–59.

Febvre, Lucien 1950: Un livre qui grandit: La Méditerranée et le monde méditerranéen à l'époque de Philippe II. *Revue historique*, CCIII, 2 (204), 216–24.

Febvre, Lucien 1953a: Avant-propos. In *Combats pour l'histoire*. Paris: Armand Colin, v–ix.

Febvre, Lucien 1953b: De 1892 à 1933. Examen de conscience d'une histoire et d'un historien. In *Combats pour l'histoire*. Paris: Armand Colin, 3–17.

Febvre, Lucien 1953c: Face au vent: Manifeste des "Annales" nouvelles. In *Combats pour l'histoire*. Paris: Armand Colin, 34–43.

Febvre, Lucien 1953d: Vivre l'histoire. In *Combats pour l'histoire*. Paris: Armand Colin, 18–33.

Fohlen, Claude 1973: France, 1700–1914. In C. M. Cipolla (ed.), *Fontana Economic History of Europe*, IV, *The Emergence of Industrial Societies*, London: Collins, part 1, 7–75.

Furet, François 1971: L'histoire quantitative et la construction du fait historique. *Annales ESC*, 26, 1 (January-February), 63–75.

Genêt, Jean 1960: *Les nègres*. Décines: Marc Barbezat.

Gerth, H. H. and Mills, C. Wright 1946: *From Max Weber: Essays in Sociology*. New York: Oxford University Press.

González, José Luis 1980: *El país de cuatro pisos*. Rio Piedras, Puerto Rico: Ed. Huracán.

Goubert, Pierre 1969a: *L'Ancien Régime*, I, *La Société*. Paris: Armand Colin.

Goubert, Pierre 1969b: *L'Ancien Régime*, II, *Les Pouvoirs*. Paris: Armand Colin.

Gould, Constance C. and Handler, Mark 1989: *Information Needs in the Social Sciences: An Assessment*. Mountain View, CA: Research

Libraries Group, Inc.

Hazard, J. 1973: *The European Mind, 1680–1715*. Harmondsworth: Penguin.

Hexter, J. H. 1972: Fernand Braudel and the *Monde Braudelien.* ... *Journal of Modern History*, 44, 4 (December), 480–539.

Hobsbawm, E. J. 1962: *The Age of Revolution, 1789–1848*, New York: Mentor.

Hobsbawm, E. J. 1978: Comments. *Review*, 1, 3/4 (Winter–Spring), 157–62.

Hofstadter, D. R. 1981: Metamagical themas. *Scientific American*, 245 (November), 22–43.

Hopkins, T. K. and Wallerstein, I. 1987: Capitalism and the incorporation of new zones into the world-economy. *Review*, 10, 5/6, supplement (Summer/Fall), 763–79.

Hunt, E. K. 1984: Was Marx a utopian socialist? *Science and Society*, 48, 1 (Spring), 90–97.

Huppert, George 1978: The *Annales* school before the *Annales*. *Review*, 1, 3/4 (Winter–Spring), 215–19.

Jones, E. L. 1988: *Growth Recurring: Economic Change in World History*. Oxford: Clarendon Press.

Keyfitz, N. 1976: World resources and the world middle class. *Scientific American*, 235 (July), 28–35.

Kinser, Samuel 1981: Annaliste paradigm? The geohistorical structure of Fernand Braudel. *American Historical Review*, 86, 1 (February), 63–105.

Labrousse, Ernest 1970: En survol sur l'ouvrage. In Fernand Braudel and Ernest Labrousse (eds), *Histoire économique et sociale de la France*. II, *Des derniers temps de l'âge seigneurial aux préludes de l'âge industriel, 1660–1789*, Paris: Presses Univ. de France, 693–740.

Landes, David 1969: *The Unbound Prometheus*. Cambridge: At the University Press.

Lefebvre, Henri 1980: Marxism exploded. *Review*, 4, 1 (Summer), 19–32.

Le Goff, Jacques 1974: Les mentalités: une histoire ambiguë. In J. Le Goff and P. Nora (eds), *Faire de l'histoire*, Paris: Gallimard, vol. 3, 76–94.

Le Roy Ladurie, Emmanuel 1975: De la crise ultime à la vraie croissance, 1660–1789. In Georges Duby (ed.), *Histoire de la France rurale*, II, E. Le Roy Ladurie, dir., *L'âge classique des paysans, 1340–1789*, Paris: Seuil, 355–599.

McNeill, William H. 1986: *Mythistory and other Essays*. Chicago: University of Chicago Press.

Mannheim, Karl 1936: *Ideology and Utopia*. New York: Harvest. (German original published in 1929).

Mantoux, Pierre 1928: *The Industrial Revolution in the Eighteenth Century*. 2nd rev. ed. London: Jonathan Cape.

Marx, Karl 1967: *Capital*. Trans. by Samuel Moore and Edward Aveling, 3 vols, New York: International.

Marx, Karl 1972: *Critique of the Gotha Program*. In Robert C. Tucker (ed.), *The Marx-Engels Reader*, New York: W. W. Norton, 383–98.

Marx, Karl 1977: Results of the immediate process of production. Published in English as the Appendix to Karl Marx, *Capital*, trans. by Ben Fowkes, New York: Vintage, 943–1084.

Marx, Karl 1978: *The Class Struggles in France, 1848 to 1850*. In Karl Marx and Frederick Engels, *Collected Works*, X, New York: International, 45–145.

Marx, Karl 1979: *The Eighteenth Brumaire of Louis Bonaparte*. In Karl Marx and Frederick Engels, *Collected Works*, XI, New York: International, 99–197.

Marx, Karl and Engels, Frederick 1942: *Selected Correspondence, 1846–1895*. New York: International.

Marx, Karl and Engels, Frederick 1982: *Collected Works*, XXXVIII, New Work: International.

Mathias, Peter 1969: *The First Industrial Nation*. London: Methuen.

Mathias, Peter and O'Brien, Patrick 1976: Taxation in Britain and France, 1715–1810. *Journal of European Economic History*, 1, 3 (Winter), 601–50.

Meldolesi, Luca 1982: *L'utopia realmente esistente: Marx e Saint-Simon*. Bari: Laterza.

More, Thomas 1975: *Utopia*. Trans. by Robert M. Adams, New York: W. W. Norton.

Morineau, Michel 1971: *Les faux-semblants d'un démarrage économique: agriculture et démographie en France au XVIIIe siècle*. Paris: Armand Colin.

Myrdal, Gunnar 1930: *Vetenskap och politik i nationalekonomien*. Stokholm: Norstedt.

Myrdal, Gunnar 1944: *An American Dilemma*, with the assistance of Richard Sterner and Arnold Rose. New York: Harper and Row.

Myrdal, Gunnar 1954: *The Political Element in the Development of Economic Theory*. Cambridge, MA: Harvard University Press.

Myrdal, Gunnar 1957: *Economic Theory and Underdeveloped Regions*. London: Gerald Duckworth.

Myrdal, Gunnar 1958: *Value in Social Theory*. New York: Harper.

Myrdal, Gunnar 1968: *Asian Drama*. 3 vols, New York: Pantheon.

Myrdal, Gunnar 1969: *Objectivity in Social Research*. New York: Pantheon.

Myrdal, Gunnar 1972: *Against the Stream: Critical Essays on Economics*. New York: Pantheon.

Myrdal, Gunnar 1975: The equality issue in world development. *Swedish Journal of Economics*, LXXVII, 4, 413–32.

Myrdal, Gunnar 1976: The meaning and validity of institutional economics. In K. Dopfer (ed.), *Economics in the Future*, Boulder, CO: Westview, 82–89.

Myrdal, Gunnar 1981: What is political economy? In R. A. Solo and C. W. Anderson (eds), *Value Judgment and Income Distribution*, New York: Praeger, 41–53.

Nef, John U. 1943: The industrial revolution reconsidered. *Journal of Economic History* III, 1, 1–31.

Nolte, Hans-Heinrich 1982: The position of eastern Europe in the international system in early modern times. *Review*, 6, 1 (Summer), 25–84.

O'Brien, P. K. and Keyder, Caglar 1978: *Economic Growth in Britain and France, 1780–1914*. London: George Allen and Unwin.

Ollman, Bertell 1971: *Alienation: Marx's Conception of Man in Capitalist Society*. Cambridge: At the University Press.

Polanyi, Karl 1957: *The Great Transformation*. Boston: Beacon Press.

Pomian, Krzyzstof 1977: Cicli. In *Enciclopedia Einaudi*. vol 2, 1141–91.

Pomian, Krzysztof 1978: Impact of the *Annales* school in Eastern Europe. *Review*, 1, 3/4 (Winter-Spring), 101–18.

Pomian, Krzysztof 1979: The secular evolution of the concept of cycles. *Review*, 2, 4 (Spring), 563–646.

Prigogine, I., Allen, P. M. and Herman, R. 1977: Long-term trends and the evolution of complexity. In Ervin Laszlo and Judah Bierman (eds), *Studies in the Conceptual Foundations*, New York: Pergamon, 1–26.

Prigogine, Ilya and Stengers, Isabelle 1979: *La nouvelle alliance*. Paris: Gallimard. (English translation: 1984: *Order Out of Chaos*.)

Prigogine, I. et al. 1982: Openness: a round-table discussion. *Family Process*, 20 (March), 57–70.

Prigogine, Ilya and Stengers, Isabelle 1984: *Order Out of Chaos*. New York: Bantam Books.

Randall, J. H. Jr. 1940 *The Making of the Modern Mind*. Cambridge, MA: Houghton Mifflin.

Schumpeter, Joseph 1939: *Business Cycles*. 2 vols, New York: McGraw Hill.

Stein, Lorenz von 1959: *Der Begriff der Gesellschaft und die soziale Geschichte der Französischen Revolution bis zum Jahre 1830*. 3 vols, Hildesheim: Georg Olms Verlagsbuchhandlung. (English translation 1964: *The History of the Social Movement in France, 1789–1850*.)

Stein, Lorenz von 1964: *The History of the Social Movement in France, 1789–1850*. Totowa, NJ: The Bedminster Press.

Stoianovich, Traian 1976: *French Historical Method: The Annales Paradigm*. Ithaca, NY: Cornell University Press.

Supple, Barry 1973: The state and the industrial revolution, 1700–1914. In C. M. Cipolla (ed.), *Fontana Economic History of Europe*, III, *The Industrial Revolution*, London: Collins, 301–57.

Thompson, E. P. 1978: *The Poverty of Theory*. London: Merlin Press.

Tillich, P. 1948: *The Protestant Era*. Chicago: University of Chicago Press.

Tilly, Charles 1978: Anthropology, history and the *Annales*. *Review*, 1, 3/4 (Winter-Spring), 207–13.

Wallerstein, I. 1974: *The Modern World-System*, vol. I, *Capitalist Agricul-*

ture and the Origins of the European World-Economy in the Sixteenth Century. 3 vols, New York: Academic Press.

Wallerstein, I. 1979: *The Capitalist World-Economy*. Cambridge: Cambridge University Press.

Wallerstein, I. 1980a: The *Annales* school: the war on two fronts. *Annales of Scholarship*, 1, 3 (Summer), 85–91.

Wallerstein, I. 1980b: The future of the world-economy. In Terence K. Hopkins and Immanuel Wallerstein (eds), *Processes of the World-System*, Beverly Hills, CA: Sage, 167–80.

Wallerstein, I. 1980c: *The Modern World-System*, vol. II, *Mercantilism and the Consolidation of the European World-Economy, 1600–1750*. 3 vols, New York: Academic Press.

Wallerstein, I. 1982: Crisis as transition. In S. Amin, G. Arrighi, A. G. Frank and I. Wallerstein (eds), *Dynamics of Global Crisis*, New York: Monthly Review Press and London: Macmillan, 11–54.

Wallerstein, I. 1983: *Historical Capitalism*. London: Verso.

Wallerstein, I. 1984: *The Politics of the World-Economy: The States, the Movements and the Civilizations*. Cambridge: Cambridge University Press.

Wallerstein, I. 1989a: The French Revolution as a world-historical event. *Social Research*, 57, 1 (Spring), 33–52.

Wallerstein, I. 1989b: *The Modern World-System*, vol III, *Second Era of Great Expansion of the Capitalist World Economy*. 3 vols, San Diego, CA: Academic Press.

Wallerstein, I. 1989c: 1968: Revolution in the world-system. *Theory and Society*, 18, 4 (July) 431–49.

Index